The Greatest War Ever

Freda Lemuel

Bible verses are taken from the Authorised King James Version unless otherwise stated.

Books can be obtained from the following sources:

Steps to Life (Australia): www.steps.org.au
Amazon: www.amazon.com.au
tgweplus@gmail.com

Also available in MP3 audio and ebook formats.

Published July 2022

Copyright: Permission can be gained from tgweplus@gmail.com. It is given under the condition that they are not sold for profit and no changes are made to the contents.

Layout and Design: Revealer Media (www.revealermedia.com)

Disclaimer: The talks transcribed in this book are the writer's own journey in trying to make sense of this complicated world we live in. Everything said has come from years of study and is expressed in a creative way based on Earth being a planet-stage. Information is presented but readers can check the references and do their own further research. It is the author's desire that this book be a springboard for the reader to want to find out more. So much information is readily available today and readers can form their own opinions. This book is merely the author's findings.

Cover design: Colours have been chosen because of their positivity, hope and significance for a victorious life during and after the Greatest War Ever. Blue stands for the divine Law which sets the royal standard and brings true peace, safety and security. Scarlet represents the offering of blood as sacrifice and payment for humanity breaking the Law. Purple is a combination of red and blue symbolising the true, original divine Royalty coming down to mix with humanity to show the Way, the Truth and the Life. Gold is for testing and refinement of character in the process leading to perfection. White is for purity and restored, right relationship between mankind and the Creator. The words in the background have been taken from the text of the talks and represent words warring in a mental battlefield.

Table of Contents

Preface and Acknowledgments — 7
Part 1 – Act 1: Setting the Stage, the Script & the Sophists — **8**
  Setting the Stage — 9
  The Script of Sophistry — 12
  Scene 1. The Sophists — **15**
    Greece — 16
    Sophistry and Democracy, Education and Law — 19
    Rome — 20
    Definitions – Sophistry and Sophisticated — 26

Part 2 – Act 2: Timelines and History
  Introduction and Review — 29
  Scene 2. Timelines — **35**
  Scene 3. History and the Storyline — **38**
    Subjectivity and Objectivity — 40
  Scene 4. Chapters in the Storyline — **45**
    Testimony — 48
    Basic Timeline of Earth's History — 49

Part 3 – Act 3: The Performers
  Introduction and Review — 51
  Scene 5. Players and Actors Before the Flood
    Adam, Eve and Cain — 53
    Enoch and Noah — 55
  Scene 6. Nimrod, Semiramus and Tammuz
    First Babylonian Empire and Nimrod — 59
    Semiramus and Tammuz — 63
    The Terrible Trio's Legacy — 65
    John's Book of Revelation and the Three Angels' Message — 70
  Scene 7. Simon Magus
    The Great War Rages On — 71
    Simon Magus — 73
    Conclusion — 75

Part 4 – Act 4: Simon Magus, Two Simon Peters & First Bishop/Pope
  Introduction and Review
  Scene 8. Samaria And Background of Simon Magus — **78**

Samaria
Five Tribes: *Babylon; Cuthah; Hamath; Ava; Sephervaim* 75

Scene 9. First Meeting of the Two Simon Peters   84
Simon Magus Peter and the Origins of Peter
Headquarters in Rome   89
Planet-Worship   90
Janus and the Keys of the Kingdom
Summary   94

Scene 10. First Bishop of Rome Revealed   95
Evidence
First Meeting of the Two Simon Peters   97
More Scriptural Proof   98
Word Origins of Pope   100

Scene 11. Simon Magus' Mistress   101
Helena
Conclusion   105

Part 5 – Act 5: Simon Magus' Death & Legacy of Gnosticism   108
Introduction and Review

Scene 12. Death of Simon Magus & His Legacy   110
Death of Simon Magus
Simon Magus' Legacy   112
The Future of Simon Magus   115

Scene 13. Gnosticism   116
Meaning of Gnosticism   117
History and Background
Two Types of Science: *Meaning of Science;*   120
Trust in God or Man;   122
Gnostic Science/Knowledge
Examples of Gnostic Beliefs: *Humanism; the Sethian Sect;*   124
Valentinius; Dualism

Scene 14. Gnosticism and Today   131
Quotations about Gnosticism
Five Consequences of Gnosticism: 133
1. Effects on Youth
2. Effects on Eve And Humanity   134
3. Education and The Three Degrees of Knowledge
4. The Roman Catholic Church   135
5. Covid Plandemic   136

Table of Contents

Conclusion	138

Part 6 – Act 6: Word Examples of Sophistry — 140
Introduction and Review

Scene 15. Six Word Examples of Sophistry — 142
1. Antichrist
2. Universal — 148
3. University — 154
4. Basilica
5. Allegories — 164
6. Other Languages: Numbers and Signs
Conclusion — 166

Part 7 – Act 7: Blasphemy & Techniques of Persuasion — 168
Introduction and Review

Scene 16. Blasphemy — 171
Biblical Examples
Origin of the Word Blasphemy — 172
The Process and Effects of Blasphemy — 173
Words to Remove from the Vocabulary — 175
Related Features of Blasphemy: — 176
  1. Tone of Voice
  2. Humour
  3. Body Language — 177
Toned Down Blasphemy
Targets of Blasphemy: — 178
  1. Physical Body – Internal and External (The Blood)
  2. Invisible Parts of Humans — 182
  3. Procreation
  4. Relationships (Father Mother, Children) — 183
Satan and Blasphemy — 187
How Can We Combat Blasphemy? — 189
  1. Our Goal
  2. Our Missions
  3. Our Weapons — 190
God's Instructions and Reminders — 191

Scene 17. Fifteen Techniques of Persuasion — 193
Conclusion — 200

Part 8 – Act 8: A Glimpse of the Future – Hanok's Story   **202**
    Introduction and Review
    Testimony   207
    Hanok's Story – Prologue/Introduction

Panorama 1– Hanok's Background and The Journey   **207**
    Overview of Hanok's Life
    The Transformation
    An Old Friend   209
    The Flight
    Kesil-Orian   212
    Superman   214

Panorama 2 – The Homecoming Welcome   **216**
    Sea of Glass
    Meeting The Prince   216
    Royal Garments: *The Crown; The Harp; The Palm Branch;*
        Music and Hanok's Song   218

Panorama 3 – Royal Tour Through Ouranos   **220**
    The City: *The Walls; The Gates of Pearl; Gold Streets and*
        Buildings; Nature
    Mount Siyon–*The River of Life; The Tree of Life*   225

Panorama 4 – The Temple of Miqqedas   **228**
    The Grandest Musical Welcome
    The Holy Place: *The Table of Bread and Juice; The Candlestick;*
        The Altar of Perfume

Panorama 5 – The King and His Story   **232**
    The Most Holy Place and the Throne
    The King's Song
    A Royal Meeting   229
    The King's Message of Hope   234
         237

Panorama 6 – A Personal Assistant, the Mansion & a Surprise   **238**
    Personal Assistant
    The Mansion, The Wreath and a Furry Friend   240
    The Thinking Room   242

CONCLUSION   **243**

Preface and Acknowledgments

Originally, this series of talks was planned to be a single one-hour presentation. It all began with a short lively discussion with a friend and I was invited to give a talk on a particular subject. While preparing, I soon realised there was too much information and the talk became a 'living organism' growing into three, then six and finally eight. It has been a sheer privilege and blessing to bring together much information collected over the years.

In the beginning, there was no thought whatsoever of making a book and audio book. However, the 'growing organism' developed after many suggested that these should be produced so more people can receive this information which is so relevant to current events. My prayer is that the information will plant seeds wherever it spreads. I hope that listeners and readers will be able to see a bigger picture of our uncertain world than the one we see from our limited human viewpoint. My desire is that all will be encouraged and hold on to the great hope of a glorious eternal future.

I am extremely grateful for many friends and zoom listeners near and far, who have encouraged, supported me and asked for more talks. There are many people to acknowledge and I won't name them. You know who you are and how much I appreciate from the bottom of my heart your support, prayers, advice, encouragement and financial assistance. A special thank you to my technical team which has attended to the production. They have flattened out many of the mountains which loomed in my mind.

Above all, I wish to thank my Father-God and His Son Jesus Christ for strengthening and enabling me to complete my part of the project. This is my small mission in the Greatest War Ever—to use weapons of words to fight back in a war of words. I am just planting the thought-seeds and leave it up to the Creator of the universe to nurture them, to cause the seeds to grow further, and bring forth good fruits for others to harvest. I hold onto the promise given in Isaiah 55.11.

> 'So shall My Word be that goeth forth out of My mouth.
> It shall not return unto Me void,
> but it shall accomplish that which I please;
> and it shall prosper in the thing whereto I sent it.'
> F.L.

Part 1–Act 1: Setting the Stage, the Script and the Sophists

Introduction

The title of this series of talks is–'The Greatest War Ever.' It will attempt to cover many topics. I know I am probably trying to cover too much. However, everything is connected with each other. You could say this is a 'special fried rice' presentation with everything mixed in together. I hope and pray that what I have to say will be clear, simple and easy to understand.

I want to try and show how very little has changed over the 6000 years of earth's history and that the main changes have been only in intensity as the earth groans like a woman in labour about to give birth. The contractions and pain become more frequent and intense as the great expectation and climax of a new life loom closer. In this period of time as the Lord's second coming approaches in the very, very near future, it's like a mother giving birth. It is a time of great expectations, positivity, faith and hope that all will go well and we will be given a new life. But it is all mixed up with pain, suffering, agony and trials. The contractions become more intense.

Romans 8:22 *'For we know that the whole creation groaneth and travaileth in pain together until now.'* Jesus described these days as a *'time of sorrows.'* We are trapped by time in the midst of this labour and there is no escape around the process. Just as a mother cannot avoid the labour, we can only charge straight through with preparation, prayer, perseverance, and trusting in God that we will be delivered safely. A brand-new life is about to begin. We are so close.

We can see this time as a positive exciting one and we can and must rise above the doom and gloom. Romans 8:18,21 *'For I reckon that the*

Setting the Stage, the Script and the Sophists

sufferings of the present time are not worthy to be compared with the glory which shall be revealed to us...' 'Because the creature itself also shall be delivered from the bondage of corruption into the glorious liberty of the children of God.' Life can't get any better than that!

I always like to focus on the Big Picture of things and then zoom into the smaller pictures. It is far too easy to drown in the details and lose sight of reality. The saying goes that 'The devil is in the details.' And it is so true because he does not want us to look upwards and learn the truth. So, let's zoom outwards, take a peek from the viewpoint of someone literally off the planet, an outside objective observer. Then we will zoom inwards and look at just a few details of a few small pictures. Let's escape from this COVID cesspit and see it for what it really is. In the big scheme of things, it is just a one step closer to the Lord's Coming. I want to set a stage.

In this first talk, we will look closely at the setting up of the stage ie the platform for the show. We will analyse the script, discover the plot and drama and meet some actors. The show is not in chronological order because we will flit back and forth through the 6000-year timeline of the earth to see how the past still influences today.

So, now let's set the stage.

Setting the Stage

It has been written many times that the church and the earth are like a theatre. 1 Corinthians 4:9 says, '... for we are made a spectacle unto the world and to angels and to men.' Hebrews 10:33 tells us, '... ye were made a gazing stock.' We are being gazed at and closely watched. In Acts of the Apostles page 12 we read, 'It (the church) *is the* theatre *of His grace*...' In Education page 622, it says, 'the world is a theatre, the actors, its inhabitants, are preparing to act their part in the last great drama.' And in 6 Bible Commentary 684 we read, 'This whole world of ours is a stage *on which the conflict between sin and righteousness, truth and error, is being carried on before an intensely interested audience composed of the inhabitants of the universe.*'

This is the biggest picture or panorama of what is going on today on planet earth. Doesn't that make us feel so small! Nevertheless, we are extremely precious in the eyes of God.

So now, I want you to see yourself in outer space amongst the vast audience of angels and inhabitants of other worlds watching the greatest show on earth. It is the most spectacular show ever to be played out on the planet-stage. The Author of the play and Producer of the show is God the Father sitting on his Producer's seat, His throne, in heaven. He sends His Son, Jesus onto the planet-stage as Director. The Director is also co-Author involved in writing the script for the story. The Prompter behind the invisible curtains is the Holy Spirit quietly speaking in the hearts of the players on the earthly stage. His job is to remind and guide them of the parts they are supposed to be playing in the storyline whenever they forget and lose the plot.

Originally, the planet-stage was in full view with open contact and communication between the Producer and Director and the first two players, Adam and Eve. The show was going according to the first script. Glorious light lit up the whole globe-shaped stage. It was the latest new creation in the universe with a special purpose. The players were different to all other inhabitants because they were made in the image of the Creator-Author-Producer-God. Their purpose was to show how they could use their gift of free will to live according to the universal Law of Great Love in the theocratic government with God the Father at the head.

Everyone in the universe already knew this. But you see, a problem had occurred in heaven when one angel decided he wanted to do things his way. He rebelled and led others astray. So, now the Head of the government had to show everyone that His way was still the best. The ever-loving Head of Government, our Father-God, could have easily killed the rebels and got them out of the way. But His heart of Great Love would not let Him because that would only create fear in all His angels and children in other worlds. They had never seen death.

So, a fresh new type of creature was created who had not lived in the universe before, but would prove that the gift of free will and the Law of Great Love worked perfectly. After all, until this rebellion, everyone had lived perfect lives in perfect bliss for past eternity. The audience

Setting the Stage, the Script and the Sophists　　　　　　　　　11

was now experiencing some confusion because so many angel friends had been lead astray, and were now involved in a Great War. The Great Cosmic War began. The angels were naturally extremely interested and focused on this little new world, just one among countless others in the universe. This is why the audience gazed at it very intensely. What would happen? How would these new creatures called human beings behave?

In all human theatre shows, there is drama and tension in the plot and this is what happened. After the perfect beginning of this earthly show, a veil or curtain came between the visible stage and the invisible audience. It was a curtain of secrecy, mystery and confusion as lies mingled with truth, cast shadows and darkened the stage. Only the truth of God's Word and the original script could bring back the light. In Education page 173, it says, 'But in the Word of God the curtain is drawn aside and we behold behind, above and through all the play and the counterplay of human interests and power and passions, the agencies of the all-merciful One silently, patiently, working out the counsels of His own will.' God wants His theocratic government back because it is THE perfect way to rule.

In this show, the drama and tension arose when an angel, the saboteur author called Satan interfered. He began by changing the script to suit his own purposes. He had and still does covet the Producer's chair with all its authority and power. He also wanted to take over the Director's job as well–and the Prompter's position - and take over the whole show. Cleverly and ingeniously, he rewrote the script by changing the language ie the words. This is where sophistry comes in.

Satan is also a Chief General of an invisible army of demons, the fallen angels hiding behind the stage curtains, operating unseen. The true Director, Jesus, became the Chief Commander of his own invisible army of holy angels. The Great War begun in heaven still continues today on earth. The Chief General uses all means possible to force humans to act out his own evil character and do his dirty deeds for him. This is why they are called actors. They take on someone else's personality. However, the Chief Commander sticks to the original script giving His human players a gift of free will to choose to play the original roles they were designed for. They are the players on the platform.

Look around us today and see how Hollywood is full of people trained to be someone else. These false personalities influence, not only adults, but also children to change and mould their little characters. News reporters, politicians and world leaders are basically actors performing the character of someone else. We will look at this in more detail later on.

So, hopefully, we can now rise above the details of a battlefield on the one black spot in the whole universe and see the grand spectacular show of this tiny world-stage we live in. Hopefully, we will see the dramatic panoramic view of the earth's timeline over 6000 years. We cannot see and know everything of course, because only the Producer, Director and Prompter know that. But we can at least get a bigger view to help us put the devastations and catastrophes of today into perspective. We can be outside, objective observers and ride above all this disaster by faith and obedience to God.

Now, let's look at the script of the show so we can follow the storyline. This is the script of sophistry versus the original script of God's Word. The show is a long, drawn-out dispute or controversy between the Godhead and its enemy. It is between the Chief General Satan and the Chief Commander Jesus.

The Script of Sophistry

We need to find out what the word sophistry means. Then we will see how the script is essentially a battle between The Word of Truth as inspired and written by God, versus human words as given by the saboteur author and director, Satan.

A theatre show is based on languages of different kinds. They can be spoken and/or musical languages combined with tones of voices and body language. Spoken words are carefully chosen and cleverly used to get a message across. Music gives words even more power. Signals from body language and all types of voice tones add extra force. This is why masks are so dangerous because it is not possible to 'read' the vital face language of smiles or frown etc. Isolation makes it difficult to see full body language. Full language becomes restricted.

Setting the Stage, the Script and the Sophists

So, let's look closely at sophistry because this is where the deception in the world originally started. As I go through the talk, keep in the back of your mind that whatever I say about the past is still happening today. As Solomon said 3000 years ago, halfway through the earth's timeline, and when sophistry was raging, he wrote, *'There is nothing new under the sun.'* And then later on, as we then look at the life of Simon Magus and discover what Gnosticism is, we will see more roots of sophistry which have spread around the globe like an invisible cancer. The roots feed and fuel the Great War between God's Word and Satan's words. This supernatural battle has never stopped in all 6000 years of the planet-stage's history. Keep in mind also, that history is His Story ie God's story. He is the true Author. His Story is not the human distorted, twisted versions found in "man's story" (from which I have coined the word, "manstory" which appears later in the text).

So - what then is sophistry? According to the Collins Dictionary, sophistry or sophism means 'false argument intended to deceive.' The Bible tells us Satan is the father of lies. He is the originator of sophistry. The word comes from the Greek word, sophisma. My own definition which I would use to teach a child is this—'Sophistry is twisting of words so you can get what you want.' That's all it is. 'Sophistry is twisting of words so you can get what you want.'

Even little children can understand this because they manipulate their parents every day trying to get their own way. Sophistry is cleverly changing meanings of words. For example, a child learns not to say, 'I want, I want' but to say, "I need, I need.' And it becomes more urgent. Sophistry presents false ideas to look like truth and to cause doubt and confusion. It is used to deliberately deceive others by cleverly presenting false arguments which distract from the truth. Distraction is one of Satan's greatest war weapons. The arguer merely skirts around the real issue and subtly avoids the main point.

Part of sophistry is something called higher criticism or critical thinking. Higher criticism arose in the 1800s when scholars began analysing dates, origins and authorship of the Bible. The Bible, God's Word, the script for the show has always been deliberately attacked in the Great War. Note that the attack is all based on logic and reasoning according to a finite human mind. Note also that the analysis focuses on skirting around the core point of the Bible which is essentially a collection of God's love letters to help and save His precious beloved human children. No wonder the enemy and Chief General wants to target and obliterate this script.

The focus of higher thinking of the 1800s, is, and still is, on the details of the validity of events and dates, or whether the characters including Jesus, really existed, or whether certain events actually happened, or whether translations are correct or not. The devil is certainly in the detail and the argument goes on relentlessly. The devil's goal is to take time and attention away from God's truths. Doubts have been cast on the validity of the Bible to the point today that God's Word is almost totally disregarded and ignored and even ridiculed and rubbished. And it is all done through sophistry. Satan twists words in order to get his own way.

Higher criticism has had devastating results on people's faith. Over the decades it has gradually insidiously led into the New Theology in the mid Twentieth Century. And critical thinking is now taught everywhere in schools. It sounds good–as if students are being trained to think for themselves. They are criticising and doubting whatever they are told. But in fact, they are being conditioned to doubt everything and not trust someone else's view, especially the absolute truths of God. Higher thinking, critical thinking and New Theology are all forms of sophistry. They are merely intellectual word games in a war of words.

In humanism, where man takes the place of God, each individual believes he has his own truth according to his own perception of the world and his own personal needs and wants. This means that there are billions of philosophers and philosophies in the world. No wonder there are so many arguments in families and wars between nations. Everyone is their own god knowing good and evil and tragically living in confusion and uncertainty and deception. It is exactly as Satan told Eve in the Garden of Eden–you will be like God and know good and evil.

So now we have the script of the show. Let's go into the first scene and meet some sophists.

Scene 1. The Sophists

Greece: The first scene of the show is about to begin on the platform of Greece. The word sophistry began in Greece in the fifth and fourth centuries BC. Sophism comes from the Greek word, sophisma. It goes back to the first Greek philosophers who were obviously called sophists.

Some examples include Protagoras, Hippias and Plato. Protagoras is generally regarded as the first sophist—apart from Satan, of course. Protagoras was the one who wrote, 'Man is the measure of all things.' What a statement that is! In other words, man decides for himself what he is going to believe and do. Do we hear an echo of this today in Alistair Crowley's words in the law which he established, 'Do as thou wilt.' And everyone does as they please because they are their own god and judge. In this way of thinking, there is no place for the one true God.

The ancient Greek sophists were professionally paid teachers for the young, wealthy Greek men. They provided an education in many areas and supposedly taught important life skills ie skills of how to live in this world—but not skills to train character and prepare for life in heaven. The sophists taught philosophy, public speaking, rhetoric, music, politics, athletics, mathematics, religion, human nature, man's origins and the natural world. Phew! This covers basically everything and has had lasting influences right up to today.

Let's focus for a few minutes on the word rhetoric and relate it to the present. Modern day sophistry stems from this. Rhetoric simply means how we communicate and how we describe reality through language ie words. Rhetoric involves understanding how language works and how words are controlled and organised in order to get a message across. It focuses more on the techniques of persuasion rather than the content of the actual words, although they are of course, very important too.

In ancient Athens, the 'demos' ie the people, learned how to effectively speak to the senate/government, to court juries and in public speeches. Rhetoric is persuasive. Students learn to think critically to discover strong or weak arguments and to attack them. Rhetoric and sophistry are the art of persuasion to motivate particular audiences in particular situations. And can't we see this today all around us!

The writings of Plato and Aristotle have influenced modern sophists who are merely power-hungry teachers using verbal 'magic tricks.' They use double-meanings of language in order to deceive and support their own reasoning in order to get their own way. They are not concerned with truth and justice but only want to gain power. They attempt to cover it under an umbrella of false truth or fake news.

Plato wrote a work called 'The Sophist.' In it, he describes sophists as instructors paid to hunt the young and wealthy. I am using the word hunt because Satan is a hunter, a roaring lion looking for human prey. In Plato's play he describes the hunt or search for people like 'merchants of knowledge, for the athletes in the contest of words and for the purgers (ie cleansers) of souls!' Plato basically concluded that sophists do not offer true knowledge but only offer opinions of things and that they only provide 'shadows of truth.' He is quite accurate here. He knows what sophistry really is.

He wrote that, to be called an authentic sophist, one had to practise 'the art of contradiction making, descended from an insincere kind of conceited mimicry. He had to be 'not divine but human,' and present a 'shadow play of words.' Plato argued that a sophist was a person who made his living through deception, whereas a philosopher loves wisdom and seeks truth.

Doesn't this still apply to today? We see sophists all around us. Think about the propaganda machine and how rhetoric and sophistry are being used to push the so-called 'vaccinations' and booster jabs for COVID-19. COVID is a perfect example of techniques of persuasion that are used to motivate particular audiences ie the masses, in particular situations ie in a so-called health crisis pandemic—or plandemic. In a later talk, we are going to examine some specific techniques of persuasion.

Sophistry and Democracy, Education and Law: Sophistry is connected with democracy, education and law. The main centre of government of ancient Greece was in Athens, and Athens was the home of democracy. Those who sought after government positions in public office found sophistry a very useful way of getting into the political system. Sophists of this time in the fifth and fourth centuries BC were very active in

Setting the Stage, the Script and the Sophists

politics. They played a large part in establishing laws and they were the first lawyers in the world because of their high levels of skills in argument.

And the situation is just the same today. Just observe the current politicians, the writers of newspaper articles, news reporters and how they can use words to sway the audience one way or another. They are all acting and spouting the words which have been scripted to them from higher levels. And they are changing laws and bringing in new ones all the time. Our premier here in Victoria is a perfect example of a sophist.

Pope Francis, is another good example. Being a Jesuit pope, he is especially trained in sophistry. In December 2021, just a month ago, he had a three-day visit in Greece, the home of democracy and the birthplace of Western civilisation. He met in Athens and spoke with nationalist politicians from various countries for a summit meeting. He said, 'Today, and not only in Europe, we are witnessing a retreat from democracy.' He said this in the very city of Athens where democracy began. He went on to say that democracy '... demands hard work and patience.' He also said, 'It is complex whereas authoritarianism is peremptory and populism's easy answers appear attractive.' Peremptory means expecting to be obeyed immediately without questioning; no provision for debate, ie dictatorial. Can you see the war of words?

The Pope also referred to the classical Greek thinkers like Socrates and Aristotle. So, the Pope has spoken, therefore authoritarianism will happen according to him. And it is already happening because it has all been planned in many countries. But note that he was careful not to actually say that authoritarianism will definitely happen. He just planted seeds and is preparing minds for that time. Note also that the Pope who is supposed to be God on earth, cleverly does not mention the truth about governments. The true government of God is a theocracy with God, the Creator at the head, not a human. It is not a democracy or socialism or communism or whatever other human-made government there is. Like a skilful arguer, Francis skirts around the issue and distracts from the main point.

Sophistry is also connected with education and law. In ancient Greek education, it was taught to the wealthy young men. In the early Western world, sophists were the first teachers in the art of speaking and writing especially in the medical area. Interesting. Aren't we in a big medical situation right now with Big Pharma, the WHO, the doctors and nurses in the medical system. All are acting out their parts according to the saboteur author's script. They probably don't even know what they are really doing. Thankfully a few doctors and nurses are speaking out the truth of what is really going on. Sadly, it is at the risk of their jobs and even their lives.

The ancient Greek teachers made their living through developing a 'science of eloquence' and teaching techniques of persuasion using sophistry and rhetoric. They taught how to argue and contradict. We see an echo of this in the 1700s with the philosopher Hegel and his Hegelian dialectic. Hegel was an expert in using contradictions to twist to a new conclusion. This is basically known as thesis (original idea) + antithesis (the opposite) = synthesis (a combination). For example, black + white = grey. Hegelian dialectic can be used in countless ways eg God created man (thesis) + man evolved through evolution (antithesis) = God created evolution (synthesis).

Many people today actually believe this to be the new truth. So today, basically in sophistry, words are cleverly used to sound good and right, but they are actually false and wrong. Lies are mixed with truth. Black becomes white and white becomes black with all shades of confused grey in between.

Note that the goal of argument was never to reach a conclusion of absolute truth. Truth evolves and changes. The goal of argument is to merely win the word battle and to gain power. Highly skilled sophists can dispute absolutely anything whether they know about the topic or not. They can instantly impress the listeners and their opponents with their carefully chosen words to support their case. Their purpose is to argue in order to influence their audience. They do not identify or focus on the truth but concentrate on proving their case. A good sophist or lawyer or politician or teacher is able to defend his argument whether it is his own opinion or the opposite, whether he believes it or not.

Can we see this today! It is everywhere surrounding us wherever we go! This is why lawyers can get their guilty clients set free today. This is why

Setting the Stage, the Script and the Sophists

we can see corruption in our justice system and governments all over the world. Listen to how politicians avoid answering the reporter's questions and evade the issue. They are all playing word games of sophistry and rhetoric. True, there are some genuine truth-seekers out there. But they are in a tiny minority and get labelled 'rogue-politicians' or 'mis-informers' or 'conspiracy theorists.'

Rome: We have jumped around in time between past and present. This early period in the fifth and fourth centuries BC is known as the First Sophist. Greece was the first Sophistic. The Second Sophistic came in the next empire, the Roman Empire. In this time, a sophist was merely any teacher of rhetoric and was a popular public speaker. Just like the Greeks before them Roman sophists had a huge impact on education, and politics, law and moral areas. The Romans developed the Greek sophistry and rhetoric further with the goal of controlling their world of the time, ie their growing kingdom around the Mediterranean Sea. But note that this verbal cleverness has never stopped as they now continue to control the whole globe.

Cicero is a famous example of a Roman sophist. He successfully combined Greek and Roman styles of language. The legacy of these two so-called great ancient empires of Greece and Rome lives on today because they had such an influence on western culture. When I was in the last two years of high school, one of my subjects was called Classical Studies. We learned about the Greek and Roman Empires and how important they were in setting foundations for today. And they certainly did.

I was at a Church of England so-called Christian boarding school in Adelaide. I say 'so-called' because I now know it was anything but Christian teaching. All we did was sing a hymn each morning in assembly and I went with the other boarders every Sunday to a high Anglican church service and did not understand a word. But it was fascinating watching the priests in the impressive robes walking up the aisle, swishing the incense around, taking their positions on their platform-stage and carry out their acting. I did not understand the Latin which was spoken. I could have been in a Catholic Church. I was not brought up in a Christian family and was not a believer, so it all went over my head. The rest of the school week was filled with worldly subjects including evolution.

There was absolutely no Biblical focus at all in any subject. Such is the influence of the ancient Greeks and Romans on education today! And it was all done over time through words using sophistry and rhetoric.

Can you see the word battles which have been going on for millenniums? Sophistry is merely a counterfeit form of truth arguing against God's Word. God's Word was spoken all through the ancient times and written down in the Old and New Testament writings. All along, Satan has been attacking it, trying to destroy it because he knows the absolute truth. During the time of the kings of Israel and Judah, the scrolls were lost for years but, praise God, they were discovered in Jeremiah's time. And for centuries, they were preserved by the Waldenses.

Definitions–Sophistry and Sophisticated: As we study the script of this spectacular show, let's now look at another word which stems from sophistry. It's the word sophisticated. Various dictionaries have fascinating definitions of what the words sophism and sophisticated mean. The dictionaries give deeper meanings which reveal what is really behind the word. These definitions are SO applicable to the sophisticated language used by advertisers, media reporters, politicians and world leaders.

Firstly, the Cambridge dictionary describes sophisticated as being, 'intelligent in a complicated way and therefore able to do complicated tasks.' Have you noticed how the COVID statistics are presented to look simple, but they are so complicated when you delve into them and find out how they have been manipulated to suit the purpose of the organisation behind them. This is sophistry hidden in plain sight for all to see.

The Macquarie dictionary says similar, but adds, sophisticated means 'changed from the natural character or simplicity; complex, intricate.' This describes well how actors in this show are acting out the character of someone else, not their natural God-given selves. The Free dictionary.com says sophistication means, 'showing much worldly knowledge or cultural refinement. Surely, this is humanism. It's about the world and man only, and not God. It also says, very complex; and complicated appealing to tastes of the sophisticates. (So now, we have two classes of humans–the sophisticates and the non-sophisticated); being pretentious and superficially wise.'

Setting the Stage, the Script and the Sophists

Can we see this pretentiousness now ie people claiming to be more important and superior than others. We see so much superficiality today in all the shallow conversations and talk about movies and sports and music and entertainments! People try to appear as if they know a lot when they don't. Words, words, words everywhere.

Dictionary.com says being sophisticated is to be 'altered by education so as to be worldly-wise and not naïve.' Look at the education system today. It's full of sophistication and complexity and nothing about God! Even so-called Christian education is often watered down to get public approval, government funding, to be accepted by all gender groups and appear to be tolerant in the name of God's love.

Collins dictionary says similar to the above. It says 'misleading, make artificial, being worldly-wise, tampering with text for the purposes of argument.' Satan is certainly tampering with the original script of the show, God's Word in the Bible. He wants to mislead and make people worldly-wise rather than Godly-wise. There is a wonderful quote from Patriarchs and Prophets page 658 which says, 'There is no insanity so dreadful, so hopeless, as that of following human wisdom ungirded by the wisdom of God.' And is this world insane today? Yes! Just look at the massive increase in mental health problems today.

The Macquarie Thesaurus has dozens and dozens of words related to sophism which reveal the truth of this evil word. In section 600.2+3 there are words such as irrational, erroneous, false, ill-founded, incorrect, self-contradiction, fallacy, mysticism, and Jesuitism. Yes, Jesuitism from the Catholic Church. Hmmm. Very interesting. I hope you are getting a clear picture of what sophistry and rhetoric are all about and how they are in full force today in the greatest show on earth?

These definitions imply many untruths. They imply that highly educated, sophisticated people are superior to others. But Paul writes in 1 Corinthians 1:19, *'I (God) will destroy the wisdom of the wise and will bring to nothing the understanding of the prudent.'* The definitions all imply that human wisdom is greater than God's wisdom. But Proverbs 3:19 tells us that, *'The Lord by wisdom hath founded the earth; by understanding, He established the heavens.'* God proves that He is the Creator of the earth, not Satan. And 1 Corinthians 1:20 says, *'... hath not God made foolish, the wisdom of this world?'* We can be certain of WHO will win this wicked war of words!

The definitions also imply that less-educated people are stupid and dumb to be treated as lesser humans, even as cattle as so many are being treated today, being held in their five kilometer bubbles and, in some countries, even restricted to their own properties. Compare this with what God the Creator says in Psalm 8:4-8. *'For Thou hast made him a little lower than the angels and hast crowned him with glory and honour. Thou madest him to have dominion over the works of Thy hands. Thou hast put all things under his feet: all sheep and oxen, yea and the beasts of the field.'* We are far more than cattle! We are sons of God, children of God. I John 3:1 makes it clear, *'Behold what manner of love the Father has bestowed unto us, that we should be called the sons of God...'* Many times, in the same book, we are called his *'little children.'*

How precious we are to Him, our Father-God! Yes, we are little, but we are much higher than the animals and all equal in God's eyes. He shows no favouritism between the more educated, sophisticated ones and the less educated and down and out ones.

But most importantly, these definitions imply, without even stating the fact, that there is an original, simple, uncomplicated, unsophisticated and absolute truth. Otherwise, how can something be altered or twisted or changed or made unnatural and worldly if there is no original absolute truth! God is real, and exists, and is sovereign above all men. There is an absolute truth that He created language in the first place. The tower of Babel proves that. There is an absolute truth that Jesus is real. This is why Satan's greatest lie is that he himself, ie Satan, does not exist - because if he did exist, then so would Jesus.

Sophisticated information also implies knowledge or light and understanding. Satan was once called Lucifer, the light-bearer. This is why Satanists prefer to call their religion, Luciferianism and not Satanism. They prefer to be seen as having knowledge and giving light rather than being the antagonist of Christ. If Satan is a light-bearer, then why are his activities associated with the colour black? Why does he hide himself? Satan did actually speak some truth. What he had told Adam and Eve was true—if they ate from the Tree of Knowledge of Good and Evil, they

Setting the Stage, the Script and the Sophists

would know both good and bad and become like gods themselves. What God told them was also true–that they would die if they ate from that tree. And that's what happened.

What a sacrifice–to give up their perfect lives and find out what evil was! What a cost! And the whole of human lives has suffered as a result ever since. But praise God, He showed us a way out to save our lives! One of the most important ways He has done this, is through His own written Word which has power over all of man's words. It is human words prompted by Satan which have concealed God's absolute truths. Words are fascinating how they can fool people's minds and trick them into unbelief.

Just a very quick interesting word about body language which we mentioned earlier. In sign language, there are several hand signals for the word sophistry. Two will be recognised immediately as signs of Satan. One is with the three middle fingers pointing inwards and the thumb and little finger pointing upwards like the devil's horns. The other sign is with the thumb, fourth and fifth fingers curled in and the second and third fingers pointing outwards as we see in freemasonry.

Just a quick little side-issue, which is actually a large issue but I don't have time for it now. It is about humour–jokes, riddles, sarcasm and mocking. These all come under the umbrella of sophistry as well. When you analyse them, they are all twisting of words and seem, very clever and very funny. It is the element of surprise which catches you unexpectedly and makes you think twice. You doubt and question what's being said. Sarcasm is actually lying because the person says the opposite of what he means. But what comes out of the mouth comes out of the heart and reveals their true self and motive. And when you dig deeper, these people often have a low view of themselves and are just trying to puff themselves up.

Suffice it to say that what Paul writes is how God wants us to speak. Ephesians 4:29 says, *'Let no corrupt communication come out of your mouth, but that which is good to the use of edifying, that it may administer grace to the hearer.'* Ephesians 5:4 lists many things we are not to do including, *'… filthiness, nor foolish talking, nor jesting…'* I've often thought of writing a book called 'The Deceit of Humour' but have never got around to it.

Today, the words, sophism, sophistry and sophisticated are usually used in negative ways and refer to misleading and deceptive arguments. So, it seems that many actually realise the truth, but sadly, they are still misled. The main thing that all sophists have in common throughout the ages is that, no matter whether they know anything about their topic of argument or not, they have enormous understanding of the power of language and how words can entertain, impress and sway an audience from one side to another. The secrecy, deception and mind manipulation become unbelievably complicated as we dig deeper into the world of words.

But God is not a God of secrecy and deception. Yes, He does have secrets but these are withheld till the right time for our own good. Like a wise, loving parent, God always tells us what we need to know when we need it. We are not meant to know precise details and dates of the future because, if we did, it would not benefit us. It is like giving a child a birthday present. The child knows he will get something good and looks forward to receiving it. If it was given to him even just one day early, the surprise and enjoyment would be spoilt. There is always pleasure and optimism in knowing and having the hope of something good happening. Likewise, God also wants to surprise us with his blessings. And this is why aren't to go time-setting and know the exact date and day when Jesus will come. We just know it will be soon. And it is good for our characters to wait and be trained in patience and to develop our trust in Him. By withholding important information, God provides an opportunity to exercise faith and trust in Him.

Deuteronomy 29:29 says, God is a revealer of secrets. Daniel 2:22 says, *'He revealeth the deep and secret things; He knoweth what is in the darkness, and the light dwelleth in Him.'* There is absolutely no room in God's Word for deception in sophistry. He is up front about His truths. And all through His Story, he gives plenty of warning—even centuries and millenniums—ahead of important events. Through Enoch He warned for about 300 years about the Great Flood to come. Then 120 years before it happened, He spoke through Noah that the time was getting close. Even Enoch knew about the Second Coming of Jesus. And all through the Old and New Testaments are written the prophecies

Setting the Stage, the Script and the Sophists

of so many key events in God's storyline. God treats us mere little people as intelligent human beings and keeps things very simple, open and easy to understand. It is only humans who complicate matters.

So, now I hope you have more insight to what sophistry is—twisting of words in order to get what you want. Sophistry is the key in understanding the whole show on the planet-stage of this earth. This first talk has been a mere introduction to paint a picture of the earth as a theatre for a show. We have met the Author-Producer-God, the co-Author and Director-Jesus, the Prompter, Holy Spirit and the saboteur Satan who is trying to take over the show. We have set the stage and seen how the planet-stage became a battlefield with the ongoing Great War. The Chief Commander, Jesus has His army of holy angels and human warriors. The Chief General, Satan has his army of demons and human agents. We have also looked at the script involving Satan's deceptive sophistry attacking God's Word of truth. The Great War begun in heaven is merely a war of words with countless battles to win over human minds and souls.

In the next talk in this series, we will meet some leading actors in the show, especially Nimrod and Simon Magus. We will learn they are other examples of the sophisticates who used sophistry and rhetoric to get their own way. We will solve the mystery of the two Simon Peters and will discover who the very first pope was. So, let's have an intermission now from the show and then come back to our seats in outer space and be ready for the next scene. I warn you it is a gripping story and not to be missed!

The date when the curtains will open again on the next episode of the most spectacular show on earth is 22 January at 2:30, Melbourne, Australia time. Be there! Don't miss it! Thank you for listening.

Part 2 – Act 2:
Timelines and History

Hello again. Welcome to the second talk in my series entitled The Greatest War Ever. If you have not heard Part One, I urge you to hear it first because it sets the foundation for the whole series. It focuses on sophism, explaining what it is and how it is Satan's greatest weapon in the battle for human minds and souls. Everything else comes under this umbrella of sophism or sophistry. We are in the midst of the Great War of Words. We learned in the first talk that sophism is simply Satan's twisting of words to get his own way. So, let's pray.

Dear Father in Heaven, thank You for another opportunity to share what You have laid on my heart. Please help me to explain clearly and to be an encouragement to the listeners in these troublesome times. Please bless this talk and help us all to get a glimpse of how You see this world. Your perfect love casts out fear and we trust You to give us strength in the days to come. Thank You for Your patience, grace and mercy towards us. We pray this in the name of Jesus. Amen.

Introduction and Review

Just a super-quick review to refresh our memories - In Part One, we covered the introduction of how the earth and its inhabitants have been described as a theatre show with a stage, a script, storyline, a drama and performers. This is according to 1 Corinthians 4:9 which says, '...*for we are made a spectacle to the world and to angels and to men.*' And we looked at many quotations describing the earth as a stage with curtains. The show is the most spectacular one ever to be played out on the planet-stage. It is far superior to all the movies and live theatre shows ever produced and put together.

We also learned that, in this spectacular grand earthly show, the Producer is God, and the Director is Jesus who came down on the stage to personally direct the show. Both are Co-Authors. The Prompter behind the invisible curtains is the Holy Spirit quietly whispering the script to

Timelines and History

the performers, guiding them and correcting them if they lose the plot and go astray. We also learned how everything in the universe before the creation of the earth, was originally governed perfectly under the theocratic government and its Law of Great Love. God the Father has always sat at the head of the government and, for eons to past eternity, life was absolute perfection and bliss. It was always meant to be like that.

We also described the performers in the show as being divided into two groups. There are the players who play the role they were originally designed to play, to reflect the character of Jesus even though they still have their own unique personalities. And then there are the actors who take on someone else's personality other than their own, and they act out a different character. Actors, whether they realise it or not, act the character of Satan in countless disguises.

We also looked in detail at the script of the show and how the original script, that is, God's Word, was sabotaged by the first rebel and father of lies, Satan the Sophist. He changed language by cleverly twisting words to get his own way. He wanted the Producer's seat, that is, God's throne in heaven with all its power, authority, glory, honour and worship. He also coveted the job of Jesus as Director. And he also tries to take on the role of the Prompter, that is, the Holy Spirit. The Holy Spirit is a mystery to us and Satan counterfeits this well by inventing his own mysteries through deception.

So, this twisting of words to deceive and manipulate, is called sophistry, and the word sophisticated comes from this. We saw how, through sophisticated language and mind manipulation, Satan originally won over a third of the angels in Heaven and became the Chief General of an army of demons. No-one actually died, so they are all fit and well and fighting furiously today. The Director-Jesus became the Chief Commander of his army of holy angels and thus, began the Great War of Words between two cosmic supernatural forces. For over 6000 years, two-thirds of the angels have been warring against one-third of the fallen angels. The Victor is obvious already. Satan has no hope and he knows it. After the Great War started in Heaven, it then flowed over onto the planet earth and is still raging today as both army leaders fight to win over human minds and souls.

The Greatest War Ever

In Part One, we zoomed in on the stage platforms of Greece and Rome and saw how the culture of their ancient empires left a humanist legacy flooding into our western civilisation today and indeed over all the world. We saw how sophistry runs all through human governments like democracy and also through such systems as education, law and medicine.

So, that is a brief review of Part One, Scene One. Now, in Part Two, we continue with Scenes Two, Three and Four. We will look at the timeline of the show to get an overview of the earth's history and find out what the true meaning of history is because it's not taught today according to God's version. This grand spectacular show on earth is like the greatest 'Whodunnit mystery' ever. We already know that Satan is the one 'whodunnit.' He is the one who committed the very first crime in the whole of God's vast kingdom called Universe, by breaking the Royal Rules in Heaven before the earth was even created. And this is the true original sin before humans even came on the stage.

This Great War is all about murder because it is the deliberate, plotted killing of human beings, of God the Father's beloved, precious human children. Mass murder of mankind has been going for millenniums in many different ways. Sophistry is the umbrella covering this whole series of talks because life and everything in it, involves words and language. Take away words and nothing exists. God's Word would not be found in His letters of Great Love and hope and encouragement for us in the Bible. Take away such words as God, Jesus, Holy Spirit, heaven, salvation - and the whole rescue plan and hope of eternal life are destroyed. This is Satan's goal—to destroy any beliefs in absolute truth.

So, again, I encourage you to hear the first talk if you have not done so and discover the power of sophistry and how it is rife and rampant everywhere today. The COVID propaganda machine is thriving on it.

I must apologise now to you because I have misled you in Part One that I would be talking about Nimrod and Simon Magus in Part Two. I had every intention of speaking about them, but one thing led to another, time ran out and there has been information overload. So I have decided definitely to include them in Part Three. My sincere apologises for this. I have all the information for this series but it seems to be a growing

Timelines and History

organism and I have to tame it and stop it running wild.

So now, let's open the curtains again of the greatest show ever on earth and watch the next three scenes. The 6000-year timeline of the story will unfold before our very eyes. We will get an overview as it looks from the outside. Remember the earth is a theatre which is being gazed upon with great interest from the outside audience of angels and inhabitants from other worlds. In our minds, for just a few precious minutes, we now leave the earthly battlefield and phase off the planet. We are now sitting in our audience's seat in outer space watching the Big Picture of the storyline.

Scene 2. Timelines

The 6000-year timeline shows us what has already happened in the past. So, so much has happened that it is impossible for us to know it all. What is most important is that God, the Author <u>does</u> know and we are to simply trust Him for the rest of the story.

I just want to present a very basic timeline which I always keep in the back of my mind. It's like an old-fashioned clothesline with a wire strung across the top with five posts holding it up. Picture this clothesline in your mind. Likewise, the earth's timeline is an invisible line with five invisible key posts holding it up. You can close your eyes for a few minutes and picture in your mind what I describe. Alternatively, and even better, you can draw the picture on a piece of paper with a pencil. If you want to do it that way, quickly grab a large piece of paper, pencil and rubber. I'll give you a few seconds to do that.

The timeline is very simple, basic and essential to following the plot. We could rely on other timelines already made, but as a teacher, I know there is nothing like doing something for yourself to learn and understand and remember.

So—here is the picture to draw. There are four tall vertical posts with a large gap in between of roughly equal length, maybe two–four inches. Imagine these posts as numbers from left to right 1 2 3 4. Then draw a fifth vertical line after the fourth, half the distance of the other gaps. Next, draw a straight horizontal line across the top from posts 1-5 like a wire clothesline pulled tight.

Each large gap represents 2000 years and the last gap is 1000 years. Creation is on the far left side at post no. 1 and today is on the right at post 4. So you can write in the words Creation and Today. The last gap is the future, the millennium to come. Above the second post, write the number 2000BC. Underneath that number, write 2000AM. We know that BC stands for Before Christ. The letters AM are used for years starting from Creation because they stand for Anno Mundi which means years after Creation. This post has an easy number to remember because 2000BC and 2000AM are the same. It's the only post where the two numbers match up–2000 years before Christ equals 2000 years after Creation. Then after Christ we use the letters AD which mean Anno Domini or 'the year of the Lord.'

I want you to remember the letters AM, BC and AD because soon we will see how Satan, the super sophist, tries to change them to get his own way and alter the history timeline and cause great confusion.

Next, on our timeline, we travel across another 2000 years and get to the third post. Above that post, write the number 4000AM ie 4000 years after Creation. Above that number draw a picture of the Cross. This is where BC starts.

The next 2000 year gap uses the letters AD. So above the fourth post write the numbers 2000AD and 6000AM below it. We are now in year 2022 just to the right of the fourth post so you can draw a little stick figure of yourself.

So, now we see three gaps of 2000 years ie six millenniums plus a shorter gap of one millennium. You can now draw a short line halfway between the posts to mark the thousand years. And this is the whole storyline of this spectacular show. When the drama ends, the curtains close. Show over!

Can you see how close we are? And this is all true because the Bible tells us so. Now it's time to peg up just a few major events on our clothesline. We truly believe Jesus is coming again extremely soon. So, peg up just to the right of the fourth post, next to your stick figure of

Timelines and History

you, the words, Second Coming. That is how close we are. At the fifth post, write Third Coming. The First Coming is obviously at the post with the Cross. I hope you find this to be a very easy timeline to memorise. Just for a few seconds, close your eyes and picture it in your mind. See the five posts, the 2000-year gaps and the words and numbers. I hope you can do this. Well done!

Praise God that He has revealed to us the three key events, the three Comings of Christ, so we can be absolutely sure He is in control of the storyline. It is all planned because it is written in His Word. God is still the true Producer and Author. The line of His original script still stands even though it has had a few detours. Every prophecy in the Bible will be fulfilled. Time and time again, He has forewarned us. There are only a few prophecies to go.

So—this is our basic of basic timeline and storyline of the whole amazing show. I hope you find it easy to remember. As I speak of historical events, you can peg them up on your timeline by writing them in and memorising them as you go. I love timelines and have done quite a few focusing on different periods. When I first started, I was shocked to see just how long 4000 years looks before Jesus came onto the planet-stage for the first time. We have only had 2000 more years since then. And there's just over 1000 to go. God is unbelievably long-suffering and patient with us.

Now, we will hang up a few more essential pegs on the line plus a couple which I have already talked about in Part One. There have been two major events in the storyline where God has intervened in a most spectacular and mighty way in which only He could. The first is the Flood when He rebuilt the planet-stage. So, let's put a peg up with the label, Flood. It goes just to the left of the second post. But leave a little gap for a few other words. Underneath Flood, write the name Noah because he and his family were the only humans who lived before and after the Flood.

A couple of hundred years after this global event, God intervened again by changing one language into many different languages. So, in that gap after Flood, before the second post, write First Babylonian Empire and Tower of Babel. You might have to write the words one underneath the other. The Flood and the new languages were major setbacks for Satan because he has no such creative power over nature and language. He can only change and interfere with what God has made. For a short time, he was halted in his tracks but was soon again on the hunt for human prey which was increasing rapidly in its population. He very quickly learned new sophistry tricks with all the different languages. He is extremely intelligent, crafty and sophisticated.

The third major intervention of God after the Flood was when He sent His Son-Director, Jesus, onto the stage. This was at the 4000-year post where you drew the Cross - just over 2000 years after the Flood. Again, how long-suffering and patient is our ever-loving heavenly Father! And today, another 2000 years later, it <u>must</u> be time for God to step in again. Satan and his army of demons have been trying, with the help of their human agents and actors, to destroy the planet-stage and all its human inhabitants by turning it into a battlefield with death and cataclysmic destruction all around the globe. The planet-stage has almost been destroyed by his human agents. They did his dirty works for him.

The greenies and technocrats are trying to improve the climate and use technology to try and fix things up in order to make life easier, better and healthier for humanity. But, the situation only gets more complicated and worse in every area of life—government and politics, medical and health, education systems, climate and weather, families, self-identities, mental health and whatever else you can think of. It's all coming to a climax right now.

And it's all because the majority will not accept the absolute truth of God's existence. They choose not to humble themselves or ask for outside help. God appeared to Solomon and called His children to come back to Him. He said, '*<u>If</u> My people, which are called by My name, shall humble themselves and pray and seek My face, and turn from their wicked ways, <u>then</u> will I hear from Heaven and will forgive their sin and will heal their land.*' 2 Chronicles 7:14 That's not just healing the people from poor health, but also the nature, the land and the climate! God has power to do this. But—the majority would and will not give up their pride and humble themselves.

We are living in the consequences of government under the leadership

Timelines and History

of Satan, the saboteur producer, director, author and prompter of the show. It's interesting that, all the science fiction movies and books today flooding into people's minds are preparing for an enormous event when the earth will soon be invaded and conquered by aliens. But the truth is that it was invaded 6000 years ago and is virtually already conquered. The wicked saboteur prince of this world may have a lot of control, but his days are numbered and the true Prince, the Son of God will become King of the planet.

Now, I quoted a verse from the book of Solomon, so let's peg him up on the timeline at the 1000BC mark which is 3000AM. That's halfway through the story. So, it's very easy to remember that Solomon lived exactly halfway through the whole story. Nothing has essentially changed in 3000 years. Satan and sophistry are still alive and flourishing.

We know that God's perfect number is 7. To me, and many others, it makes sense that the coming 1000 or so years after the 6000AM post would be the perfect time for the millennium prophesied in Revelation. Seven is the number for new beginnings. At the end of that seventh millennium, all will be made new again. The eighth millennium is the start of life in eternity. What a thought!

Revelation describes how, during the seventh millennium, Satan and his army are left on a desolate stage with no human prey to stalk and capture. The dead saints from all the millenniums plus the remaining living ones, have risen and been rescued by the Chief Commander our Lord Jesus, and taken to Heaven. Those humans who chose to be on Satan's side are still in the deep sleep of death and know nothing. So, during that millennium, the wicked Chief General hasn't even got them for company. These 1000 years will be absolute torture for him and his demonic army with no-humans to prey upon and tempt and destroy.

Walter Veith in his talk, 'What's Up Prof? No. 98,' presents an excellent outline of these last time events. It's well worth watching. And he describes what the saints will do in Heaven. Fascinating wonderful stuff to look forward to.

Moving right along in the Big Picture of the storyline, Jesus returns with the saints after that final millennium, to the blackened, desolate earth.

The Greatest War Ever

He brings the city of the New Jerusalem down and the final judgement takes place. He has the last Word and final say and brings the show to a close. Satan, the super-sophist, the counterfeit Producer, Director, Author and Prompter and all his demons and all the human actor-agents die and become extinct forever, never to return. Note that the Bible teaches they will not suffer forever, but only for a time in the fiery lake and then they will be permanently dead. Sin will not be able to raise its ugly, monstrous head ever, ever again.

At last, the most spectacular show on earth comes to a close. And a completely new planet is built even better than this one was. Those who overcome the battles and are victorious in the Great War of Words will have a new home and harmony with God and the rest of His kingdom of Universe forever and ever and ever. The original perfect life of bliss will resume once again after a seven-millennium interruption, just a tiny glitch in eternity. The show will end but, this time, the invisible curtains on the new planet-stage will never close. There will be no veil of mystery and secrecy of sin separating us from God. We will be totally free to live the life God intended for us in the first place.

The goodies win and the baddies lose as they should in any good story. Thus, the grand drama has a perfect ending according the original true Author. Everyone lives happily ever after, for all eternity. WOW! What a show it has been! And we are nearing the end of it. The final scene of Jesus returning the second time is just about to happen and we will be rescued. We just need to hang in there, trust and obey, listen to our Prompter Holy Spirit, and stick to the original script of God's Word.

But for the present, right now, we will have to return as players onstage playing the role we were designed for ie proving to other humans and the rest of Universe that God's theocratic government is the best and only way to govern any kingdom. By using our precious God-given gift of free will, we <u>must</u> keep choosing to stay in Christ's army every day and keep up the good fight by living according to His Royal Rules according to His theocratic government.

While on this earth, we are bound by time and cannot escape this most tragic drama. It is an enormous privilege that God gives us, to be able to 'step outside the box' as they say - to temporarily phase off the plan-

Timelines and History

et-stage like we are now, and see the overall Big Picture. We can get a bird's-eye view, or rather an angel's eye view, from before the beginning, through all the past, the present and into the future. Our most wonderful, ever-loving God gives us, and all His human children, the opportunity to get a glimpse of His vast viewpoint and compare it with man's limited perspective.

I could finish this talk series right here because we have just whizzed through the whole storyline at super-speed. But we still have much to learn and many pegs to hang up on our timeline. I hope and pray you will memorise and remember it. If you had difficulty with this exercise, I have done one on computer. (Note that the timeline is now in this book at the end of Part Two on page 48.)

As we continue through the series, we will flit back and forth through this timeline. If you want to, you can later redraw it using a ruler and measuring more accurately the posts and pegs to scale. And if you are really keen, you can use graph paper. It is so much fun and will be well worth it. You probably have other timelines of your own, but big detailed timelines can be overwhelming. There is nothing like drawing up a personal one and memorising key events.

Now we move into Scene Three.

Scene 3. History and the Storyline

Now that we have the complete timeline, we are ready to understand what history really is because Satan has interfered so much with this Biblically-based timeline. He has his own counterfeit line according to his twisted and kinked script. As always, he has used sophistry to gradually make the changes to get his own way.

What is history? The word history contains the word story within it. Therefore, history is the storyline of the grand show being played out on the planet-stage. History is basically made up of stories of the past. During my years of teaching, I taught my young students a simple little poem which defines history. It goes like this:

The Greatest War Ever

> *History is His Story with a time, people, places*
> *and events that have been in the past.*
> *God is big; man is small; God delights to hear us call.*
> *History and man may falter, but our God will never alter.*

From this little song, we can see that a story has basically four features in order for it to make sense. It has time, people, places and events. We have looked at time and drawn our own timeline and put some basic events on it. We just need to fill in some of the stories by adding a few more people ie the actors and players in the show. There will be different platforms which represent various empires and nations on the stage. So, let's quickly write on our timeline just a few well-known people. Remember, this is a basic timeline so the pegs will not be perfectly accurate.

We have already pegged up Noah under the Flood, and the platform of the First Babylon Empire just left of the second post. And then we added Solomon. Later on, not now, you can add where people like Abraham, Moses and the time of Judges fits in between 2000 and 1000BC. But I'll leave that up to you for later. I want to focus on what is relevant to this presentation.

In the last talk, we heard about the ancient Greek sophists, so now you can add the Greek Empire just to the left of the post with the Cross ie 4000AM. Later on, if you want, you can squeeze in the other key empires from the book of Daniel - Second Babylonian and Persian Empires came just before the Greek, so they will go immediately to the left of the Greek. The Roman platform or empire officially began 63 BC just to the left of that post but there may not be much room to write there. So, it can go immediately to the right of the Cross post. And that lasted right through the next 2000 years until today. It still exists.

We now have just a few key performers and platforms and events in the show. The little poem said at the start, 'History is His Story...' It all depends on how you pronounce the word and if you break it down into two words or not. What is the difference? 'History is His Story...' Who is 'His'? God of course. His true version of the timeline emphasises certain dates and people, so it will look very different to man's version as we are about to see. Man's story of the human past events is called history.

Timelines and History

I like to call it manstory because it is not God's story.

Manstory of the earth's timeline is always biased. It goes according to what humans see and understand from their tiny, ant-like perspective from ground level of the global stage. Humanist historians constantly look to other people and archaeology. They record how <u>men,</u> and women, but especially men, have influenced the course of events. They do not look up to the one true God and His Word to try and find out an outside objective viewpoint. Some historians acknowledge religion as part of cultures and may write about spiritual influences. They may go into detail about the various counterfeit gods of thousands of different kinds according to the nation.

This is <u>not</u> the story that God, the true Author, wants us to focus on. Another point is that there are so many humanist historians with so many varying and confusing ideas about what the truth is. Compare these with His Story which has only one simple view of absolute truth.

Manstory also glorifies human leaders and not God because its main people and main events are different to the ones the Bible emphasises. The Author-God sees the entire planet-stage from His Producer's seat far, far away in outer space in Heaven. He sees and knows everything– absolutely everything. 2 Chronicles 16:9 says, *'For the eyes of the Lord run to and fro throughout the <u>whole</u> earth…'* No human, despite all the technology today, can do that.

Humanist historians only see from their little corner of the planet where they live. They depend on the experiences and writings of others who have died or live elsewhere on the globe. Each writer has his or her own biased version of the past. No matter how hard they try not to, it is still biased because each writer chooses his own words when writing his books. If they are not in Christ's army with minds submitted to the Chief Commander, then who is guiding their minds?

Benjamin Franklin once said, 'Give me 26 lead soldiers and I will conquer the world.' The 26 soldiers are the 26 letters of the alphabet. How true this statement is. Benjamin Franklin was a founding father of America with a very good reputation. But there are two ways of understanding his quote.

Not everyone knows Franklin joined freemasonry in 1731. He was actually one of Satan's human agents and in this statement he was really saying that sophistry conquers the world by using letters to make words and twist ideas in order for his Chief General to get his own way and gain power. What perfect weapons words are in the hunt for souls! How mightily Satan is using them today in the propaganda machine forcing his evil schemes on human minds and brainwashing them about these deadly injections.

When I was a child, I learned a little ditty—'Sticks and stones will break your bones, but words will never hurt you.' Oh yes, they will! Solomon told us in Proverbs 18:21 *'Death and life are in the power of the tongue.'* Benjamin Franklin may have said, 'Give me 26 lead soldiers and I will conquer the world.' But the real truth is, 'Give me Jesus and His Word, and He will conquer the world.'

We know that humanist historians put man above God. Therefore, they serve Satan whether they know it or not. They actually rewrite the script of the grand show according to his sophistry genius. They don't realise they have submitted their minds to him and not to Christ. However, in contrast, Godly writers who record His Story put God above man and gain more perspective from the outside Big Picture. The whole storyline of this grand global show and Great War of Words, involves Satan's words in manstory pitted against God's Word in His Story. The writings of any historian depend on whether they are being objective or whether they are subjective. Let's look a little closer at these two words.

Subjectivity and Objectivity: I used to get these two words confused so I did an in-depth study of them and it is very revealing. This is a summary of what I learned. Subjective simply refers to the writer or one's Self being the subject looking from the inside to the outside at something. Therefore, his view is based on his personal experiences, opinions and preferences.

We know that Satan's biggest problem is Self and Pride. He always puts Self first and wants humans to put themselves foremost and above God. So, being subjective is associated with Self. When being subjective, there can often be something called 'confirmation bias.' This means that the writer chooses evidence in his research which leans towards his

Timelines and History

own personal opinion. The evidence can look very convincing, logical and persuasive.

A quick Wikipedia search for the meaning of the word, subjective, reveals some truths just how deep it goes. It says, 'subjective exists in the mind of a person and pertains to his viewpoint…. Subjectivity is subject to personal interpretation and is biased. Human philosophies are subjective because <u>they relate to something as it exists in the mind.</u>' Wikipedia said that.

Isn't this whole Great War of Words a battle for the mind to change our view away from God! Therefore, humanists must know they are being subjective because their worldview centres around themselves. It has to if they don't seek God's outside objective view.

This is why the Author-God wrote through Paul, '*Be transformed by the <u>renewing</u> of your mind.*' Romans 12:2 We are not to focus on Self and our opinion. Renewing implies an original mind was changed or brainwashed. And our minds are easily changed and brainwashed through sophistry. In 2 Corinthians 10:5 Paul also said, '*Casting down imaginations and every high thing that exalteth itself against the knowledge of God and <u>bringing into captivity every thought to the obedience of Christ</u>*.' And what is Satan doing? He exalts himself above God and the knowledge of God, and lets his imagination run wild in his own rebellious evil mind.

This Great War of Words is all happening in the mind. It starts in the heart and which army side we choose to enlist in. Then it flows into the mind and becomes thoughts and words, and these determine our actions, whether they be of God's Great Love, or the actions of Satan's Great Hate. Suffice it to say once again that, being subjective comes down to self, self, self. Remember all the 's'. **S**elf is the **S**ubject giving a perspective looking from the inside to the outside. **S**atan also starts with 's' and his problem is with **S**elf.

That is enough about being subjective. Now, what does objective mean? It is much simpler. Being objective means something is observed from the outside. Think of the letter of objective - 'o.' An **O**bject is being **O**bserved from the **O**utside. An **O**utsider is **O**bserving and giving his perspective. The Word, God has an 'o' in the middle of it and He is the **o**utside **O**ne who we can rely on and trust for accurate perspective from His side of the story. He is our 'Triple O' - our **O**utside **O**bjective **O**bserver we can call on at any time to help us understand His Story and not manstory.

Objectivity is not based on personal human opinion or preference. It is not based on feelings and experiences, but facts from observations, reports from studies and unbiased analysis. Objectivity is more general, universal because it is seen from God's perspective and is scientific. It relates to something which exists <u>outside</u> the mind in the true reality of the Big Picture as seen from God's throne in Heaven. In contrast, subjectivity relates to something existing <u>inside</u> the tiny little human mind on earth.

How do we become objective when looking at events of the past? We study the storyline from God's Word, His true original script in the Bible, and find out what is really going on behind the scenes. We <u>can</u> 'phase off the planet' just like we are right now as we sit in the audience of angels and inhabitants of other worlds. And we gaze down intensely along with them on this sad, sad story of the one and only sin-sick, black spot in the whole wide universe. We <u>can</u> be objective and not subjective. We just need to think outside the box that we are being forced into by the worldly powers that be. That box is a mental cage or snare which Satan is trying to trap us into through sophistry and propaganda. As they say, 'It's all in the mind.'

Scene 4. Chapters in the Storyline

Let's look a little closer at our timeline and see how man organises the earth's timeline subjectively compared with God's version, objectively. Satan has done enormous damage to make a simple straight storyline crooked. Stories have smaller sections called chapters which make them easier to follow and understand. So it is with this grand storyline, of His Story. We call them time periods. Let's see how Satan has changed them.

Manstory has different dates and time frames for the earth's timeline. Manstory also uses different names for time periods rather than those

Timelines and History

given in the Bible. The names in manstory start with the Ancient Times which is supposedly millions of years not thousands. Then comes the Middle Ages also called Dark Ages, Renaissance, Classical Period, Romantic Period, Late Nineteenth Century, and various names throughout the Twentieth and Twenty-first Centuries like Modernism, Post-Modernism, Post Truth. It's all very complicated and sophisticated and I am not bothering to give you the dates and details. You can find that elsewhere if you want.

I want to make a short comment to show how the ancient Greek and Roman empires left their legacy in the humanist version of manstory. The word Renaissance means rebirth and describes a rebirth of ancient Greek and Roman humanist philosophies, and styles of art, painting and architecture. It was a rebirth in the 1400-1500s. It came straight after the dark Middle Ages in which there was suppression of light and knowledge for the masses. In the 1700s, the Classical Period is also named after the ancient Classical Greek and Roman Empires because of more revival of the old styles.

Humanist historians will label their time periods based on their ancient humanist beliefs. Who knows what future writers will call this time we now live in, ie if there is enough time left for future historians! We will soon find out that God has already got a name for this current period which we live in now.

During the Renaissance and Classical Periods and other time frames, God still had His people all the way through. He sent His players onstage for such times as they were destined for. He was always in control. At the same time that humanism rose up in the Renaissance Period in the 14-1500s, the Reformation happened with Luther, and all the reformers fighting to stick to God's script. In the 1700s, the Classical Period was a time of supposed enlightenment because of the increased scientific knowledge. So, it is also called The Enlightenment. But at this time, there was also a rise in spiritual knowledge called the Great Awakening with John and Charles Wesley and others. So, all throughout the time periods, the goodies and the baddies kept battling on against each other in the Great War of Words.

Let's move on or we could get seriously side-tracked following that path. It is interesting that, for millenniums, manstory has still based the dates of its time periods according to the first coming of Christ. We have BC, Before Christ, and AD, anno domini ie in the year of our Lord. Coins are disappearing from the money system now, but every time someone has bought something with coins, they have admitted Christ's existence because the date is on the coins. Every time someone writes the date, they inadvertently admit Jesus is real! We cannot get away from that Cross post.

However, someone has woken up to that fact and has tried to get rid of the letters BC and AD. The letters have been changed to CE, Common Era and BCE, Before Common Era. Common is a very popular word today, isn't it–everything has to be done for the common good of the global population. Spiritually, we hear the word common applied in the ecumenical system which is combining all belief systems into one common purpose. They say, 'Let's stick to the points in common.' School books have been gradually changed to include these new letters.

This is an excellent example of Satan's sophistry–changing words to get what he wants–ie to get rid of Jesus. But–God still has control over time. The numbers of the years still centre around Christ and acknowledge He is real. Satan cannot fully get away with his plans to change the story timeline. But unfortunately, he can cause terrible confusion by distracting masses of minds.

It is also important to note in manstory's version of the earth's timeline, that humanist historians can only name a period of time <u>after</u> it has happened. They just invent names when they see certain characteristics which might define that period. They are always <u>behind</u> the times. But believers in God have the precious knowledge that has been foretold thousands of years ago. Believers and readers of the prophecies in God's Word are always <u>ahead</u> of the times because they learn from the original Author of the story. God has used His players such as Moses and other Old Testament prophets and writers to be His scribes to pass on His messages and warnings. Their writings include amazing true details about the future. God wants us to know what will happen so we can be prepared.

The main periods which God wants us to know were written down 2600 years ago in the writings of Daniel and also in John's book of Revelation 2000 years ago. We have been forewarned of what is happening right

Timelines and History

now. Dates of BC and AD are obviously not given in Daniel's books because Jesus had not come then, but the numbers of years are given according to certain events. Ever since Jesus' first coming, we can now calculate the dates.

So, the names of these prophecies use numbers such as 2300-year prophecy, 1260 years, 1290 years and 1335 years, and the shorter 490 years. There are also the seven churches in Revelation which represent seven time periods since Christ's First Coming. At some stage later, you might like to add these to your own timeline.

We have already put in a few key players and events that God wants us to remember. Now let's look at the very end of the timeline. We are 22 years past 2000AD/6000AM. What does God call this present time we live in? Many times, the Bible calls it, the 'End of the World.' How simple is that? All the signs Jesus foretold in Matthew 24 are falling into place. He told us, *'And if I go and prepare a place for you, I will come again and receive you unto myself that where I am, there ye may be also.'* We have had 2000 years plus warnings and hope.

Yes, the show's Director, our Chief Commander, Jesus, is coming down to the stage very, very soon, in just a few short years, to rescue His true and faithful players. These are the ones who have stuck to the original script of keeping the roles they were designed for. These are the ones who have obeyed the Royal Rules, the Ten Commandments, and kept the faith of Jesus. Daniel and John's prophecies of the kingdoms alone, are proof of God's existence and power because almost every single prophecy has come to pass. Yes, we are truly in the period the Bible calls the 'End of the World'.

And God has prepared us well for it in His Word so we can be ready. Romans 15:4 says, *'For whatsoever things were written aforetime (ie before they happened) were written for our learning, that we through patience and comfort of the scripture, might have hope.'* God wants to give us hope for a bright and better future. Psalm 119:52 says, *'I remembered Thy judgements of old, O Lord, and have comforted myself.'* God wants to comfort and reassure us that He is still in control and will have His way in the end. All good stories have goodies and baddies, and the goodies should always win to make a happy ending, and let the listener or viewer leave feeling good and happy. This grand spectacular show on earth is a good story because we can be sure it will have a positive ending. God has said so in His Word, so it <u>will</u> happen.

So—that was a super brief summary covering the earth's timeline of seven millenniums. We have looked closely at the timeline of the earth and can see that the periods in the timeline of manstory are totally different to His Story. In the next talk we will move deeper into the drama. In Scene One in the first talk, we covered the lives of the ancient Greek and Roman sophists and connected their teachings with the present day. In this talk, Scene Two was about Timelines. Scene Three was about history and His Story. Scene Four was about the chapters or time periods.

Next time in Scene Five, we will look closer at some important performers ie the players, actors. We will definitely meet two major villains in the show, Nimrod and Simon Magus. They are only two of all the 'whodunnits' in the murder mystery of mankind. We will hear about Simon Magus' background and life and his female companion. We will also learn about the foundations of the Roman Catholic Church, solve the mystery of the two Simon Peters, and discover who was the first religious leader of the Roman Catholic Church. This will prepare us for the later talk on Gnosticism which originated at the time of Simon Magus in the first century AD. It is a most fascinating story you won't want to miss.

But, right now, the invisible curtains are drawing across the planet-stage to close Scene Four of the drama. There will be a two-week intermission and the curtains will open again on February 5, 2022 at 2:30. Be sure to come back to your seat and be in the vast audience in outer space with the rest of the angels and created beings of other worlds. And be sure to bring your timeline, pencil and rubber so we can hang up some more pegs.

Thank you so much for being with me on this journey. May God keep us all strong as we go back onstage in the Great War to fight the good fight of the battle for the minds. May God keep sending His angels to protect us from the enemy's daily bombardments and temptations until our Lord comes to rescue us and take us home very, very soon.

Let's pray and thank our almighty God. Thank You God for Your Word which says, '*We can do all things through Christ who strengthens us.*'

Timelines and History

In You Lord, we <u>can</u> stay strong and be mighty warriors in Your army whether it be in big or little ways. We thank You for this time of rest in outer space and for increasing our faith. We praise Your holy name and give all glory and honour to You. Amen.'

(Note: A decision was made here by the listeners to allow the writer to go ahead and share a testimony.)

This testimony applies so much to this talk.

Testimony: I want to take a few moments to share a testimony of how I have personally been affected and led up the garden path with detours along the crooked wide way. But God led me back onto the straight and narrow way. I have always loved history but now I love His Story even more. My early information or lack of it, came from what was taught in school and university and my early teaching years. I was not a believer in those days, so the little I learned was from the humanist subjective perspective. Perhaps some of you went through a similar experience.

All I can remember from school years was snippets about the Middle Ages and the Greeks and the Romans from two years of Classical Studies in my final years at school. Overall, very little history was taught and it came under the subject called Social Studies which covered many other areas as well. I am a trained music teacher and learned a bit more about historical periods as I had studied them in order to understand different music styles and pass exams. Then I started teaching in various schools in Melbourne. At one school all I taught was music history and was frantically learning days and weeks to be ahead of the lesson and try to sound intelligent. I relied totally on history books and, of course, there was no Biblical, Godly Outside Object Observer viewpoint. There was just some general information about the styles of religious music, not any Biblical content.

When I was 30, after another long story which I won't go into now, I finally received the Lord Jesus Christ as my Saviour and this changed my life dramatically. He opened my eyes to the humanism in all I was doing and I found I could not teach that way anymore. I prayed in desperation one day and said, 'Lord, I'll give up teaching unless you show me how you want me to teach.' Well, He picked me up out of the miry clay and, over the next thirty years, He showed me and guided me gradually and gently, bit by bit.

I had a lot of unlearning to do as I grew as a Christian. Eventually, I wrote my own Biblical music curriculum for a piano course and a home-schooling general music/theory/history course. Originally, I wrote the books just for my own students to get me out of a deep, deep teaching rut. But word of mouth spread and the whole course grew and got published. The Lord blessed me enormously with students, training teachers, travelling to New Zealand, Singapore and Malaysia, giving talks. But that's another story for another day.

Despite all these most unexpected blessings, there was still a long way to go in my spiritual journey. I was a Sunday worshipper for 25 years, therefore whatever I read and learned was based on the confused Protestant writings which were influenced by the Roman Catholic and Jesuit views, which, as we have seen, came from humanist philosophies of the Ancient Greek and Roman empires. The history I included in my books covered from Creation to Twentieth Century and I was very proud of this. But of course, it centred round the manstory time periods and their names and dates. Incredibly, without realising it, I had already mentioned the four main empires, Babylonian, Persian, Greek and Roman in the first edition without even knowing Daniel's prophecies.

I can see now much more of the sophistry and cleverness and subtlety in how the Jesuits operate in the education systems at all levels to confuse millions of students and teachers. Even though I was a strong believer, I still didn't know enough truth. I could only write what I had learned from a defective education system.

One day a lady saw my books and looked at a huge timeline stretching around two walls of my music studio. She asked, 'Where are the Waldenses?' I told her that the Waldenses were followers of Peter Waldo in the 1100s. She kindly said, but in very strong terms, that I must read B J Wilkinson's book called "Truth Triumphant". Well, my books were already published and selling well and I stubbornly didn't want to know. Self and Pride stepped in. Praise God, this lovely lady, who I still keep in touch with, kept reminding and nagging me about this book.

I finally read it and was absolutely shocked. I had never heard such history before. Then another great shock hit me. My books were wrong. It

Timelines and History

took two years to do a second edition and change all the history sections. That meant changing the main text books, the student workbooks and the test books. It was massive job but afterwards, I felt so good. I had done the right thing by God.

I'll cut another long story short. Eleven years ago, my learning curve, shot up to a vertical straight line, especially in the area of His Story and prophecy. My brain felt like it would explode as truth and reality set in. God had been so patient and forgiving and merciful towards me all those decades of teaching incorrectly. Firstly, I had taught subjective, humanist manstory for ten years. Then for the next twenty-five years, I taught confused Christianese-flavoured history. Finally, I began to teach His Story. Deeper and deeper I can see the sophistry in all those years of learning and teaching. All glory to God for bringing me through!

And that's my testimony. Thank you.

The Greatest War Ever

Basic Timeline of Earth's 6000 Year History

AM: Anno Mundi, years since Creation
BC: Before Christ
AD: Anno Domini, in the year of our Lord

Please note that this is only a very basic timeline.

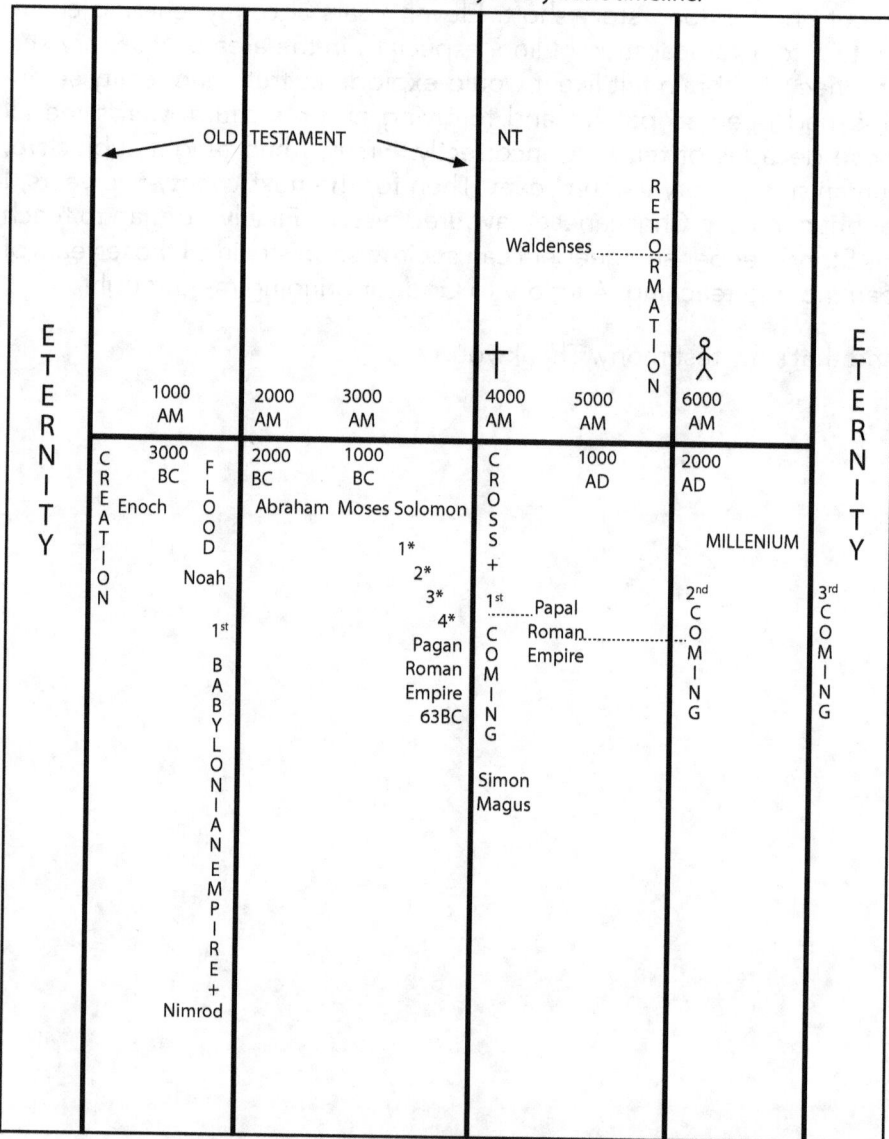

1.* 2nd Babylon Empire 605-538BC   2.* Persia-Mede Empire 538-331BC
3* Greek Empire 331-63BC   4.* Roman Pagan Empire 63BC-476AD

Part 3 – Act 3: The Performers

Welcome back to our series of talks called The Greatest War Ever. It is a war of words and the battle for the minds. So far, we have had the enormous privilege of being able to zoom off the planet to take a seat in the vast audience of angels and other created beings in God's kingdom called Universe. Before the curtains open on the next scene, lets pray.

Our dear Father in Heaven, we thank You for anther opportunity to come together and learn a little more about Your side of the world's timeline. Please let my words be Your words to encourage the listeners and bring us all peace and calm and objectivity to be able to look way beyond what is happening on the earthly battlefield. We pray this in the name of Your Son, our Chief Commander, Jesus Christ. Amen.

Introduction and Review

We have had the privilege to sit in outer space and get a few glimpses of pieces of the Big Picture, of the global theatre and the greatest show ever on earth. We have been able to see a little of what God, our Outside Objective Observer, our Triple 0, is seeing on the planet-stage in the global battlefield of the Great War of Words which began when Satan rebelled in Heaven. Satan then came to earth with his army of one-third of the angels and the War has never stopped.

Every theatre show has essential features and we know the true Producer of this show is God, the Creator and Father. His Co-Author and Director is His Son Jesus, and the Prompter is the Holy Spirit quietly speaking in the hearts of the performers to keep them to the original script. We saw in an earlier talk how there are two types of performers. Actors take on someone else's personality and act out their character, which is ultimately Satan's character in an infinite number of disguises. This wicked, saboteur, counterfeit producer, counterfeit director and counterfeit prompter hides behind the scenes getting his human agents to do his dirty work in a mass murder of mankind spreading out over millenniums.

The other type of performer is the players who play the role they were designed for ie to reflect the character of Jesus and prove to the rest of Universe that God's government of theocracy and the gift of free will is the best and only way to govern any kingdom.

Back in Heaven, God could have easily destroyed Satan and the demons in one swift blow. But He chose not to because that would have created fear in all his other beloved beings. His heart of Great Love could not bear for them to experience this most dreadful feeling. He put Himself on trial so all those in His kingdom of Universe could decide if His method of theocratic government under the Law of Great Love and its gift of free will, was best or not.

We also learned that the original script for the show is God's Word, the Bible, but the saboteur script-writer Satan interfered with his own counterfeit, sophisticated, deceptive language called sophistry—the twisting of words to get his own way. And he also uses techniques of persuasion called rhetoric. In Scene One, we set the stage and looked at two platforms, the ancient empires of Greece and Rome in particular, where the ancient sophists laid the foundations for western civilisation today. Of course, Satan was the first sophist in Heaven before the earth was made, because he manipulated the minds of the angels. In Part Two, Scenes Two, Three and Four, we looked in depth at the timeline of the story.

I hope you have your timelines with you today so you can follow along and peg up some more characters and events. Maybe you have memorised it. That would be marvellous.

In Part Two, we also saw how Satan has tried to interfere and change His Story ie God's Story. His Story became history or rather, manstory. We learned a little poem:

> History is His Story with a time, people, places
> and events that have been in the past.
> God is big; man is small; God delights to hear us call.
> History and man may falter, but our God will never alter.

We have also learned how Satan has changed the letters AD (Anno

The Performers

Domini, the year of the Lord) to CE (Common Era). And he has changed BC (Before Christ) to BCE (Before Common Era). And through his human agents, ie humanist historians, he also changed the names of the time periods in God's storyline. In the Bible, they are dates of prophecies and the names of the seven churches. But today the time periods are given totally different names such as Ancient Times, Middle Ages, Renaissance, Baroque, Classical, Romantic, Modernism etc. These are based on human subjectiveness ie seeing from the limited and biased perspective from Self inside the mind, and looking outwards.

In contrast, God is the Outside Objective Observer, The Triple 0, and has a realistic view of what is going on. After all, He is sitting on His Producer's seat, His throne in Heaven. He sees the whole Universe while humans are only on ground level on just one tiny planet. The rest of the inhabitants in other worlds on other planets in other galaxies, all live in perfect harmony and bliss according to the theocratic Law of Great Love. But humans are being bombarded with enemy attacks left right and centre, to confuse the minds with many different philosophies of life. And they all centre around man.

In Part Two we looked closely at the meaning of subjectivity and objectivity and compared the two different ways of organising the chapters or time periods in the grand story.

Now in Scene Five, we will focus on certain players and actors before the Flood. In Scene Six we will focus on Nimrod and his wife Semiramus and her son Tammuz. In Scene Seven we will finally be introduced to Simon Magus, the one we have been waiting for. Don't get too comfortable in your celestial seats. It won't be long and you will be sitting on the edges. The plot of the drama gets thicker and darker as the tension and suspense rise. So—let's jump right in.

Scene 5. Players and Actors Before the Flood

Adam, Eve and Cain: The curtains open once again onto the platform of the original one great continent of the earth. Now we are at the far left of our timeline, right back at the very beginning when the first two players, Adam and Eve, were cast onto the planet-stage. The Great War of Words begun by Satan, flowed down from Heaven onto the newly-created Earth. As a result, sin and death entered the planet, not just in humans, but anything with life such as animals and plants. After Adam and Eve gave in to the enemy's temptation and ate from the forbidden tree, they did not die immediately. God mercifully kept His promise that they would multiply and spread out into the world. He always keeps His promises. Descendants soon came, and the Great War of Words quickly spread along with sin into the hearts, minds and bodies of their children.

Cain became Satan's agent and committed the first murder by killing his brother, Abel. Cain's rebellious heart held ideas and beliefs based on Self and Pride, and put himself above God. These beliefs spread into his mind and turned into thoughts of hate towards his brother. They became argumentative words which led to the act of killing. The very first death occurred on the planet and, indeed, in the whole vast kingdom of Universe.

Through the deathly power of words, Satan had already quickly sabotaged the script of the show and changed the original storyline very dramatically. Cain was banished from Adam and Eve's family, and thus began a dynasty of actors acting out the character of Satan. This included Lamech, the first known polygamist. Adam and Eve had another son called Seth who founded his own dynasty of players which led to such mighty warriors of the Lord as Enoch, Abraham, Isaac and Jacob, the twelve tribes etc right down to Jesus' mother, Mary.

Of course, before the Flood, it wasn't simple black and white with two distinct groups of performers, because some of those in Seth's downline changed from players to actors, and some of those in Cain's downline switched from actors to players. And it all became quite messy and complicated—just like today. Human soldiers in the Great War always have the gift of free will to change army sides from the evil Chief General to the loving Chief Commander, and vice-versa.

So, over all the generations from Adam and Eve, the pattern was firmly set in how beliefs and words determine behaviour. Belief of the one true God in the heart/spirit, or no belief in the one true God, affects the mind, thoughts and words. These in turn affect the body's actions and behaviour, either for good or for evil.

The Performers

Ever since the beginning of the show, the wicked super-sophist has used his demons and human agents to carry out his wicked plans of destruction, murder and death. It is amazing how powerful words are - for good or for bad. Through mere words, Satan has caused six millenniums of the most devastating destruction and countless human deaths possible. The deaths within the last hundred years caused by Hitler, Stalin, Pol Pot and others are mere drops in an ocean of blood. They are mere details in the Big Picture of the Great War. But praise God, that His Word is far more powerful than Satan's, and His Word will come to pass and have final victory.

Words, words everywhere; God's Word will win the War! Let's not get side-tracked and get back to the pre-Flood era.

Enoch and Noah: For over sixteen centuries since the global stage was built, things got worse and worse on the stage battlefield. The Great War flared up in spot battles around the continent. Way back then, there was a famous player and mighty warrior for the Lord called Enoch. He only lived 365 years, a short time compared with others in those days. His mission was to warn everyone about the Flood and also about a time of God's Judgement in the future. God used him as a special messenger to prophecy the Second Coming of Christ which would not happen to nearly 4500 years later.

The tiny book of Jude tells us in verses 14-15 that, *'And Enoch also, the seventh from Adam, prophesied of these saying, "Behold the Lord cometh with 10,000 (ie myriads) saints to execute judgement upon all and to convince all that are <u>ungodly</u> among them, of their <u>ungodly</u> deeds which they have <u>ungodly</u> committed, and of all their hard speeches which <u>ungodly</u> sinners have spoken against Him."* Four times, the word ungodly is used here. If there were a lot of ungodly people before the Flood, there must be many, many more now.

So, you now can write Enoch halfway between the first two posts on your timeline.

After the death of Enoch's son, Methuselah, the Producer-God stepped in and intervened because the drama was becoming too wild and twisted, and the script had to be brought back into the straight and narrow line. Noah was another key player in the show. Time and time again for 120 years, he gave warnings of the imminent flood, a great water cleansing of the planet-stage. And it's very interesting that, just over 120 years ago from today, another important messenger-player was sent onstage to give warning after warning to us about terrible times of trouble to come, and the imminent arrival of Jesus.

The Flood is the first example of such miraculous, divine intervention on the planet-stage. God spoke out His all-powerful Word to change the course of nature causing the Great Flood to put an end to the devastation of humans. Only eight people were saved, even though there could have been many more, _if_ had they chosen to. There _was_ room in the ark. Everyone had the gift of free will, so the choice was theirs. Tragically, many millions perished because of unwise decisions to serve in Satan's army.

Even then, God still showed mercy on His wayward precious children —they all died within a week. It was very quick. There was no long suffering and they went straight into the deep sleep of death knowing nothing and in no pain. They are still there as if in a deep, deep coma, just like the faithful loyal ones before the flood occurred. All except one —Enoch never died but was translated and taken straight to heaven. It is fascinating to think that, as we sit among the audience, Enoch is somewhere here with us!

For the eight saved living humans who were left behind, rescued and safe in the ark, there was still great hope in the new world. The Flood was a massive setback for Satan and his army of demons. It proved just how little power he had over nature and the planet. And it proved Who the real Creator was.

So, that was a short scene on the great continental platform lost during the Flood. We now move along the timeline to just a couple of hundred years after the Flood. The next platform is the newly created earthly stage. Once again, it was one massive continent.

Scene 6. Nimrod, Semiramus and Tammuz

First Babylonian Empire and Nimrod: We are now in the First Babylonian Empire. On your timeline this is already pegged up between the Flood and the 2000AM/2000BC post. You can write in Nimrod's name under 1st Babylonian Empire.

The Bible describes Satan as a roaring lion. Very soon the revengeful lion was on the hunt again for more human prey. As the population increased, he was able to cleverly tempt with his sophistry and rhetoric, many more, fresh, new and naïve humans into his own army. One of his greatest human agents who has gone down in record books was Nimrod, the great grandson of Noah through Ham, then Cush. Nimrod was the founder and ruler of the first Babylonian Empire. His kingdom included the vast area around, and in between the Tigris and Euphrates Rivers, from the Persian Gulf up to Turkey. This was called Babylonia, Mesopotamia and Assyria. It includes the land we know today as Iraq.

Like Satan, Nimrod was a mighty hunter. In his early years he was famous for hunting animals. Statues and pictures of him which exist today, often show him holding an animal. Before long, however, he was hunting human souls in order to expand his empire and gain power and control over people, to make them his slaves. Like his wicked Chief General, Nimrod wanted a One World Order with himself at the head of government. Of course, Satan was the higher invisible, supernatural authority above him.

It is fascinating that Nimrod had a secret headquarters in a place called Sturnia named after the planet Saturn. We will come back to Sturnia very soon. But first, just a quick tiny side-issue which links this with today and is an example of Satan's sophistry:

Just over 2000 years after Nimrod, the ancient Romans named the seventh day of the week Saturday after the planet Saturn, the Roman god of wealth. Therefore, people today unknowingly still acknowledge the worship of the planet Saturn every time we call the seventh day of the week Saturday. It's like unknowingly worshiping the sun by going to church on Sunday, the first day of the week, named after the sun-god, Nimrod.

Such is the enormous influence of the ancient Roman Empire on today's western civilisation. And beliefs and culture of this civilisation originated further, way back in the First Babylonian Empire.

Back to the actor-Nimrod. He was the instigator of the rebellion in defiance of God by having the Tower of Babel built. The Bible says in Genesis 11:4 *'Go to, and let us build a city and a tower whose top may reach unto heaven; and let us make a name, lest we be scattered abroad the face of the earth.'*

Cities were never ever in God's plans for man. His instructions to Adam and Eve were for their descendants to spread abroad all around the earth, in all the countryside. When people live together in cities, they are easier to control, like cattle being herded into paddocks. Cities originated with Cain.

When Cain was banished from Adam and Eve's family, he was driven by fear that someone from his old family might hunt and kill him. He was the very first one to start building cities. They were fortresses with strong walls were built for protection against unseen enemies. Fenced in cities also allowed more control over humans to make them dependant on Cain's leadership.

It's interesting to see that fear and the control of humans was a driving force way back then, and today, nothing has changed as we can see in this Covid crisis. This all has to originate in Satan who continues right now using fear of an invisible enemy, a so-called virus pandemic, to coerce masses into becoming dependant on the medical system and pharmaceutical companies and the powers that be above them. Our cities may not be fortressed, but masses of people are dependent on the workplace and services provided in them. They willingly want to live in them. And it's all done through sophistry with its propaganda using words and rhetoric.

Suffice it to say that, fear, force and control were, and always have been, Satan's methods to get his own way. He's just a big invisible bully. We could get very side-tracked here, but we must return to Nimrod and his fortressed city of Babylon.

The Performers

The Tower of Babel stretched far into the sky with large rooms at the bottom for priests to live in and chambers at the top for Nimrod and his wife. From these great heights, the king and queen would be able to gaze over their kingdom, offer human sacrifices and carry out disgusting, most wicked practices. The tower was supposed to reach up to the clouds and be a refuge if ever there was a flood like the last one. Obviously, Nimrod did not trust God's promise never to flood the earth again.

The scripture says Nimrod wanted to *'make a name'* ie build a reputation for himself, be famous and have all the glory, honour and worship. Like his invisible Chief General, he wanted to be the Most High. Nimrod certainly did that, because in pagan cultures to follow, he was deified as god of the sun and father of creation, a counterfeit one true God. But, for those who know the truth, Nimrod left a very bad name and bad reputation. He may be remembered for his power and founding the first empire after the Flood, but he receives no glory, honour and worship from true believers.

Nimrod was known in many cultures with many different names such as Marduk, the king of all gods in Babylonia; in Assyria he was called Nirmada, in Sumer he was known as Amarutu. The Canaanites named him Baal, and the Romans called him Bacchus. A mountain near Mt Ararat was named Mt Nimrod. The Caspian Sea was once called Mar de Bachu or Sea of Bacchus. A chief city in Assyria was called Nimrud.

Nimrod was very much into astrology and we have seen how he worshipped Saturn. In the place called Sturnia, he communicated with Satan and his demons and received instructions for his growing empire. Where was Sturnia? It just happened to be near seven mountains in the boot-shaped land jutting out into the Mediterranean Sea which was later called Latium or Italia. Today we know it as Italy. That is a fascinating study we don't have time for right now, but you can read more in Alexander Hislop's book, "The Two Babylons."

Suffice it to say that the wicked invisible Chief General has always had his hidden headquarters in that country. Today, he still rules the whole planet from his throne there in a tiny country of the Papal States in the middle of Italy. The Bible calls him the 'prince of this world,' note–he's

The Greatest War Ever

not the 'king of the world', just the prince. Satan assumes to be the king and may have a lot of power and authority, but the true King is coming very soon to claim back His territory and his loyal, faithful, obedient servants.

The original goal of Nimrod, was a one world government. This was the same goal as Satan, and has never ever changed in the past 4000 years. Today it is called the New World Order, and the Great Reset is working right now to bring this about in world governments, politics, the economy, financial, medical and education systems and every area of our lives. A global pandemic in the form of a COVID virus is a very efficient means using the medical system to put this plan into action. It all comes under the cover of health, because health is vital for everyone to stay alive. The injections, supposedly to protect our bodies, are a mere subtle means to collect personal information, to get vaccination passports so humans can be traced, contacted and kept under strict control in a social system of slavery.

Another rising issue is the Climate Change crisis because weather, air, water, and soil are also crucial for human survival. Human powers have learned how to manipulate the climate and weather in order to control people. They can cause cyclones, earthquakes and natural disasters wherever they want. Google HAARP and you will find out a lot more. (High Frequency Active Auroral Research Program)

All starts with words in the mind, ie sophistry according to the Law of Great Hate enforced by the most evil, wicked head of government possible in the on-going Great War of Words. The most wonderful news we have from the gospel, is that the War will be over very, very soon. We are at the end of it and just have to hang in a little longer.

Satan keeps working today through his many human agents to manipulate minds and gain control. I know we have been jumping backwards and forwards through the timeline, but we must realise there is nothing new under the sun. Everything in the past affects our lives today. And it's all according to God's natural law of cause and effect. Consequences after consequences are occurring right now because of major events which happened centuries and millenniums ago with Adam, Eve, Cain, and Nimrod. Now we meet two more crucial actors in the show.

The Performers

Semiramus and Tammuz: Back to the First Babylonian Empire just after the Flood. Satan used two other characters besides Nimrod to be his best actors and villains at that time in the show. These were Nimrod's wife, Semiramus and her son Tammuz. There is much mythology about these actors. Satan loves this deception because it adds mystery and fascination, and tempts the inquisitive ones.

Some say Semiramus was Nimrod's mother. Others say she was a prostitute and owner of a brothel. Maybe she was both. It doesn't matter because the stories all serve their purpose to distract from the truth of God's existence. What is important however, is that after her death, statues and pictures of mother and child became objects of worship. These continued through millenniums and exist today all through the Roman Catholic Church. They are the origins of mother-child worship, Madonna and Child. After Jesus came, these became Mary and Child. Thus originated Mariology, the worship of Mary, and also the idea of God having a mother.

All are absolute, downright lies. Nimrod, Semiramus, Tammuz and Mary are all in the deep sleep of death knowing absolutely nothing and should never be idolised and worshipped or communicated with. It breaks the First and Second Commandments.

Another lie and myth is that, when Nimrod died, he went to live in the sun, but supernaturally came back and fathered Tammuz. Semiramus was a licentious, immoral woman, and anyone could have been the father. She established a complicated system of priesthood, so we will never find out who the father really was.

Tammuz died at a young age, supposedly killed by a boar. He is remembered because of his birthday on the 25th December which is the basis for the pagan tradition of Christmas today. It has become a global glittering celebration of a birthday without the Birthday Boy. But the Bible does not tell us to remember Jesus' birthday. What is significant, is His death because He was the ultimate sacrifice for our sins.

Semiramus also established forty days of mourning for her dead son and this practice has continued today in the form of giving up something for forty days of Lent before Easter eg sweets or smoking or whatever. The pagan celebration of Easter is a counterfeit of the original Passover, and began with Semiramus. Easter got its name from one of Semiramus' many titles–Ishtar. People today don't realise where Christmas and Easter truly originated.

Tammuz later became known as Mithra and this led to Mithraism, a counterfeit Christianity where he became the Saviour, a false Messiah. He and his mother are still worshipped today as Madonna and child, or Mary, Mother of God and her son Jesus. Christmas was originally a Mithraic festival worshipping the sun to celebrate winter solstice in the northern hemisphere, ie summertime down here in Australia. The beginning of longer days symbolised the so-called triumph of the sun-god Nimrod over his enemies. According to the pagan religion, Tammuz, the son of the sun-god Nimrod, was supposed to have risen and come back to life each year on December 25 when the sun was at its lowest in the sky. This is the basis of Christmas Day. Countless Christmas carols reinforce many lies.

Bible facts show that Christ's birth was more likely to be in October. But it doesn't matter when He was born at all. That is not important for our salvation. His death is crucial for the saving of our souls.

You may have read versions of these pagan stories which differ to mine. But it doesn't matter what is true or not because they are all lies mixed up with a little truth designed to cause confusion and distraction. So, we won't delve deeper into other differences. Many masses of people believe these lies and just go with the flow and the fun, and entertaining traditions.

The Roman Catholic Church has made sure that the Easter celebration always falls on the first full moon after the equinox (today's 21st March). In the northern hemisphere, the first Sunday after that is the first day of Spring. Hence, all the symbols of new life are represented in Easter eggs and little bunny rabbits representing the queen of fertility and maternity, Semiramus, who is dead and lifeless. So many Christians today believe these symbols are to do with Jesus' rising from the grave with new life, but it's all another counterfeit, a sophisticated twisting of words. And the tempting, addictive taste of chocolate also helps to distract from the truth. The Easter or Ishtar tradition still continues today

The Performers

with Hot Cross Buns. These stem from the ancient practice of offering round cakes with an X on them to the Queen of Heaven, Semiramus. Hot Cross Buns have been so commercialised now and they appear in the shops as early as January rather than at Easter time in April. It all comes down to making money.

Note that the Biblical Passover was always held on the fourteenth day of Nisan ie our April. To the Jews, it didn't matter whether it was a Friday, Monday, Wednesday or whatever day of the week. They did not have such pagan Roman names. They just used numbers–first day, second day or third day etc. But the Easter or Ishtar tradition was developed centuries ago by the Roman Catholic Church, so that the celebration would always fall on a weekend - Friday to Sunday. And if the true Passover ever fell on a Friday, they would change it to another weekend. How wickedly devious that is!

Semiramus was extremely powerful in the military and this can be seen in unexpected ways today. Her army of priests always surrounded her and she had fortresses built around the city of Babylon for protection. These fortresses had turrets around the top for guards to stand between and keep watch. They could quickly duck behind the jutting wall if an arrow came towards them, and then step out again to fight back.

The turret-shape became the pattern for the queen's crown she wore on her head. And the legacy of crowns lives on as we see queens, princesses, kings and princes today wearing stunning, gem-studded tiaras and crowns for formal occasions. These crowns only serve to assert their authority and power. Their expensive costumes boast of their wealth and glamour. If a picture of someone from the royal family is placed on the front page of a magazine, people will flock to buy it. The fascination and mystery of royalty lives on. The crown goes right back to the turrets on the fortresses and are only symbols of Semiramus, the ancient pagan goddess. Every queen we see today is a type of Semiramus to be looked up to, respected and admired, even adored. Queen Elizabeth II is a perfect example.

Semiramus was known as the queen of a thousand names. These included Ashtoreth, Astarte in Israel, Ishtar in Sumaria, Isis in Egypt, Artimus or Diana in Ionia, Demeter or Aphrodite in Greece, and Venus in Rome.

Each nation and culture around the world has their own version in statues of her with a child. There are also symbols of fertility such as having many breasts with the milk of life, and she holds baskets of fruit or grain.

When Semiramus died, she supposedly went to live on the moon near her husband in the sun. So, she became known as Queen of the Moon as well as Queen of Heaven and is often represented standing on the crescent moon with twelve stars surrounding her head. Note that the twelve stars can be seen in many places today eg the European blue flag has twelve stars in a circle shape of the moon. The ancient Romans named the second day of the week after her–Moonday or Monday - because she supposedly lived in the moon. The first day was called Sunday after Nimrod who was supposed to be in the sun. Sun and moon worship began with these two actors and satanic agents. They are acknowledged unknowingly every day as we use those names in our language.

The halo circle of the sun is seen in many artworks and sculptures around the heads of Mary, saints, and pictures of Christ. This originates from sun-worship of Nimrod and moon-worship. Semiramus was remembered as the Queen of Heaven and lives on in countless statues, idols and mythology. She was the model for every goddess and female cult of ancient and modern worlds. She is the basis for mother-child worship in the Roman Catholic Church, and the idea of the mother being the go-between, a mediator, interceding for the people to the father-god, Nimrod. She is still represented today in countless statues in and on top of cathedrals.

In Mozart's opera, The Magic Flute, she is called the Queen of Heaven. This opera is full of freemasonry symbols because Mozart was a freemason. In another opera called Aida by Giuseppe Verdi, Semiramus is worshipped under the name, Isis. That show is full of ancient Egyptian idolatry, beliefs and rituals. Today, audiences love these operas not knowing who and what they are accepting. Opera is merely words set to music and acting. Music is a most powerful means of manipulating minds. And combining music, words and body language in the form of entertainment, Satan gains even more power and control. But–we won't go down that path because it far too long and complicated for now.

Semiramus was also the one who established the hierarchy of priests

The Performers

and priestesses giving false teachings to direct worship to Satan. She also started the disgusting and immoral paedophilia behaviours all through the story timeline right up to the churches today, to the Roman Catholic Church and other denominations, to Satanic churches and cults. The sacrifices of babies, children and young virgin women is still rampant through freemasonry.

Right now, you can google and find teenagers and women giving their testimonies of the horror and torture they have experienced with those in high authorities of royalty and government, and the wealthy ones living in palaces and mansions. I googled a couple and they were horrendous. Tens and tens of thousands of young ones go missing every day around the world and no-one knows where they are. They are either dead or suffering most terribly. All because of Semiramus. Yes, she was a most foul, evil woman and one of Satan's best ever human agents.

This horror is part of the terrible legacy left by this trio of Nimrod, Semiramus and Tammuz. It's too horrible to dwell on.

Terrible Trio's Legacy: There is less known about Tammuz because he died at a young age. However, he, his mother and Nimrod left a most awful legacy for us today. I call them the Terrible Trio. The most spectacular show on earth is truly a most fascinating and amazing drama. The plot just gets thicker and thicker, darker and darker as the storyline unfolds. These three names have changed thousands of times throughout the millenniums. But their Satan-like characters they once acted out, have lived on in countless other human agents, and are in full force, hidden in plain sight this very day.

Sadly, as time went on after the Second Babylonian Empire, some of these actor-agents included nearly every king of Israel and Judah in the Old Testament, plus a few queens. These rulers were from God's chosen people who were supposed to be the example of His theocratic government based on the Law of Great Love. Other nations were supposed to see the blessings and want to copy and be part of a worldwide, kind, loving theocracy with God at the head, the way it was always meant to be. But super-sophist Satan, the Triple S, continued to abuse God's created language through spoken words, through the language of music, body language and techniques of persuasion.

The Greatest War Ever

The enemy also changed language in other secretive ways. He loves numbers, codes and various shapes and symbols, eg triangles, pentagons, circles within circles, all-seeing eyes, obelisks etc. He has always used magic or sorcery, mysticism and astrology, communicating with demons and believing they are dead ones come to life. In reality, they are as dead as a door-knob and cannot know or speak anything. Demons impersonate them. Just as God's holy angels can transform into helpful humans, demons can also take on human form.

All these things took off from the First Babylonian Empire of Nimrod and continue today in countless ways. The majority of people are blinded and fooled, unaware of what is happening and the traps they have fallen into. And they wonder what is wrong with the world now.

Today, Satan's abuse of <u>all</u> types of languages still exist and are hidden in full sight for everyone to see. If we open our eyes, we will recognise them everywhere in advertising, pictures of popular musicians covering one eye, or putting a finger to their mouths as if to say, 'Sh, don't tell anyone. This is a secret.' We see the secret language in hand gestures of leaders as they tuck one hand under their coat near their heart promising to keep some great secret. Freemasons love to boast silently and publicly of the secret club they belong to as they communicate with each other without words. Through silent symbolism, they can recognise who is in their club or secret society. Hundreds of signs and symbols are found in statues, obelisks, ornaments, jewellery, fashions everywhere. They are so common, once again hidden in plain sight, that the majority doesn't even notice them.

The legacy of the Terrible Trio has never ended. The great fortressed city of Babylon may be physically gone, but it never went away spiritually. Its satanic foundation based on fear, force and deception lives on. Fear, force and deception lead to suffering, and this is what is ruling so many countries today.

But all is not lost. Let's gain some hope now from a mighty warrior and player on the stage-battlefield called John. John wrote the most encouraging words in his Book of Revelation and gives to us the Three Angel's Message.

The Performers

John's Book Of Revelation And The Three Angel's Message: John was inspired to write the Book of Revelation with all its warnings. Interestingly, that was written just over 2000 years after the fall of the Tower of Babel. It is also 2000 years since our time. God is warning us in this book so we can be prepared in advance of these end times which are right upon us. How good is our ever-loving Father-God to encourage us and give the great hope of a happy ending to this long, painful, drawn-out saga.

John wrote in the second angel's message in Revelation 14:8, '*Babylon is fallen, is fallen,* (notice that he repeats and emphasises this fact that Babylon is defeated), *that great city because she made all nations drink of the wine of the wrath of her fornication.*' John is saying that the legacy of Babylon is about to be destroyed, because out of it came lies and false teachings from her spiritual adultery.

John repeats similar words with a strong powerful voice of the fourth angel's Message in Revelation 18:2 '*Babylon the great is fallen, is fallen and is become an habitation of the devils, and the hold of every foul spirit, and a cage of every unclean and hateful bird.*' These awful birds are the demons, the deceptive false Holy Spirits working in mysterious ways to trap human prey into their snares or cages.

He goes on to say, '*For all nations have drunk of the wine of her fornication, and the kings of the earth have committed fornication with her, and the merchants of the earth are waxed rich through the abundance of her delicacies.*' There is so much to learn from these verses. Let's just glean a little from them.

Who are the kings, the great men on the earth? They are a large group of the mega-super rich we call 'The Elite.' There are world leaders of governments, kings, queens, princes, presidents, prime ministers, sheiks, sultans, emperors, Imams, chiefs and whatever name they are given. In the Bible, they are all simply lumped together as kings, ie counterfeit kings of the One True King of the earth, Jesus Christ. God, the head of His theocracy, never ever intended humans to have their own kings under whatever name.

We know that Satan is called the 'prince of this world.' He has his throne at the invisible peak of a tyrannical, pyramid-shaped government. His army of demons operates all around the globe he rules over. We have learned that his throne is in ancient Sturnia, now known as the Papal States in Italy. From here, the papacy is the highest, visible, earthly, human level. There are four popes ie *'kings of the earth.'* They are called grey, black, white and red. You can google them to find their names and see pictures of them. They are all alive and well, operating through the Jesuit organisations underneath them. More kings and many merchants are in the levels just below the Jesuits.

Who are the merchants? These are also super-wealthy business people with great authority over even more levels underneath them in the humungous pyramid government. Like those above them, they are greedy for money, power and control just like Nimrod, just like their invisible Chief General, Satan. I won't mention all the names here because there are far too many and we know a lot of them anyway. But we've all heard of the Rockefellers, the Rothschilds, Bilderbergs, Bill Gates and Anthony Fauci.

Some are seen all through the media propaganda machine forcefully pushing their agenda on the population, while others are hidden behind the scenes. All are actors using sophisticated language of sophistry, rhetoric and propaganda to carry out the dirty work and sorcery of Satan. They are not far from the top levels of Satan's pyramid-shaped government.

Back to the Book of Revelation - what mighty words John wrote in Chapter Eighteen. God is crying out to us when John says, *"And I heard another voice from heaven saying, 'Come out of her my people, that ye be not partakers of her sins, and that ye receive not of her plagues, for her sins have reached heaven, and God hath remembered her iniquities.'"* Our true Author of the show was always in control of the storyline in John's day, and still is. His Word says so.

Again, we could easily get side-tracked here but I will just pick out one more verse which describes Babylon and is so relevant to now. Revelation 18:23 describes the COVID situation perfectly. It says, '… *for thy merchants were the great men of the earth; for by thy sorceries were all nations deceived.'* We now know who the merchants and great men

The Performers

of the earth are. The verse says all nations were deceived by sorceries. The Greek word for sorcery is pharmakiah, the origin of the word pharmacy today. Through Big Pharma, sorcery is being cast over the masses through incredible sophistry and deception. These merchants are definitely waxing rich through the abundance of the delicacies and profits from pharmaceutical companies, the injections and masks, PCR and RAT tests and everything associated with the so-called protection against the virus, all supposedly for the common good and the benefit of our loved ones.

Again, we could get side-tracked and talk about the guilt and pressure pushed on the free-thinking, unjabbed ones, but we'll leave it there. You know what I am referring to.

The devil is in the details and these side-issues would be the distraction he would love us to take. Personally, I find it too distressing and depressing to dwell on the details. Information is sent to me every day and is overwhelming and I don't get to watch it all. But I trust in my God who knows every single detail of the Big Picture. The most wonderful thing is that our Father-God in Heaven had His Word written down by John 2000 years ago for our benefit today. Yes, God, the Author is still in control.

Satan's agents, ie the rulers of the darkness of this world, the demons, the kings and merchants are like puppeteers in high places all pulling the strings on the 'people-puppets' below. They are the false, counterfeit shepherds trying to herd their human prey into the city-paddocks and treating them like 'sheeple-people.'

But, we free thinkers must hold onto the strong cords of faith linking us in our hearts to Christ, our true Shepherd. We must cling to them firmly for the sake of our very lives. Sophistry is in full force right now and we are on the edge of the climax of the Great War of Words. We must hold tight to those cords of victory.

Remember we are free thinkers. What does this mean? It means we <u>still</u> have the gift of free will to think for ourselves, outside the box, off the planet, like we are at this very moment. Jesus separates or sanctifies us, so we can be free from the tyranny going on all around. We are free when we submit our minds to Christ, and we can think what He wants us to think. We are free to phase off the planet and see more of the Big Picture from the viewpoint of our Triple O, the Outside Objective Observer. We were created as intelligent human beings, not like the dumb beasts of the earth. We were not created to be changed and genetically modified into robot-like puppet slaves.

Anyway, let's get back on track and learn a bit more from Nimrod and the Terrible Trio. We can clearly see how the city of Babylon has always existed through the earthly timeline ever since their day. We can see how their legacy continued through the Roman Catholic Church forcing every nation and denomination to believe the 'wine' of her false teachings which only stem from the father of lies. These false doctrines are founded in that legacy.

The three actors committed spiritual adultery by seducing the bride. The bride is the church of believers in God. The Terrible Trio has led her away from the true Husband, Christ, in a counterfeit belief system, a mixture of watered-down doctrines. Praise God that, all through the millenniums of His Story, there has <u>always</u> been a remnant of true believers, the true church, the pure unadulterated bride, who will soon be united with her Husband at the Second Coming. May you and I be part of this small remnant.

We are now going to leave this platform of the First Empire of Babylon. After the fall of the Tower of Babel, the Word of the Producer intervened again and caused the great continent to split into many continents. People were dispersed all over the globe. They took with them the Babylonian traditions and developed them into their own cultures and religions. But the ideas, beliefs and rituals all had the same origins and common features of the Terrible Trio.

We do not have time to go into all the variations of pagan cultures now and that would be a major fruitless distraction. However, the Bible mentions the main cultures that God wants us to know about, because they have especially continued to influence western civilisation today. And western civilisation is rapidly flowing into the smaller pagan groups. The main empires to remember in His Story are the Egyptian, Assyrian, second Babylonian Empire, the Persia-Mede and Greek Empires.

The Performers

And after these, The Terrible Trio's legacy flowed into the Roman Empire which grew into the Roman Catholic papacy in the fifth century AD. Then it started the Jesuit Society in the 14-1500s. In the 1700s, freemasonry and numerous other secret societies began and spread globally until this very day. Satan's pyramid government grew and grew as Jesuits infiltrated all nations. The base of it became wider and broader to extend originally from just around the Mediterranean Sea to cover the entire planet. Unbelievable!

This, in a nutshell, is the true timeline of His Story, God's version of the past, and what He wants us to learn from. He presents it in His Word, the true script, the Bible. The Spirit of Prophecy books add even more detail. Human flaws, warts and all are exposed, and Satan is identified as the main villain of His Story.

At the same time in this amazing Book, God, our ever-loving Father and Ruler of the whole Universe, outlines His plan of salvation right from the time of Adam and Eve, through the Tabernacle, the permanent Temple, and through the final ultimate sacrifice of Jesus. Our heavenly Father wants to rescue His precious, beloved faithful, and loyal human children from this most horrible, terrible battlefield. And of course, any others who are willing to come on His side are most welcome.

We can see how Nimrod, Noah's great grandson through Ham and Cush, was a big baddie in the show. Where were the goodies living at the same time fighting in the Great War of Words? Noah's youngest son, Shem was at the beginning of the downline leading to Abraham, Isaac, Jacob, the twelve tribes and Moses etc right down to Jesus. So, there must have been many goodies fighting for the Lord in the time of Nimrod and the centuries after.

The Bible tells us the names of some of them in Shem's downline. There were Arphaxad, Salah, Eber, Peleg, but we don't know much about them. Peleg was alive at the time of the great continental split after the destruction of the Tower of Babel, so he was a contemporary of Nimrod. More goodies followed such as Rue, Serug, Nahor, Terah, then Abraham, Isaac and Jacob and the others. Note that even these men weren't perfect and sometimes gave into human weaknesses. Oh, how merciful is our Father in Heaven towards his human family!

The Greatest War Ever

So that brings us to the end of this Scene Six about the Terrible Trio in the First Babylonian Empire. We now move onto Scene Seven and meet the next villain in the show—Simon Magus.

Scene 7. Simon Magus

The Great War Rages On: I must warn you, that unfortunately, we will not finish looking at Simon Magus in this talk. There is so much to learn from this human agent and skilful actor of Satan. But I will just give you an introduction and background. We will discover mind-boggling things about him in Part Four. The time of Simon Magus happened 2000 years after the Terrible Trio when the Roman Empire was just starting. Life on the planet-stage-battlefield had gotten so, so bad in the Great War. The storyline of the sad saga was crooked, twisted and distorted. The Producer-God, the Triple O, intervened in a most powerful way once again. He sent His Son-Director, Jesus, onstage to bring the storyline back on track.

It is interesting that Jesus came in full view to be seen, heard, touched and lived with. Unlike Satan's hidden, devious, manipulative tactics, there was no hiding or secrecy in Christ's ministry. He came as Director to do His job and guide as many people as possible back onto the right narrow path to salvation and eternal life. And He did this with the help and power of the Prompter, Holy Spirit, who worked in His wonderful, mysterious, invisible ways. Absolute truth was revealed to thousands and thousands of human hearts. Many were converted from being actors and became players on the good and narrow track.

The Chief Commander showed incredible Great Love and many people young and old, willingly, without coercion, enlisted into his holy army. And then, by dying and rising up from the grave, Jesus, Chief Commander proved He had power over death. The fear of death lost its sting and humans knew the certainty of eternal life in heaven. This was another major setback for the enemy Chief General, Satan. He was livid.

Within a very short time, the master-sophist and saboteur-director started interfering and tampering with the script again. He just never gives up. He attacked and blasted humans with his old clever tricks and sophisticated word weapons in the Great War.

The Performers

We now finally meet his next key human agent—Simon Magus. In my opinion, Simon Magus is in the same class as Nimrod because he gave the ancient Babylonian legacy a massive boost. The first and second Babylonian empires may have physically been destroyed, but the spiritual city of Babylon continued to thrive.

A few years after Jesus returned to Heaven, God inspired John to write in enormous detail about Babylon the Great in the Book of Revelation chapters 17-18 which we mentioned earlier. We have had 2000 years of serious desperate warning to be prepared for current events right now. World history, ie manstory as recorded by humanists, does not focus on such key people as Nimrod and Simon Magus. It does not base its knowledge on what the Bible teaches. In fact, it deliberately tries to disprove Bible truths, to rubbish them and say the stories are mere myths and fables.

So, Simon Magus came on stage at the same time the Director Jesus was also there. 4000 years of Satan's sophistry had gone by plus all the unknown years of sophistry in heaven. Satan had plenty of practice and was an expert by now. This time period of the First Coming was a pivotal point in God's version of the show which the world tries its best to avoid, but can't. Simon Magus acted out a crucial role in the Great War of Words. Let's meet the man.

Simon Magus: Simon Magus was a result, a product, a culmination of everything that had gone on ever since the first Babylonian empire. In his education, he had been taught a wealth of knowledge and lies from a great pot of smouldering ingredients of false doctrines we could call 'true misinformation.' This had accumulated from the Assyrians, then the second Babylonian Empire under the rule of Nebuchadnezzar and Belshazzar and others. As well, fake truth was thrown in by the Egyptians under all the pharaohs, then the Persians under Darius and Xerxes, then the Greeks under Alexander the Great. As well, the beginnings of the Roman Empire under the Caesars threw in all their gods and lies.

Into this great cauldron of lies, and misinformation and fake truth, was thrown true truth of Judean teachings about the coming Messiah. Simon Magus became a major stirrer of the putrid pot of soup with his magic spoon.

He was born and raised in the town of Gitta in Samaria, southwest of the Sea of Galilee, between the Mediterranean Sea and the Jordan River. He was trained in a false, religious environment. It was full of counterfeits of God's truth. Acts 8:9-10 tells us that people believed he was divine and God Himself. They called him, *'great one... the great power of God.'* That's how powerful he had become.

Who do we know today who claims to be divine and God on earth? This living person right now, always dresses in white robes like an angel of light, the light-bearer-Lucifer? And the whole world is worshipping him right now believing him to be the *'great one... the great power of God.'* There is only one—the White Pope called Francis.

Simon Magus was the equivalent of this man. Simon Magus was Satan's right man for that time just like Nimrod was for his time. He must have had a highly intelligent, sophisticated brain. Through language, like his invisible sophist Chief General, Simon Magus blended all the pagan lies he had learned, with Judean truths and influenced as many minds as he could. Gnosticism would develop out of his false teachings and we will look at that very closely in another talk.

It is interesting that, in the Bible, there are only four verses mentioning Nimrod, but there are twelve about Simon Magus. We know many more details about this new actor—so many that the next talk will centre around him. But for this brief introduction, suffice it to say in the words of the Bible from Acts 8:9-12, *'But there was a certain man called Simon, which beforetime in the same city* (ie a city in Samaria) *used sorcery and bewitched the people of Samaria giving out that himself was some great one; to whom they all gave heed, from the least to the greatest saying, "This man is the great power of God." And to him they had regard, because that of a long time he had bewitched them with sorceries.'* This is the Bible's excellent description of Simon Magus.

Verses 12-24 describe how Philip went to Samaria to preach the gospel. He had such success that Peter and John were sent up to help. Peter was doing miracles, baptising people, and they received the Holy Spirit. Simon Magus saw this, and offered money for the same power to do miracles. But Peter saw into his heart and knew that he had what Bible calls, *'the gall of bitterness.'* This is an Old Testament phrase meaning

The Performers

to go to idols and the abominations of the heathens. Peter knew Simon Magus' heart and he foresaw danger. I suggest, if you have time, to read Acts 8: 9-24 before the next talk in preparation for an in-depth study of this man.

Conclusion: I apologise to you once more for holding off on Simon Magus—but time has run out. This is what they do in the movies - they keep up the suspense by leaving the audience in a cliff-hanger. Please come back to your celestial seats with the outside audience of angels, the inhabitants in other worlds and Enoch for the next episode of the greatest show on earth. It becomes even more spectacular as the Great War of Words spreads and the plot gets darker and murkier.

Just a quick preview—like a movie trailer to whet your appetite: in the next talk, the drama continues as more confusion floods in with many details of this new actor. You will be introduced to two characters of the same name—Simon Peter. We will see how Satan used them through the usual sophistry to deceive and confuse. It is a gripping episode and not to be missed. And if we get time, we might meet Simon Magus' mistress. It would make a sensational movie, but I don't think that the Jesuit theatre of Hollywood would allow it to be produced. So—on that cliff-hanger, as one of the biggest villains in the show steps on stage, the curtains close.

For now, we must return to the planet-battlefield, hopefully as players and not actors. It is always our choice as to which army side we fight on in the Great War of Words. Do we fight for the Lord and Chief Commander who is the guaranteed Victor with two-thirds of the angels? Or do we serve the Chief General, Satan, who is the guaranteed loser with only one third of fallen angels? The choice is ours. There is no other army to choose from.

And as we return to our daily lives, look out for examples of sophistry all around you. Just one huge blatant example—look at the media, the suppression of true news, the glossing over of the truckies protest in Canada and Australia, the protests in many European countries and the UK. In a later talk we will analyse techniques of persuasion used.
Beware the sophistry! Beware the sophistry!

The Greatest War Ever

Next time we meet, bring your seatbelts with you because it is going to be a rocky, rough ride. May our ever-loving God be with us all and keep us safe and strong as we fight the good fight until Jesus comes and takes us home. Curtains open again on February 12 at 2:30pm.

Let's close with a prayer. Father in Heaven, we claim Your promise that you will never leave nor forsake us in these desperate times. Please bless us and protect us and guide us all as we go back out into the battlefields of our own lives at ground level on the planet stage. Please keep the holy angels of your army encamped around us, protecting and guiding us each day. We thank You from the bottom of our hearts for being the true Author of your story and are always sovereign and in control. You always teach truth and not misinformation. We thank You for your Son and Director, our Chief Commander. And we thank you for the Holy Spirit, the Prompter, quietly whispering in our hearts to keep us on the narrow path of Your Script. And we thank you for your unseen angels who stay close to each and every one of us. I pray this series of talks will not discourage or depress anyone, but encourage us all to keep looking up to You, and not get overwhelmed with the details of the devil. We pray these things in the most beautiful name of our Lord Jesus. Amen.'

Part 4 – Act 4:
Simon Magus, Two Simon Peters and the First Bishop

Introduction And Review

Here we are again sitting comfortably in our celestial seats eagerly awaiting the next scene of the greatest show on earth. What a story it has been so far as we've zoomed back and forth across the 6000-year timeline, and looked at a few significant events and people of the past, and connected them with the present world situation. Thank you so much for coming to the fourth talk in this series, The Greatest War Ever. Welcome to another 'off the planet' experience, with the vast audience of angels and inhabitants from other worlds. Before the curtains open, let's pray and ask for the Lord to prepare us to learn even more of His truth.

Our dear Father in Heaven, Author of this amazing story, we ask You to open our minds and hearts and eyes to understand Your truths and to see this world more from Your objective perspective. Thank You for your Script in Your Word and prophecy. Thank you for placing us on the earthly stage at this most significant time in Your Story. Help us to stay awake and be alert during the show, and especially in our daily battles in the Great War of Words. Help us learn more and more of Your side of the story. In Jesus name we pray, Amen.

So now, with great interest and intensity just like the angels, we are watching in our minds the most spectacular show ever to be performed. It is far better than any Hollywood Jesuit theatre could ever produce, because it is based on absolute truth, and not lies or deception. At this point in our superfast journey through over six millenniums, the timeline passes before our very eyes. In this talk, we will zoom in on the platform of the beginnings of the Roman Empire at the time of Christ's First Coming. By now, some new human members have joined the audience. Enoch is somewhere out here with us. And so is Moses who died, but came to life again and was taken to heaven.

The Greatest War Ever

From our outer space viewpoint, we are situated very comfortably and much closer to the Producer-God, the Director-Jesus, who are both Co-Authors, and are guiding the saga with the help of the Prompter-Holy Spirit. We have learned a great deal already in the previous talks. This Creator Trio rules their kingdom of Universe which they created by simply speaking out their all-powerful Word. We know their government is a theocracy founded on the Law of Great Love with its gift of free will to every created being in their vast kingdom of countless galaxies and planets.

We have seen how, when the Great War broke out in Heaven, Satan, once called Lucifer the Light-bearer, became the Chief General of his army of fallen angels, the demons. Christ became the Chief Commander of His own army of holy angels. A war between two mighty, powerful supernatural foes followed and has continued ever since on planet Earth.

Earth was created as a type of stage where a court case is being held and the Father-King Himself willingly put Himself on trial. What an act of Great Love! It is up to the jury of His children to decide if His way of government is the best or not? Human beings were created in the image of the Royal Trio to prove once and for all, to the rest of those worlds in Universe, that it is the only way to rule. After all, it had worked successfully and perfectly for eons into eternity in the past. Until Satan's rebellion, everyone in the Kingdom of Universe lived in perfection, bliss and sheer happiness with a servant-like love and respect for each other.

But, for some reason unknown to man, Satan allowed Self and Pride to puff up in his heart and all the trouble began. With sophisticated techniques of sophistry and rhetoric, he became the original source of sin and the first rebel to revolt against the theocratic government. We have seen how he and his army attack humans so that two groups of performers are now on the stage. There are the actors acting out his wicked character of Great Hate. And there are the players reflecting Christ's character of Great Love. At the time of the Roman Empire and the Chief Commander-Jesus' arrival on the planet-stage-battlefield, the Great War of Words had been raging 4000 years—plus the time back in heaven.

Simon Magus, Two Simon Peters and the First Bishop

In the previous three talks, we looked closely at the earth's 6000-year timeline and saw how the time periods of the Bible are very different to Satan's way of organising them. His human agents, the humanist historians, have been doing a successful job of this. In the second talk, we drew a very basic Biblical timeline, so if you have it with you, you can peg up some more names and events as we go along.

We have also seen the script of the show and how God's Word is battling against Satan's sophistry, as arrows of word war weapons shoot around the earth. Words, words everywhere; which ones will win the War?

We have also studied the difference between history, ie manstory, and His Story, ie God's Story. We learned about subjectivity and objectivity and how our Heavenly Father is the Triple O–our **O**utside, **O**bjective **O**bserver. Satan could be called the Triple S–the **S**ecret, **S**ubjective **S**ophist because he hides and only sees things from his self-centred, prideful point of view. He manipulates human minds to do the same.

And we have watched the performances of certain characters. There are always goodies and baddies in a show. We met just a few of the goodies—Adam, Eve, Seth, Enoch, Noah and then John who wrote the Book of Revelation with its warnings from the Three Angel's Messages. Some of the baddies we met were Cain, and the Terrible Trio—Nimrod, Semiramus and Tammuz. There are countless others we have not got time to meet them in this series.

However, today we are about to focus especially on one new goodie, Simon Peter, the apostle, and one big baddie, Simon Magus. I believe this topic is extremely important because we are going to fight Satan with our war weapons of words and expose more of who he really is. We are going to attack the roots which the very foundation the Roman Catholic Church claims to be founded on. Today, we will sit through four, maybe five scenes if we have time. Scene Eight which follows on from the previous talks, will be about the background of Simon Magus. Scene Nine solves the mystery of the two Simon Peters. Scene Ten reveals precisely who the first bishop or pope of the Roman Catholic Church, and hopefully we will get time for Scene Eleven and meet the mistress of Simon Magus.

So, are you ready for the next gripping episode? Fasten your seatbelts and get ready for a rough, rocky ride. We are now at the post on your timeline marked 4000AM with the sign of the Cross. Our first scene takes us to a little platform on stage in the small land called Samaria just southwest of the Sea of Galilee. This little place is on a larger platform of the Roman Empire which is in its very early days and gradually expanding around the Mediterranean Sea.

Scene 8. Samaria and the Background of Simon Magus

Just in case you may be wondering where I am getting my information from, I have a bibliography at the end of this book on page 107. Briefly, much of the information I am about to share comes from a lengthy article written by two men - Ernest L Martin and John D Keyser. It is published by the Hope of Israel Ministries Ecclesia of Yehovah. It's very long–58 pages - and quotes from many valid sources. It's well worth reading. If you want a copy of this article go to: www.hope-of-israel.org/magus.html.

I am just giving a very brief summary here. Whatever I am about to share, is <u>not</u> made up by me or a figment of my imagination. This is <u>not</u> conspiracy theory, but conspiracy fact from what I believe to be reliable trustworthy sources. The facts are there. Now, let's zoom in on this little land of Samaria.

Samaria: Samaria was in Israel, part of the northern kingdom of the old promised land of Canaan. Remember that Canaan was the land especially set apart for God's chosen people. They were supposed to be the example for the rest of the world of how to live under the theocracy of God's government, its Law of Great Love and gift of free will.

In the last talk, we were introduced to Simon Magus who had the privilege of being born in this very promised land of Canaan. We saw how he was born in the town of Gitta and was raised up in a false, counterfeit religious environment. We looked at the Bible verses from Acts 8:9-10 saying, he *'used sorcery and bewitched the people of Samaria giving out that himself was some great one.'* People young and old listened to him and said, *'This man is the great power of God.'* They regarded him as being divine and God on earth.

But he was merely a magician in the style of all those magicians from the previous empires of Babylon, Assyria, Egypt, Persia and Greece. He was a false prophet and Babylonian priest. He was a fraud, a trickster, a liar, a deceiver skilfully acting out the character of his invisible Chief General, Satan. And he was one of Satan's best ever agents used to capture the minds and souls of human prey.

When Simon Peter, the apostle of Christ, came along to Samaria, Simon Magus discovered new things he was unable to do, like raising the dead, and healing the sick in the name of Jesus. He tried to become a member of the apostle's group by being baptised and also offered money for the power. But Simon Peter saw through his motives.

This rejection led Simon Magus to form his own version with his own Messiah/Saviour/Redeemer. And he would see to it that he himself was at the head of his religious organisation. His ultimate goal was to overthrow the one and only original truth of God's existence. Satan would use this man to carry out his most evil plans and to leave his own special mark or signature on the earth, and cause as many as possible to worship him, not the true Creator or His Son. How did Simon Magus do this? We know he did it through sophistry.

At this point in time of Christ's First Coming, the cosmic Great War of Words began a whole new phase in its development. Satan was livid and revved up with revenge. The fiery flames of words flared up so insidiously without the majority of the masses realising it. The effects over the next 2000 years would prove to be horrendous beyond accurate description. Many writers have written sordid details, but God knows there were even more horrors we don't know because He sees absolutely everything. What an ever-merciful God we have who is unbelievably patient and did not blot the earth out of existence long ago. It's only by His grace that we are here today.

Five Tribes: We are now going to look a bit closer at the land of Samaria. Oh, how it had changed since the glorious Golden Age of King Solomon and the United Kingdom, when all twelve Israelite tribes lived under one God-appointed monarch. After Solomon, the kingdom divided

The Greatest War Ever

into two, north and south. Then, the Assyrians conquered the northern kingdom and the Jews were scattered in other nations. Some Israelites stayed behind. Only the Southern Kingdom of Judea remained intact. 720 years passed by before the Chief Commander came onstage. Samaria was now in the old Northern Kingdom. Idolatry flooded in as never before. By the time of Christ, there were endless political troubles.

2 Kings 17:23-24 tells the story of how the Assyrian king brought five tribes of people from Babylon, into Samaria. Verse 24 lists them as Babylon, Cuthah, Hamath, Ava and Sepharvaim.

These people brought with them their own Babylonian and Assyrian gods. Over centuries, their tribes intermarried, increased in numbers and naturally passed on their beliefs and traditions. They practised the same old paganism of ancient Babylon, and carried on the legacy of the Terrible Trio, Nimrod, Semiramus and Tammuz, but with new variations and different names. These people from the mixture of the five tribes became known as the Samarians.

At one time, the Samarians were attacked by savage lions. They thought they must be doing something wrong in this promised holy land of Israel and were being punished. In desperation, they asked for a local Israelite priest to teach them about Jehovah, the true God. They wanted to be saved. Tragically however, for the previous 200 years, the remaining Israelites in the old northern kingdom had still been worshipping the two golden calves set up by their first king, Jeroboam. So, the priests were not Levites as they should have been. They were ordinary people who had become important. Consequently, the Samarians got an Israelite priest who did not teach or practise God's truth. He was just as idolatrous as they were. As a result, the Samarians falsely called themselves 'People of Jehovah' but still continued downright paganism.

Can we see this happening today? Don't some people still take on the name of Jehovah, call themselves Christians, followers of Christ, but unknowingly and willingly continue pagan abominations? Like the early Samarians, they genuinely believe they are doing the right thing by God. Such is the deception and sophistry of the evil Triple S.

Babylon: One of the many idols worshipped in Samaria was a goddess called Succoth-Benoth, also known as Venus. Essentially, of course, she was Semiramus. Her name meant 'tabernacles of daughters.' So, tabernacles, chapels, or tents of worship were made from tree boughs which the men of Babylon transported into Samaria and erected in honour of Venus. Their daughters continued to be prostituted, and babies and children were sacrificed just as they had originally been in Babylon. This evil has not stopped since and has spread around the whole planet.

Cuthah: Another idol to be worshipped was Nergal of the tribe of Cuthah. This name means 'the great man,' the great hero,' or the 'god of the chase,' ie the hunter. So, Nergal was a form of Nimrod, the hunter-god from the ancient city of Cuth which belonged to Nimrod. Nergal was worshipped in Samaria, and its citizen Simon Magus, would also prove to be a hunter of souls just like Nimrod, and Satan. Revelation 18:9-13 tells how the *'souls of men'* are being hunted, bought and sold today by merchants of the earth. But God has already told us of a time soon to come when these *'merchants of the earth shall weep and mourn over her* (ie Babylon) *for no man buyeth their merchandise any more...'*

In the last talk we saw who some of the 'kings and merchants of the earth' are today. We saw how they are the Elite high up in the pyramid hierarchical government with Satan at the very tip and the masses of population at the bottom. Very soon these merchants and the kings of the earth, rulers of nations, will finally see the truth of how they have been deceived. The masses are already beginning to understand how they are treated like sheeple-people and puppets to be manipulated by the puppeteers above. It won't be long before the kings and merchants of the earth meet their Maker and come to their fate. They are doomed already. How do we know for certain? Because the Authors of the story have written it down in their Script, the Bible. It <u>will</u> happen in the fullness of time.

Hamath and Ava: Back to Samaria: In the third tribe, the Hamathites from Hamath worshipped the god, Ashima. He was the god of propitiation or the one who carried the guilt of his worshippers. He was a pagan redeemer just like Osiris in Egypt. This practice of having a type of priest as a mediator between man and God, still goes on today in the Roman Catholic Church. It is a counterfeit of the true High Priest, Jesus, who is in Heaven right now interceding for us as our One and only Mediator.

In the fourth tribe of Ava, the Avites followed Nibhaz, the god of Hades, the underworld or afterlife. The Avites also adored a goddess called Tar-Tak, the 'mother of gods.' According to legend, Tar-Tak was the mother of the Assyrian people. Of course, she was just another form of Semiramus. The concept of God having a mother is still believed by many today as Jesus' mother Mary, is called the 'Mother of God.'

Sepharvaim: The fifth and final Babylonian tribe was Sepharvaim which worshipped two gods. One was called Adram-Melech and the other was Anam-Melech. Adram-Melech was the 'god of fire,' the Sun or Baal ie yet another form of Nimrod, the sun-god. The second god called Anam-Melech was the 'god of flocks.' He is the same as the Greek god Hermes, the good shepherd. But we know who the real Good Shepherd is—our Lord and Saviour Jesus Christ.

All of these ancient gods from the five tribes brought in from Assyria, stemmed from deities of the First Babylonian Empire and the Terrible Trio. Through Simon Magus and later church leaders, these gods would be very cleverly woven into a new, massive, complicated, global, counterfeit belief system.

500 years before Simon Magus came onstage, the Lord and Chief Commander used a mighty player and warrior called Daniel to write down a prophecy. Daniel lived in the time of the Second Babylonian empire and actually lived in the city of Babylon. He knew full well about the sorcery and wickedness going on. His prophecy describes in great detail about three beasts and a fourth monster-beast with ten horns and a little horn rising up with great power.

The animals represent four kingdoms. God the Author, had Daniel write it all down as part of <u>His</u> script, therefore this prediction <u>would</u> be fulfilled. By the days of Simon Magus, the first three empires had come and gone. The lion of Babylon, the bear of Persia-Media and the leopard of the Greek empire had all fallen and were in the past. Only the fourth, the monster-beast of the Roman Empire, remained. And that had already begun when the Romans conquered the Greeks about 63 years before the Lord Chief Commander arrived on the earth.

Simon Magus, Two Simon Peters and the First Bishop

The monster-beast was so hideous that Daniel could not find words to describe it. At the time of the Cross, the monster beast in Daniel's dream was just beginning to stir and come to life. Today, words still fail to fully describe the extreme monstrosities and wickedness that this beast would carry out for over 2000 years.

Back to Samaria—In the days of Simon Magus, the first century AD, the Samarians were called Samaritans. Simon Magus became known as Simon the Sorcerer or Simon the magician. He was one of the most influential men of the eastern world. His last name, Magus, is the Persian/Chaldean word for priest. He would prove to be the major link between the ancient Babylonian system and the new mixed up counterfeit belief system which would later develop into the Roman Catholic Church. Nearly 500 years after the Cross, Roman paganism would become the Roman papacy.

In the second century, 152 AD, Justin Martyr wrote a book called "Apology". Four times, he mentions the name of Simon Magus and calls him the 'founder of Simonianism.' Justin Martyr describes him as a Samaritan born in Gitta and a magician who was in Rome in the days of Emperor Claudius in 45AD. He wrote that Simon Magus made such an impression that he was honoured as a god. A statue was erected in his honour on the Tiber River between two bridges with the inscription 'Simon deo Sancto' (ie Simon, the holy god). In the days of Claudius, it would have been illegal to erect a statue to any man as a god or an honoured person unless it was accepted by the senate. And then it would still have to be agreed to by the emperor. Obviously, permission was given by the senate and by Claudius. The statue was still standing in Justin's day in the second century AD and people were worshipping it. Records show that Simon Magus prophesied that Rome would be the crowning of his glory and he would be adored as a god. And he made sure he was.

So, now we have a brief cultural background to Simon Magus, and the genes and knowledge he inherited from his ancestors in the pagan nations going right back to the First Babylonian Empire. This is why he was, who he was. Spiritual Babylon lived on through him. This is a summary of the sophisticated, complicated, deceptive soup-like concoction of counterfeit belief systems that led up to Simon Magus, the supposedly divine one ie God on earth. And–he was born and raised up in the very promised land of Canaan which was supposed to be model of theocracy for the rest of the world. What a twist in the storyline! Unbelievable, but true. Not conspiracy theory, but conspiracy fact.

The whole Great War of Words all began with Satan's conspiracy, a controversy, and plot to overthrow the King of Universe. And it is enacted in miniature form on the one tiny black spot of Universe–planet-earth. To put things into perspective, God's vast kingdom called Universe has no borders and is filled with a glittering glorious works of art filled with sparkling stars and colourful galaxies. Planet-earth is a mere blot, like an ink smudge. We tiny humans are like ants scurrying around the outer crust. No–we are even smaller than that. We are more like microscopic atoms.

But, let's not get side-tracked and return to the tiny platform of ancient Rome.

Scene 9. The Mystery of the Two Simon Peters.

In the first century AD, there were two Simon Peters. Over the coming years, Satan, would display his mastery of sophistry once more, by confusing Simon Peter, the apostle with Simon Peter Magus, the sorcerer. We will soon discover why Simon Magus was also called Simon Peter. But let's analyse the apostle's name first because that is shorter and simpler.

Simon Magus Peter and the Origins of Peter: John, the mighty warrior we met last talk, tells us about the first meeting of Jesus and Simon. In John 1:42 we read, "... *And when Jesus beheld him* (He saw Simon), *He said, 'Thou art Simon, the son of Jona.'*" Jesus also told Peter, "*'Thou shalt be called Cephas' which is by interpretation, a stone.*" Jesus used the Aramaic word, Cephas, meaning stone, pebble or small rock. Matthew 16:16-19 tells us that, later on, Simon said he believed that Jesus was "*the Christ, the Son of the living God.*" Jesus replied by saying, "*And I also say unto thee, that thou art Peter, and upon this Rock I will build my church ...*" This time, Jesus used the Greek word Petra which also meant rock.

But He was actually talking about <u>Himself</u> as the foundational Rock of

Simon Magus, Two Simon Peters and the First Bishop

His church, not Simon Cephas Peter. The Roman Catholic Church has deliberately misused Matthew 16:18 as evidence that Simon Cephas Peter was the rock which its church was built on, and not Jesus. This is pure sophistry and twisting of words at its best. Consequently, there is still confusion today about the two Simons. We will now learn how Simon Cephas Peter could never ever have been the rock foundation of the Roman Catholic Church.

The second Simon Peter was Simon Magus. How did he get the name of Peter? Once again, in order to understand the present, we must go back into the past. We have to look at the word origins of the name, Peter.

The word Peter had a most significant meaning way back in the First Babylonian Empire of Nimrod 2000 years earlier and also in the Persian Empire. The first mention of a "Peter Temple", is in this huge area of Mesopotamia. Within 200 years after the great Flood, men were already rebelling against the truth. They built cities and brought in idols. Temples were erected and culminated in the Tower of Babel. The pagan gods were known as Patres or Peters. In early civilisations, chief pagan gods were generally known by one of these two names, or a variant such as Pator or Patora.[1]

The interpreters for the pagan magicians were called Patres and they had power to interpret heathen mysteries. The Hebrew Lexicon written by Davidson shows the word PTR with no vowels. P-T-R. It means 'to interpret.'

What is an interpreter? He is someone who goes between two parties? Who were the two parties Satan used? They were himself the counterfeit king, and the people. The Patre was a mediator, a 'go-between,' translating and passing on messages from the supernatural. This would develop as a counterfeit of Christ, the Mediator who is the true 'Go-between' the true Father-God and the people.

We know that Semiramus set up an elaborate priesthood of mediators underneath her. About six centuries later, things had gotten so bad on

---

[1] Ancient Mythology by Bryant Vol 1 pg 354; and The Ultimate Source of All Super Natural Phenomena by R R Wlodyga

the planet, that God instructed Moses to build a tabernacle/temple where He could dwell among His people. Moses was told to set up a system of priests with one high priest starting with Aaron as mediator and continuing through his descendants. After Jesus died, rose again and went back to Heaven, He became our One and only divine High Priest and Mediator. True believers have the enormous privilege of being His human priests who can turn and pray to the One High Priest who intercedes for us right now to our Father-God in the heavenly Temple.

Tragically, alongside this divinely designed system of mediation between two parties, Satan's counterfeit organisation of priests has continued for over 4000 years from Babylon right up to today in the Roman Catholic Church. It still uses ancient sophistry, sorcery, demonism and magic tricks.

The name Peter was also one of the earliest pagan gods lasting up to the Greek and Roman Empires. By this time, the name had also taken on a widespread secular meaning of father or parent, but that was not its main meaning of being an interpreter. In many ancient religions, the father was the chief priest of the family. Consequently, the head of the family was known as the Pator or father. The Pator/Father had a priestly position and was also called the Ahpator or Patriarch. Abraham is an example. But originally, Pator meant interpreter.

Each pagan country had its own Peter oracle and temple with its own names. In Greece, the Pethor Temple was in the city of Delphi. The ancient Greek author, Homer, had used this word Pator in his stories. In Egypt, the Pethor Temple was in the city of Ammon. The ancient Egyptians called their interpreters or priests PETR that is, PETER.

Peter temples were always built on high places. Why would this be? Well—Satan knows that the original Temple of God is on a mountain in Heaven. He was once the light-bearer Lucifer, who stood <u>inside</u> the Most Holy Place of the Temple as a covering cherub beside the Ark of the Covenant. Consequently, temples built by humans were always in high places, yet another counterfeit of the original Temple in Heaven. Satan had known the gloriousness of the heavenly Temple.

All through the Old Testament books of the Bible, we read of idols

Simon Magus, Two Simon Peters and the First Bishop

and temples being built in the high places. Cathedrals and churches throughout the centuries have always been built on the highest or a high place of a town or city. Satan knows that God's glorious light shines down from the original temple in Heaven and is on a mountain, because he was there. He also knows that it is still there and exists this very day. He likes to think that he has the same authority and power as God. His goal has always been to be like the Most High.

We could get very side-tracked here about St Peter's Basilica. I started a little research on it to check something, and dozens of cans of worms opened up, but I will leave that to the next talk. Let's return to the origins of the word, Peter.

When Moses wrote about the ancient Egyptian magicians, he said they would peter or patar ie make interpretations. Deuteronomy 23:4 tells how the prophet Balaam *was the son of Beor from Pethor of Mesopotamia...* Balaam was the chief Peter, (interpreter) from the Pethor (Peter Temple) on the Euphrates River in Mesopotamia, the very home of idolatry and counterfeit religion. I always thought Balaam was a weak, comical man because of the story about the talking donkey. But no—he was such a powerful, influential prophet with a wide reputation, and that is why the Moabites summoned him to curse the Israelites. They even ignored their own gods.

In Semetic language, the word Balaam meant, 'Conqueror of the people.' Balaam saw himself as sitting on the very same seat of authority as Nimrod, the great hunter of souls. We could say that Balaam was also the equivalent of Simon Magus, and—of the current pope today. When the Moabites summoned Balaam from Pethor of Mesopotamia, they knew they were going to the highest authority of Peters ie interpreters.

Josephus wrote about this false prophet saying, 'Balaam, who lived by the Euphrates, was one of the greatest prophets of the time.'[2] Balaam was a successor of Nimrod, and was the greatest priest or chief high priest of his time. The Romans would later use their Latin words to call this position, Pontifex Maximus. Balaam's headquarters were in the Pethor Temple, the equivalent of Saint Peter's Basilica today. So, he was not the weakling I thought he was.

2 Antiquities IV, 6, 2

The Greatest War Ever

The gods Artemis and Bacchus we mentioned in the previous talk, were also called Patora or Peter-gods. Artemis is often shown standing by a stone pillar called the Patroa or Peter and this pillar is a phallic symbol representing creation and life-giving seeds. Phallic Peter-stones were, and are all still over the world in the forms of obelisks and pillars. They were sacred stones rising up as shrines for various gods. The word Petra came to mean large rock, specifically the sacred Peter-stone. In Greece the sacred book was called 'Book Petroma' ie 'Peter-Roma' or 'Peter's Book' meaning the 'Book of the Grand Interpreter.' Pagan temples were called after their Peters or interpreters. One temple in Greece was called Petron. Another was Petraessa, and another Patara. The oracle was called Patareus. Patrae was an ancient town where the goddess Diana had a temple.

How many variations of a word can you get! But the common letters are always PTR. The word, 'interpreter', is most interesting. The first half of it is 'inter' and means between, ie between two parties. The second half 'preter' is extremely close to the word Peter and contains the three key letters—PTR. Maybe we should accent a different syllable and pronounce it <u>INTER</u>-preter and not in-<u>TER</u>-preter. Hmmmm. I cannot find any evidence to prove a connection, but isn't it a fascinating coincidence? But, let's not get side-tracked.

In Greece, the word Nicolaus also meant 'Conqueror of the people' and refers back to Nimrod just like the name Balaam. Those who followed the doctrines of Nicolaus ie Nimrod, were called the Nicolaitanes. Jesus said He hated the doctrines of the Nicolaitans, and He praised the church of Ephesus because they hated them too. That comes from Revelation 2:6,15. In verse 14, Jesus also refers to *'Balaam who taught Balac to cast a stumbling block before the children of Israel, and to eat things sacrificed to idols and to commit fornication.'*

Both names, Balaam and Nicolaus, point to Nimrod, the originator of paganism. All of the heresies in the seven churches of Revelation refer to paganism. Therefore, they also refer to all the counterfeit gods called Peters. We know the seven churches represent seven historical periods from Christ till today. Therefore, paganism and Peterism have never stopped. Spiritual Babylon is thriving right now. Satan never gives up his fight in the Great War of Words.

Simon Magus, Two Simon Peters and the First Bishop

Headquarters in Rome: Back to the platform of the Roman Empire. Rome became the headquarters of paganism. We can now understand why Simon Magus was also called Simon Peter–a god and INTER-preter. How easy it would be in the coming millenniums for Satan to confuse multitudes about the two Simon Peters. The monster-beast of Daniel's dream was only just beginning to come alive and rear up its ugly, head with ten horns and a hidden little horn. We can see how, in the very first century AD, Simon Magus Peter, high priest, god and magician, was the one who brought together the doctrines from many empires of the past into the Roman Empire.

Simon Magus Peter shifted the headquarters of idolatry from ancient Mesopotamia and established the new headquarters in Rome. Rome was known as the 'city of gods.' How many gods did the Romans have–hundreds, thousands? All were a sophisticated, complicated distraction from the One true God. Rome was now the world's headquarters of pagan religion and it remains so this very day.

But remember in the last talk we learned that, back in Nimrod's day, Satan had set up his own invisible headquarters in the area of Sturn or Sturnia (named after planet, Saturn). This was near where Rome is situated. So, for over 2000 years before Simon Magus appeared on the planet-stage, Satan was already ruling invisibly and secretly over the whole globe from this hidden place.

Therefore, central Italy was already the headquarters for <u>all</u> pagan religions which developed in <u>all</u> the continents over the planet. Satan's army of demons have been flat out working <u>all</u> over the globe ever since the population spread with the continental split. This is why there are so many different belief systems round the world, whether they be in small native tribal village or large nations. But each one has something in common with all others–their religions are a distraction from the one true living God.

In Simon Magus' day, there were beginnings of developments of an open visible headquarters, not hidden or secret. There were and still are Peter-gods everywhere, Peter temples, obelisks, statues, rituals, sacrifices and everything that goes with the mystery of paganism. In the fourth century, Roman Emperor Constantine would have a new large cathedral built in Rome. Later, in the 15-1600s, it would be replaced by St Peter's Basilica, and be regarded by millions as the greatest of all churches in Christendom. The headquarters was always, and still is, located there right along with Satan's own invisible throne where he has ruled from the top of his invisible pyramid and his hierarchical, tyrannical government. What a blasphemy!

Today, he rules the world with secrecy, mysticism, sorcery, fear, force and deception from this counterfeit temple and seat of authority. Under the Vatican, there are levels upon levels, tunnels and more tunnels where old records are kept, and Satan worship and sacrifices are still being carried out. Very few people know this. Just read the stories of Alberto Riveira, an ex-Jesuit who left the Jesuit Order and revealed the wicked truth. You will find horror story after horror story. We don't have time to go down that path right now.

Suffice it to say that, however grand and magnificent this modern Peter Temple looks, it is nothing compared with the ginormous most glorious Temple in Heaven. And one day very soon, God-willing, we will have the opportunity to see it. But for now, in the earthly show, let's have a little look at planet-worship of the ancient Romans because this would develop into traditions still practised today.

Planet-Worship: In this first century AD, many planets were worshipped. The ancient Romans used the word Peter in their names. There were Neptune-Pator, Saturn-Pator, Mars-Pator. These were the three chief gods. The Romans took the Greek god, Zeus-Pater, the father of all the gods, and renamed him Ju-Peter, or as we know it, Jupitor. This name incorporated Pator meaning god and father. Surely, this is a counterfeit of our original true Father-God.

And now the plot of the story just gets thicker. Jupitor was the main god along with another one called Janus-Pater. The statue of Jupitor is still worshipped in Rome and represents Janus-Pater. But Janus-Pater and Jupitor were actually two separate gods with different roles. How complicated it gets!

Janus and the Keys of the Kingdom: Who was Janus-Peter? The Roman author, Plutarch, told the story of the life of Janus who was supposed to be an ancient prince reigning since the beginning of the earth. He was the first to build cities and conquer people and establish government over them. Hmmmm. Who does this remind us of–Nimrod? The god, Janus-Peter, supposedly brought humans out of a barbaric, savage primitive life into a logical, more civilised system.

Again, I say hmmm. Isn't this what our present Age of Technocracy is still trying to do–make us more civilised, healthier, live longer and be better human beings. And this is called 'progress.' So many are being taught to believe that man is evolving into a better species. However, nothing has changed in the last 2000 years since Simon Magus, or even the last 4000 years since Nimrod. Spiritual Babylon is alive and well today. Perhaps the only difference is that the means and methods have changed. There is nothing new under the sun. If anything, humanity is not progressing, but is regressing and falling into a worse state because the spread of sin, the breaking of God's laws.

Janus-Peter was in charge of many religious activities. As an interpreter, ie priest, god, he prophesied the future. He was also the keeper of the gates of Heaven and Earth. The word Janus means gates. He is shown with a key in one hand to symbolise his control over the gates and highways and, of course, the 'pearly gates' of Heaven. Are alarm bells beginning to ring in your head? There was also a goddess called Cardea who also had a key. These two keys came to symbolise the 'keys of the kingdom of heaven.' And don't we see them in symbols all throughout the Roman Catholic Church?

After Janus' death, he became deified and was worshipped as a god called Pator or Peter. So, Janus-Pater could only refer back to the father of paganism, Nimrod, but with a new name. Yet another example of Satan's sophistry and confusion. He constantly changes names and twists meanings of words in to order get what he wants–to be like the Most High with all authority, power and control. He is relentless.

Let's move on to the same Roman platform, but nearly 400 years later. The Roman Empire split into two - the west and the east. The seat of Rome was moved to Constantinople in the East. But before long, Constantinople became a threat to Rome. About 378AD the pope 'suddenly and conveniently' became the heir to the two keys of Janus and

Cardea, who now had been renamed Cybele.

These two keys symbolised the two main deities of Rome—Jupiter and Janus. The pope used them to claim that he was Simon Peter's successor and therefore had more power. It was all esoteric—ie a hidden mystery. This claim was timely revealed in 431AD when the pope publicly declared he had possession of the two keys and convinced people to believe the lie that he had the keys to the gates of heaven.

Oh, how the plot of the storyline thickens. The true salvation plan through Jesus, our Mediator, is distorted and abused. According to the Catholic Church, only through Saint Peter, could humans be saved ie salvation came only through the pope who was the one supposedly in the papal line from Simon Peter. Which Simon Peter do you think is being referred to? According to their tradition, it was Simon Cephas Peter, the apostle. But we know that could not possibly, logically be, and very soon, we will prove it without a doubt. It had to be Simon Magus Peter, the link between paganism and the catholic, counterfeit version of Christianity.

Back to Janus-Peter, the gate-keeper, and the keys. The drama gets even more exciting. Note that, as well as having keys, gates also have hinges. The word cardinal means hinge. Therefore, the pope (symbolising the gate) is able to turn and operate on these hinges, the cardinals. In the Babylonian times, there was a pagan College of Pontiffs or priests or cardinals, with its chief high priest called the Pontifex Maximus. Today, the pope is still called the Pontifex Maximus.

So, we have all these words associated with each other in such a sophisticated way—Janus-Peter/gatekeeper, keys to Heaven/chief high priest/Pontifex Maximus/pope/Peter/Patre, Pator, Patora, Pathor, Patar, Petra, Patara, Petraessa, Petron, Pethor, Patareus—'Peter Piper picked a peck of pickled pepper.' Oh, can you see how hot and peppery the storyline is getting. Satan's use and abuse of language gets quite ludicrous.

I'm sorry, but that funny tongue twister popped into my head as I was practising saying all the 'p' words. I could not resist putting in a little sense of humour into such a serious topic. It's good to have a belly laugh occasionally because if we don't laugh, we would cry as we look around us and see what is happening. I don't know about you, but at times, as I read and write these talks, I feel sick in the stomach.

And who is having the last laugh over language when pentecostals are talking and singing in tongues, their non-sensical, goobledy-gook language of the demons? Satan is laughing with glee to see God's intelligent language being so abused. I attended a Pentecostal church for two years and know exactly what goes on. It is ludicrous.

The dictionary explains that ludicrous means, absurd, laughable, eccentric, stupid, unreasonable, ridiculous and foolish. God's word in Proverbs 14:8 says, *'The folly of fools is deceit.'* This is Satan to a tee. Testimonies to Ministers page 409 says, 'Satan laughs at their folly for he knows the truth.'

Anyway, we've had a little chuckle at how ludicrous Satan is in his sophistry. It lightens the serious drama a bit. Suffice it to say, all those PTR words mean one and the same in the language of sophistry. They mean god with a lower case 'g', Satan's counterfeit of God. We have sidetracked quite a bit, but this is actually still very relevant because it comes under the umbrella of sophistry.

Back to the pope-gate and the cardinal-hinges. We learned last talk that there are now actually four popes (grey, black, white and red), so the plot gets even murkier within the last few centuries. They all still operate through their hinges, the cardinal-priests. But Satan just can't stop there. He loves his war word weapons, and his triangle pyramid shape of government with all its levels of hierarchy. More names were added to the list–primates, deacons, patriarchs, metropolitan bishops, etc each with their own levels of authority and power over those below them. Words, words everywhere; the more, the better to confuse! Suffice it to say, they all essentially originate with the word PTR–Peter-interpreter-'INTER-preter'-god and father. Satan's government pyramid gets broader and broader as it builds from the top down. The plot of the storyline just gets more and more intricate. The saying goes, 'the fish rots from the head down.' And so it is.

Now let's go back to Janus-Peter. Janus was also in control of the calendar through his priests. People would consult him about the calendar because Janus supposedly had authority over time. Consequently, the first month of the year was named after him—January. The Catholic Church still feels it has the same authority over time and the calendar today. Didn't the little horn of Daniel's monster-beast 'think' to change times and laws? That's from Daniel 7:25. The word 'think' is most important because Satan knows he cannot change time, because he could never create time in the first place. He only can change the numbers, words and dates and let the people believe his tricks are truth.

For the Jews, the first month of the year was always the month of Nisan, also called Abib, which is our April. But today we use the Roman calendar. In 46BC Julius Caesar started the Julian calendar named after him, but over the centuries, that was chopped and changed. Then in 1582, Pope Gregory XIII established the Gregorian calendar named after him, which we use today. Such is the power of Satan who thinks and claims to change times and laws. But he doesn't because God's seven-day week with its Sabbath, has never stopped since the seven days of Creation.

Interestingly, Satan still cannot get away from the First Coming of Christ, the pivotal point in the storyline. Every time someone writes the date, they acknowledge Jesus Christ is Lord over time, Sabbath and everything else. The best-known example of the Roman monster-beast thinking to change times and laws, is when Emperor Constantine legally changed the Sabbath from the seventh day to the first day of the week, in the year 321AD. We keep getting side-tracked, don't we? Let's move on.

It can easily be seen how the Roman Catholic Church claims to sit in Peter's chair and why its chief temple is called Saint Peter's. Incidentally, the chair was never actually Peter's. It was a throne given as a present to Pope Gregory by King Charles the Bald, grandson of Emperor Charlemagne in the ninth century AD. The throne is full of traditions, symbols, rituals and legends—all major distractions leading one up the garden path and round the bend.

Summary: After all this explanation, it can be understood why the early pagan church of Rome gave Simon Magus the name Simon Patres/Peter. Consequently, it stands to reason that Simon, son of John, an apostle and a true believer in Jesus, should really be called Simon Cephas rather than Simon Peter just to avoid confusion. It is true that Simon <u>was</u> called Peter by Jesus, but he was never a god to be worshipped like Simon Magus was. Yes, he was a saint in the sense of being in the general priesthood of believers under the authority of Christ. But the Catholic Church tried to counterfeit that authority and made him their own saint. All the while, under the cover of Christ's apostle, it acknowledges Simon Magus Peter as god. How wickedly evil and deceptive! Pure, pure sophistry.

So now, hopefully the mystery of the two Simon Peters is solved. Simon Cephas Peter was a player in the Chief Commander's army playing the role he was designed for–to spread the gospel, to defend his Father-King and prove that the gift of free will and Law of Great Love are always the best and only ways to govern a kingdom. In contrast, Simon Magus Peter was an actor in the Chief General's army, acting out the character of his leader, Satan with the goal of destroying the gospel, and forming a one world government ruled by fear, force, deception and the Law of Great Hate.

Scene 10. First Bishop of Rome Revealed

Evidence: If the above is not enough evidence, let's prove once and for all from Scripture, the Spirit of Prophecy and by checking dates, that the apostle, Simon Cephas Peter could never have been the St Peter of St Peter's Basilica. He was never the first pope/bishop of Rome, the supposed rock foundation of the Catholic Church, and founder of Christianity.

Let's briefly get introduced to another mighty warrior and player for the Chief Commander, Christ. His name is Paul. Paul was another apostle at the same time as Simon Peter and Simon Magus. He made it clear that his own mission was in Rome, the city of gods with its uncircumcised gentiles. And he made it clear that Peter's mission was with the Jews (the circumcised). In Galatians 2:7 Paul wrote, '... *the gospel of the circumcision was unto Peter.*' In Romans 1:1,7; 11:13, 15:15-16, Paul stated that his mission was with the gentiles, especially in Rome. If any Jew should have been the first bishop/pope of Rome it should have been him because he spent so many years there. But he was not popular, and was arrested and killed because he preached the true gospel. Peter's

The Greatest War Ever

travels did not go west to Rome until the end of his life when he felt he had to counteract the deception of Simon Magus Peter.

We are told this in the book "The Story of Redemption". It reads -

'The apostles Paul and Peter were for many years widely separated in their labours, it being the work of Paul to carry the gospel to the gentiles, while Peter laboured especially for the Jews. But in the providence of God, both were to bear witness for God in the world's metropolis, (Rome), and upon its soil, both were to shed their blood as the seed of a vast harvest of saints and martyrs. About the time of Paul's second arrest, Peter was also apprehended and thrust into prison. He had made himself especially obnoxious to the authorities by his zeal and success in exposing the deceptions and defeating the plots of Simon Magus, the sorcerer, who had followed him to Rome to oppose and hinder the work of the gospel. Nero was a believer in magic and had patronised Simon (ie Magus). He was therefore greatly incensed against the apostle (ie Peter), and was thus prompted to order his arrest…. Peter, as a Jew and foreigner, was condemned to be scourged and crucified.' That quote is from "The Story of Redemption" pages 315-316.

So, how could Peter have been the first bishop/pope of the Roman Catholic Church? His travels took him east to the city of Antioch in Syria, and to the Hebrews in Babylon to spread the gospel and to encourage the believers there.

Another important player and soldier in the Lord's army was also living at this time. His name was Luke. About 31 years after the Lord's crucifixion, Luke wrote the Book of Acts in 62AD. His book describes many events which affected the early church. No thanks to Simon Magus, false belief systems were already rising in the West (Rome, Greece), in the north (Asia Minor) and in the south in Alexandria, Egypt with the gnostics. God used Luke to warn the people of the time, about dangers which were beginning in Rome. And his writings were also for future believers like us today.

By 62AD when Luke was writing, Simon Magus was causing so much trouble and confusion among early believers. Many thought the sorcerer was a genuine follower of the Lord because he had been baptised

Simon Magus, Two Simon Peters and the First Bishop

and claimed to be a follower of Christ. They accepted him as one of the apostles and the chosen leader of the new church. Luke wanted to show people that Simon Magus Peter was NOT a genuine member of the new group of believers, and he exposed the real Simon Peter, the sorcerer.

It is so sad to think that deception had begun within only a few years after the Lord returned to Heaven. Satan would not give up his fight even though he knew he was doomed. The Great War of Words flared up and raged as never before. Satan was really desperate.

First Meeting of the Two Simon Peters: Let's look briefly at the first meeting of the two Simon Peters. Acts chapter 8:9-24 describes the first meeting between the two Simon Peters. It was just after the stoning and death of Stephen, that Philip went to a city in Samaria and proclaimed the gospel there and did miracles. People were healed and there was much joy and many baptisms. For many years, Simon Magus had been bewitching these people with his sorceries. But now, he saw in Philip's ministry, the power and miracles and people being converted. So, he decided to be baptized. However, this was just an external show because his heart did not repent or change.

When the apostles in Jerusalem heard that Samaria was receiving the Word of God, Simon Cephas Peter and John went up there. The two apostles prayed and laid their hands on the people so they would receive the Holy Spirit. Simon Magus asked to have this same power and offered to pay money for it. He coveted the top position of being an apostle, if not <u>the</u> leading apostle, and thought money would buy it for him.

However, Simon Peter refused the offer and told him that his heart was not right in the sight of God. Simon Magus first had to repent of his wicked ways and pray to God for forgiveness. Simon Cephas Peter saw a '*gall of bitterness.*' This was a well-known phrase meaning the person turned to idols and abominations of the heathens, and was in bondage to sin in a state of unrighteousness. Simon Cephas Peter knew that Simon Magus would combine pagan beliefs and customs with the truth in order to deceive.

After this first meeting, Simon Cephas Peter, John and Philip left the city to preach in other villages. Despite baptism, Simon Magus never did change his beliefs and ways. Right there and then, Satan was already preparing a counterfeit gospel. He had seen Christ's victory over death at the crucifixion in Jerusalem and immediately prepared to develop his fake religion and counteract the rise of the Lord's faithful followers. Simon Magus would become a top human agent, the leading villainous actor in the show. The fresh new pagan Roman Empire would flourish because of this man and his lying philosophies.

About 50-51AD Paul warned in his second letter to the Thessalonians 2:7, that there were already antichrists around ie those taking the place of Jesus. He wrote, *'For the mystery of iniquity doth already work...'* Who was the mystery of iniquity? It was the father of lies of course, Satan and his mysterious, deceitful ways of attacking using war weapons of words in sophistry. He was incredibly skilful at playing the word games to hunt as many human souls as he could.

About 250 years after Christ came, Jerome 340-420 AD wrote about Simon Peter, the apostle. He said that Peter, 'in the second year of Claudius goes to Rome to oppose Simon Magus, and there for 25 years beheld the sacerdotal chair until the last year of Nero.' (The sacerdotal chair is the same as the episcopal cathedra, the throne where the priest is the mediator between God and man.) So, Jerome claims that Simon Peter was in Rome for over twenty years including 14 years of Nero's reign. He was supposed to be the head of the early ecclesia/church from 54AD-68AD. But, looking at the facts, how could we believe this. Let's see what Scripture says and compare dates.

More Scriptural Proof: Today, the Catholic Church and its doctrines is based on the single claim and lie that Simon Cephas Peter was its first bishop-pope and founder. Their story goes that Simon Cephas Peter went to Rome and was successful in thwarting Simon Magus' plans and then assumed the title of bishop until his death in 68AD. 'The Book of Pontiffs'[3] claims that Peter was the first Bishop of Rome who, "occupied the episcopal cathedra (ie the bishop-pope's throne) for 25 years, 2 months, three days. He was bishop in the time of Tiberius Caesar, Gaius, Tiberius Claudius and Nero." Note that the length of his rule is very specific

---

[3] Translated by Raymond Davis and published in 1981.

Simon Magus, Two Simon Peters and the First Bishop

right down to the very day.

Many scriptures disprove this lie. They include the following five points.

1. We saw earlier that Rome was Paul's mission, not Peter's. It was Paul who wrote the letter to the Romans, not Peter. Paul was the one who established a faithful ecclesia or fellowship gathering in Rome. Galations 2:9 tells how James, John, Paul, Barnabas and Simon Cephas all agreed that Paul and Barnabas should go to the heathen, and James, Peter, John and Simon should go to the circumcised ones, the Jews. And that is what actually happened.

2. Paul went to Rome about 55-56 AD. If we go according to Catholic sources, Peter should have already been bishop-pope for over ten years. This does not make sense.

3. Acts 28:16-24 describes how Paul was put into prison in Rome. And afterwards, the community of new Christians and some Jews went to meet him and he shared the gospel. Surely, Peter should have been mentioned. Why not? Because he wasn't there!

4. While Paul was in Rome, he wrote to the Ephesians, Philippians, Colossians, Philemon and the Hebrews. He mentions other believers in Rome, but never Simon Cephas Peter. Why? Because Peter wasn't there!

5. Where was Simon Cephas Peter at the time Simon Magus went to Rome in 45 AD? He was in Jerusalem having been put into prison in 42AD. Acts 12:1-5 tells us that King Herod put him in prison intending to kill him. In 49AD Peter was back in Jerusalem attending a Council meeting. About 50-51AD he was in Antioch in Syria. In 52 AD he left Antioch for Asia Minor. 52-56AD, according to 1 Peter 5:13, he was travelling further east through Pontus, Galatia, Cappadocia, Asia and Bithynia. He met up with his brother Andrew in Sinope on the south shore of the Black Sea. In 65-66AD Peter is in the city of Babylon with Jews. How could he possibly have been the first bishop-pope of the Roman Catholic Church!

So, what is the conclusion from all this evidence? Peter could never ever have been the first pope of the Roman Catholic Church. He was too busy travelling to many other places. He didn't go to Rome until his last years. Who then, was the first bishop-pope of Rome? It had to be none other than Simon Magus Peter who had gone to Rome in 42AD and took the seat for 25 years teaching Babylonian mysticism and carrying out his own mysterious, secretive, priestly duties.

Now that some facts about the true situation have been established, let's see more of how Daniel's monster-beast cleverly began a whole new counterfeit belief system which would grow and thrive for the next 2000 years. Sophistry was the key because the whole show has always been about the Great War of Words.

Let's briefly look at the word 'pope.'

Word Origins of Pope: The very word 'pope' summarises everything. Pope simply means papa. Papa is an affectionate term for father or patriarch, the head of a family. The papa-pope is associated with the original word PTR through all its variations of the Peter-gods we mentioned earlier. The word pope also has roots in the original meaning of Peter which is interpreter or INTER-preter. So, in a Catholic sense, Saint Peter is the correct title for the first pope of Rome. But it is NOT Simon Cephas Peter, the apostle.

The key word is Peter, not Simon. In the word, pope, all that is left from the original word PTR is the P, but it still has a profound meaning. What an unbelievable and clever example of sophistry. What a genius Satan is at using words as war weapons, in twisting words and individual letters to get his own way. He deceptively used two names, Simon and Peter, to deliberately cause confusion. Tragically, there is no confusion today in the minds of most people because they don't even question the lie that Simon Cephas Peter is the rock and foundation of their church. It is blindly accepted today.

However, we now know that the mystery of the two Simon Peters is solved and the true first pope is completely revealed. A blurry piece in the Big Picture becomes clearer. It's like watching a magic trick. Once the secret of how it is done is revealed, all mystery and power fades away. The magician is seen for what he is—a fraud and deceiver. By revealing who the true first pope was, we have attacked the very foundation of the Roman Catholic Church. If everyone knew this information, I wonder if they would still believe that Pope Francis is God on Earth. How many more cracks would appear and break the system down?

I hope and pray this all makes sense to you. It's lot to take in, but is a perfect example of the skilful sophistry which operates in our world today and still influences millions of minds. Has your jaw been dropping like mine did as I wrote this talk? Has your stomach been leaping up into your throat like mine has been? These truths are sickening. Perhaps you have had enough for now?

(A short discussion was followed by a group agreement to continue the next section.)

Now, let's meet Simon Magus' mistress.

Scene 11. Simon Magus' Mistress

Helena: Let's side track a little to learn about the female companion of Simon Magus. In every gripping story there is an element of romance. This one is no different. But this one was a bit more than romance. The saying goes, 'Love makes the world go round.' But what sort of love? Is it God's agape Great Love that rules His kingdom of Universe? Is it physical human love on planet earth based on feelings, passion and sensuality? Or is it the worst possible love of all—Satan's love of hatred, destruction and death. Simon Magus and his mistress are a perfect example of the third type.

In every pagan religion, there are male and female deities ie copies or replicas of Nimrod and Semiramus. In paganism, there always has to be at least one male and a female. This is an earthly phenomenon because earth is the only planet in Universe where males and females are able to reproduce and continue life. This did not happen until Adam and Eve came, because they were created in God's image and able to create new life from their seeds. The Bible tells us that, in heaven, there is no marriage. The sinless inhabitants of other worlds do not need to reproduce because they all live forever and ever. Paganism in its many variations, is a belief system which only exists among humans on earth. Paganism does not exist anywhere else. In Satan's government, there always has to be a type of Nimrod and a Semiramus, because there has to be someone who created the world and people in the first place. His version of creation is a mere evil counterfeit of the true Creator Father-God.

We have seen how Nimrod certainly left his legacy of paganism from after the Flood. Semiramus, the woman in his life, did the same in her own way as can be seen in the lives of such women in the Bible as Queen Jezebel of Israel who seduced Israel into worshipping Baal. Then there was her daughter, Queen Athalyah of Judah, who carried on the foul customs. In the days after Christ's first coming, we see the legacy continue in a woman called Helena - the mistress, partner and companion of Simon Magus.

All these women were immoral and wicked seducers, the equivalents of Semiramus. You could not get a more appropriate type of woman to teach and tempt people to commit physical and spiritual fornication and adultery.

This is why John calls Babylon in his book of Revelation 17:1, '.... *the great whore..*' In verse 2 he says '... *with whom the kings of the earth* (and we know who they are) *have committed fornication and the inhabitants of the earth have been made drunk with the wine* (ie the people have becomes senseless because of false teachings and lies,) *of her fornication.*' He goes on to describe how she sat '*on a scarlet-coloured beast full of names of blasphemy having seven heads and ten horns.*' (ie the Daniel's monster beast) In verse 5 he says that '*... upon her head was name written MYSTERY, BABYLON THE GREAT, THE MOTHER OF HARLOTS AND ABOMINATIONS OF THE EARTH.*' In verse 18, he reveals that the woman '*is that great city* (Rome) *which reigneth over the kings of the earth.*' These are words from Revelation Chapter 17.

The women mentioned–Semiramus, Jezebel, Athalyah and Helena all represent Babylon and how Christ's bride, His church of believers, has been seduced and tempted away from Him to commit spiritual adultery by worshipping idols and other gods. It is like when a husband or wife leaves the other to love and adore someone else and share the same bed. This is human, physical adultery. When people call themselves Christians and love and worship idols in their religious practices, they have left the true Husband, Jesus. This is human, spiritual adultery.

Let's find out more about Helena. In a book called 'Pagan Rome and the Early Christians,' by Stephen Benko, it tells of a second century writer called Irenaeus. Irenaeus wrote about Simon Magus taking a woman called Helena out of slavery. She had been a temple prostitute in the city of Tyre, Phoenicia on the border of Samaria where Simon Magus grew up. The goddess, Succoth-Benoth or Venus, was worshipped there and it was the duty of the slaves to prostitute themselves. This is absolute, sheer, blatant blasphemy of God's beautiful act of creation.

It is a mockery of a sacred act between one man and one woman. But Satan turned it into many sinful crimes breaking God's laws and allowing people to commit adultery, fornication, offer human sacrifices to lifeless gods and goddesses, and to abuse bodies to the point of death. Satan directly attacks the very parts of the human body designed to create life. He knows full well that he and all the angels and fallen angels cannot create life and reproduce. This is one major reason why he holds such a hatred for human beings and wants us all destroyed. We are side-tracking once again. Back to the women.

Interestingly, Jezebel had also come from Tyre to marry Ahab and she became extremely powerful committing many atrocities. Likewise, Helena came from Tyre. She travelled around with Simon Magus and she continued her prostituting ways. She used magical arts, incantations, love potions and charms. Simon Magus exalted her by calling her 'the first conception in his mind' or 'the first idea.' He even claimed to have created her. What incredible arrogance and gall!

In the third and fourth centuries (AD. 260-340), Eusebius wrote about Helena. He told how the secret rites she carried out were so evil that they could not be put into writing. They were so bad that even the men would not talk about them. Helena and Simon Magus were also mentioned in the writings of Justin Martyr. So, they were well known centuries after they died. Today, no-one hears about them.

There are other books which talk about Simon Magus including E P Dutton's book called 'The Gnostics' (NY, 1977, page 45-46). These books describe how Simon Magus travelled with a companion called Helena and how he called himself the sun, and Helena was the moon. Where have we heard that before? Isn't that a continuation of the sun-god, Nimrod and the moon queen, Semiramus? Simon Magus also called himself Zeus, the Greek god and father of all gods. He called Helena, Athene and also Luna, just as Semiramus was called the moon-queen. Simon Magus claimed to have supreme power and Helena was also Ennoia or Sophia ie wisdom.

Can you see how the number of names are increasing? They are chosen with great significance leading to more confusion and deception? When we look at Gnosticism in the next talk, we will discover much more.

In Dutton's book, he describes how the evil pair were regarded as the Father and Mother of the universe, travelling around preaching, converting, and amazing the crowds by the miracles they performed. Of course, the so-called miracles had to be assisted by demonic powers. Their followers often called them 'our Lord' and 'our Lady.' This was happening just a few years after Christ's death. No wonder Luke was so concerned and wrote to warn people.

Because Simon Magus had been baptised, he still claimed to be a Christian, so it was very easy for him to blend false pagan beliefs and mythology with the new Christ-centred beliefs. He placed himself at the head of the movement and his followers even called themselves Christians. The storyline just gets muddier and muddier. The sophistry gets more and more sophisticated.

Justin Martyr wrote, 'And almost all the Samaritans and a few among the other nations, acknowledge and adore him as the first god. And one Helen who went about with him at the time, who before had had her stand in a brothel, they say that she was the First Thought that was brought into being by him (Simon Magus).'[4] Note that Justin himself was a Samaritan and would have certainly known the traditions and how Simon was regarded as a god. So, we can see why Simon Magus was called the *'great power of God,'* and was believed to have creative powers including creating Helen who he elevated to a goddess. This is one of many lies the wicked couple taught everywhere they went and

4 Encyclopedia Britannica quoting Justin.

Simon Magus, Two Simon Peters and the First Bishop

fooled masses of minds, all under the name of Christianity.

Simon Magus had a strong influence on Felix, governor of Judea and Samaria. Felix was an older man and a cruel one who committed adultery with a young beautiful Jewess. Her name was Drusilla and she was happily married to her own husband with no reason to leave him. But the SDA Bible Commentary tells us, 'Through the deceptive arts of Simon Magus, ... Felix had induced this princess (Drusilla) to leave her husband and become his wife.... The satanic devices of the conjurer and the betrayer succeeded, and Felix accomplished his purpose.' [5]

Consequently, two new names of Simon Magus and Helena, representing Nimrod and Semiramus, were added to the list of thousands already used for centuries in Babylon, Syria, Persia and Egypt. Their teachings would develop further through Gnosticism and the Roman Catholic Church. We continue to see how Satan uses sophistry by twisting words to cause doubt and confusion in order to get what he wants ie the glory, honour, power and worship from every human being. He hates humans so much because we are made in the image of God able to reproduce life. He wants none of us to go to Heaven and have the perfect happiness of eternal life which he lost. The sour grapes get more sour and bitter in his revenge on the Creator-King and His Son, Jesus.

Conclusion: It's time for the curtains to close on the dark, blackened battlefield of the planet-stage in the greatest show ever on earth. At this point, the two supernatural foes, Chief General Satan and Chief Commander Christ increased their intensity in the Great War. Once again, we leave our celestial seats and return to the battlefield-stage in the suspense of another cliff-hanger. Gnosticism is an amazing story.

Here is another little trailer to whet your appetite and encourage you to come back for the next episode. Next time you will see the death of Simon Magus and the legacy he left in the form of Gnosticism. Gnosticism will be the main focus of that talk. It's a topic not to be missed.

In the meantime, **Beware the sophistry! Beware the sophistry!** Look around you to see it hidden in plain sight and it will leap out at you. Just another current example from current events is the growing Truckies

---

[5] SDA Bible Commentary Vol. 67, p.1066

protests in Canada, Australia and now New Zealand. Notice how the mainstream media, the propaganda machine owned and controlled by levels above in the pyramid hierarchy, is reporting the news. It skirts around or glosses over the main points of the protests which is the mandatory injections and loss of human rights and freedoms with passports. It focuses on damage to the economy, people not going into shops, interviews with people who are supposedly suffering from lack of services, including medical and supplies, the noise of the horns in Ottawa and local residents' complaints. They don't mention that farmers have joined the truckies and police are supporting them, and that nurses and doctors and ordinary people and families are among the protesters. They show isolated pictures of violence which are usually done by those planted to stir up trouble. And the many thousands of protesters are called a fringe minority not representing the majority. Enough side-tracking or this talk will not finish.

Curtains open again for Part Five of this series, in two weeks' time, on February 26 at 2:30 pm sharp. Be there early to get the best seats with the best view.

Let's close with a prayer to the true Author of the show who is still in control of the torn and battered storyline.

Our dear ever-loving, ever-patient and merciful Heavenly Father, how long-suffering You are. Whatever suffering we are going through down here is nothing compared with what You must be feeling and what Your Son went through when he came down to the battlefield. Father-God, we praise your mighty name and give You all glory and honour, Creator of heaven and earth and the seas and everything in them, including us little human beings. Father, we are so miniscule in the whole of your kingdom of Universe, yet You still call us beloved and your precious 'little children.' Lord, on our own we cannot survive in this world. The devil's temptations are so great and we ask you to forgive our sins when we have gone astray. Please cleanse our hearts and keep us in right relationship with You. Work on our characters and make us fit for Heaven when Jesus comes to take His loyal soldiers back home with Him. Please keep your holy angels encamped around us, and protect us till next time when we meet for the next talk. In the name of Jesus, our Lord and Saviour, Chief Commander, Amen.

References:

- The Real Story Behind Christmas, Easter and Halloween–Vance Ferrell
- DVD: Voices of a dying Planet–Brian Neumann
- DVD: Rekindling the Reformation–Walter Veith
- rmi-ministries.com/Simon-of-the-Roman-Church.htm - Author: founder, Reuben ben Gershom (an orthodox Jew who spent seven years studying only Hebrew and Greek in the OT and NT with no outside references from man's writings at all) NB: rmi = Return Movement International
- 'Simon Magnus and the Origins of the Catholic Church' Ernest L Martin and John D Keyser : www.hope-of-israel.org.html
- The Two Babylons–Alexander Hislop
- www.britannica.com/biography/Simon-Magus
- A weekly series well worth watching is 'What's Up Prof' with Walter Veith and can be found on his website–www.clashofminds.com There are many excellent talks and series on this website to keep one up to date with current events with a Biblical perspective.

Part 5 – Act 5: Simon Magus' Death and Legacy of Gnosticism

Introduction and Review

A warm welcome to you all to Part Five in the series called The Greatest War Ever. Firstly, I wish to request that, if you recommend to your friends and family to listen to the series of talks on the CD, please tell them to start from Part One and listen in order. Otherwise, it's like reading a book and starting from the middle and missing out on basic foundations.

So, it's now time to sit back in your seats and hold on tightly for another rollercoaster ride. And let's be encouraged in all our trials during the last week. I don't know about you, but my week has been full of spiritual attacks from unexpected directions. I am very happy to phase off the planet for an hour and take a breather. Let's all be blessed by having a time of rest and refreshment from wherever you have come from on the battlefield below. Just for a few moments, enjoy the feeling of being a spectator along with the audience of angels - plus Enoch and Moses. The difference now though, is that there are even more humans sitting in the audience with us.

In the last episode, we were mostly observing the post marked Cross on our basic timeline. And we watched the early Roman Empire, the time of Christ's First Coming, and His return to Heaven. So, when He returned to His Father, He took with Him hundreds of those who were raised to life from the graves. These were the first fruits and were more miraculous evidence of Jesus' victory over death. They are a symbol of the final harvest of human souls to be taken to Heaven when the Chief Commander soon comes for the Second Time. We don't know the names of these loyal faithful soldiers, but they are also with us right now in the audience, watching intensely. They must be so relieved to be off the battlefield.

Simon Magus' Death and Legacy of Gnosticism

Let's pray and get straight into it. Our dear Father-God, our Creator of heaven and earth, the seas and all in them, we humbly acknowledge You as the One and only true God of Your kingdom of Universe. We give You all glory, honour and praise and worship. Lord, please forgive us our sins and blot them out of your Book of Iniquity. Please cleanse our hearts and clothe us with your robes of righteousness, so we can be in right relationship with You. May we please, by your mercy and grace, be among the second harvest of souls, the last fruits to be soon taken to Heaven and live with You in your Great Love forever in eternal bliss. And as we go through this next episode, please help us to understand a little more from Your outside, objective observation point. Please help me to explain simply and clearly some complex details of this mighty story. Please let me be an encouragement to the listeners. In Jesus' mighty name we pray, Amen.

In the last episode, we had a rough, rocky ride meeting the villain, Simon Magus, solving the mystery of the two Simon Peters, and discovering who the first bishop/pope of the Roman Catholic Church was. If you like a good show, you had all the features of goodies, baddies, drama, plots, whodunnits, trickery, seriousness, humour and even a bit of romance. We gasped, and groaned, laughed and cried. Sorry to say, but the road does not get any smoother. There's still a long way to go before we can say, 'And they all lived happily ever after.'

In this series, we have been looking at the Great War of Words raging all around our home planet-stage of Earth. We have seen how sophistry is Satan's main war weapon and how he has distorted the original storyline. But God's Word is the strong woven thread holding the intricate tapestry of life together. I think by now we understand very well that sophistry means the twisting of words to cause confusion and doubt, in order to get what one wants. And that is precisely what Satan has been doing for the last 6000 years after he was banished from Heaven and cast down here with one third of the fallen angels. He is the Triple S, the Secret Subjective Sophist. And we have exposed many of his tricks in events from the past up to the present day.

I am not going to do a long review to refresh your memories of the previous talks, except to say that we've touched on many topics and often got side-tracked into others which are very relevant. I think by now, we all have a mental picture of the earth as a globe-shaped stage with human performers. Human actors act out the character of their Chief General Satan. Players play the roles they were designed for, to reflect the character of the Chief Commander Jesus. The players' role is also to prove to the rest of Universe that God's Law of Great Love is the best and only way to rule any kingdom.

And I think we also understand how God is the Triple 0, the Outside Objective Observer, who is still in control of His Story, despite the interference of manstory by humanist historians. And I think we understand the most amazing act of love by our Father-God of allowing Himself to go on trial, to let the jury of all His created beings in Universe be the judge of whether His methods of theocratic government are best or not. Our Heavenly Father-God Almighty is allowing His enemy, Satan, to have a just a temporary time of power over the Earth. He is allowing sin to run its full course for a purpose. He wants everyone to see very clearly the difference between His Law of Great Love with its gift of free will, and Satan's Law of Great Hate with its inflictions of fear, force, deception and destruction. God wants no-one to have any doubts whatsoever, as to Who is the rightful Ruler of His kingdom of Universe.

We have also met a lot of players and actors, goodies and baddies and I won't go into their names again except to say that in the last episode, we were introduced to Simon Magus. Wasn't that an eye-opener - a real shocker! Today we will look at his death and legacy of Gnosticism. We will go deeper into Gnosticism, its background, some examples of its beliefs, and how they counterfeit the truth, and affect our lives today. So, let's go!

Curtains Up! Lights On! Let The Show Continue!

Scene 12. The Death of Simon Magus and the Legacy He Left Behind

Death of Simon Magus: There are different versions as to how Simon Magus, the first bishop/pope of Rome, died. One story goes that he requested to be buried alive and would demonstrate his power over life. He claimed he would rise to life in three days. Of course, this was a hopeful counterfeit of Christ's recent resurrection and did not happen.

Simon Magus' Death and Legacy of Gnosticism

Another popular story says that, when Simon Cephas Peter, the apostle, went to Rome, there was a contest over whether Simon Magus had miraculous powers or not. Simon Magus planned to fly up to heaven crowned with a laurel, a wreath of leaves on his head, and in sight of the Roman emperor to make a good impression. Apparently, some demons called Menons would support him and carry him off. So, he flung himself off a tower. But according to the story, Simon the apostle knelt down and prayed commanding the menon-demons to release him. Simon Magus fell to the ground and broke his legs. Another version of his death says he was dashed to pieces.

Today there is a stone which Catholic tradition claims is the exact stone where the Simon, the apostle, knelt down. It is seen as a sign of proof that the event actually happened. Sounds like just another Catholic relic to me, to be worshipped and used as evidence that Simon Cephas Peter was divine and was the first bishop/pope of Rome.

Yet another story says that Simon Magus died under the hands of unskilful doctors after his fall. Other records state that he lived a good old age and was buried in Rome in a sacred cemetery on Vatican Hill. Catholic tradition has it that his remains lie directly under St Peter's Basilica. The Catholic Church claims however, that the bones are from Simon Cephas Peter, the one they say is the foundation and rock of their church. There is an engraving on a door of the Basilica, of Simon Magus attempting to fly off a tower in front of the emperor and the people. One carved plaque in the Basilica shows Simon Magus falling off a cross. And inside the Basilica is a section entitled 'Episodes in the Life of Saint Peter.' But which Peter?

In the previous talk, I mentioned a long article by Ernest L Martin and John D Keyser called 'Simon Magnus and the Origins of the Catholic Church.' This is where I got much of my information about Simon Magus (or Magnus) from. The article has many details of the story of the bones of Simon Magus and how, in 1942, less than a hundred years ago, a skeleton was discovered underneath the high altar in the Basilica. It was wrapped in a royal purple and gold cloak. The bones were assembled, but the feet were missing. This strongly suggests that they were from Simon Magus, the one who jumped off a building, broke his legs, had a botched operation and probably had his feet amputated. Later in 1968, Pope Paul VI made a fascinating announcement that the bones of Saint Simon Peter, the apostle had been found right under where the high altar stands in the Basilica. Hmmm. What a lie! Today, privileged visitors can enter the small silent chamber under the high altar to pay homage and respects to what they believe is the final resting place of Simon Peter. The bones are encased in transparent boxes and can be seen through a narrow opening.

Wouldn't Simon Magus' death make a fascinating movie? All these tales add to his mystery, and they add to the confusion and distraction away from God. To go into all the gory details of Simon Magus' death would be a major distraction right now. But you can read it for yourself and the whole article by googling www.hope-of-israel.org/magus.html.

So, all in all, the mysteries over Simon Magus and Simon the apostle are a part of the mysticism and secrecy of the counterfeit Roman Church system founded on paganism. All the stories play their parts in the battles of the Great War between Satan and Christ. Whatever the truth is, Catholic tradition still lives on. The two Simon Peters have been confused ever since and the lie is not even disputed because millions believe it. How does Simon Magus affect us today?

Simon Magus' Legacy: Simon Magus left a legacy which spread like wildfire. For a time, his followers were called Simonians and soon became known as Christians as they flocked to the temple in Rome on Vatican Hill. By the end of the first century, there were over fifty sects of Simonians, but their headquarters was always in Rome. In the second century, the heresy spread east and west in different gnostic schools. In the third to fourth centuries, the historian, Eusebius, wrote how people fell down before pictures and images of Simon Magus and Helena as they were portrayed in the statues of Jupiter and Minerva. By the fifth century, all sects had been absorbed into the Roman Church. These are of course, just a part of the ongoing legacy of Nimrod and Semiramus way back in the First Babylonian Empire.

After the Chief Commander, Christ, left the planet for Heaven, there were many mighty warriors fighting for Him. We have met Luke, Paul and John who fought courageously with other disciples. They used their

Simon Magus' Death and Legacy of Gnosticism

word war weapons as they travelled and preached. Some wrote down what was going on, and gave warnings and advice to all who would listen. In the Book of Acts 8:9-21 written about 62AD, Luke warns strongly about the origins of Simon Magus which we looked at in the last talk. These twelve verses identify Simon Magus the sorcerer, as the founder of the Roman Catholic Church. People said, *'This man is the great power of god.'* They saw him as being divine just like Pope Francis today.

Paul also referred to Simon Magus in his letters to Timothy and Titus and gave more details of the false teachings and activities going on. Although they do not specifically mention the name Simon Magus, the lies would have stemmed from him. Paul's words also apply to those deceivers among us in these last days. He writes, they are *'traitors, heady, high-minded, lovers of pleasure more than lovers of God, having a <u>form</u> of godliness but denying the power thereof...ever learning and never able to come to the knowledge of truth.'* 2 Timothy 3:5-8

People in Paul's day were no different and just as easily fooled as people today. In 2 Timothy 4:3-4, Paul describes a time when, *'they will not endure sound doctrine but, after their own lusts, shall they heap to themselves teachers, having itching ears, and they shall turn away their ears from truth, and shall be turned unto fables.'* Today we will discover how Gnosticism is full of fables, fantasy, fiction, myths and imaginations. Paul wrote in Titus 1:16 *'They profess that they know God, but in works they deny Him, being abominable, and disobedient and unto every good work reprobate.'* This describes today as well.

John, another warrior, also saw what was happening and later wrote very strongly about the false Christianity of Simon Magus. He actually writes more to clarify the truth about the Samaritans than did Matthew, Mark and Luke.

John's Book of Revelation, with all its symbolism, warns of the counterfeit belief system we are to be aware of. He prophesised the history of the seven churches throughout the coming centuries until the coming of the Messiah. At the same time, his writings show how the true Church would come into contact with the false system and its many antichrists. This system can be traced back to those Samaritans, who we know from the previous talk, originated in the five pagan tribes brought in by the Assyrians from Babylon. Years after they settled in Canaan, they followed the false Israelite priest. Consequently, in the years just after Christ came, many claimed to be believers in the one true God. Some of these Samaritans became the New Testament so-called Christians, who were actually followers of Simon Magus, the first bishop/pope.

John writes about these antichrists. In 1 John 2:18, he says, '... *as ye have heard that antichrist shall come* (ie in the future), *even now are there many antichrists...*' In 1 John 2:22 he says, 'Who is a liar, but he that denieth that Jesus is the Christ? *He* is antichrist, that denieth the Father and the Son.' In 2 John verse 7 he writes, '*For many deceivers are entered into the world,* (ie in his time) *who confess not, that Jesus Christ is come in flesh. This is a deceiver and antichrist.*' And in 2 Thessalonians 2:7 John says, '*For the mystery of iniquity doth already work...*'

This was happening well within the first century after Jesus came to the planet as Saviour. Satan wasted no time in sending out his agents pretending to be types of Christ.

The Great Controversy page 511 tells about these days. It reads, 'During the time when Christ was upon earth, evil spirits manifested their power in a most striking manner. And why is this? Christ had come to enter upon the plan devised for man's redemption, and Satan therefore determined to assert his right to control the world. He had succeeded in establishing idolatry in every part of the earth except the land of Palestine. (Note that this includes all the nations and tribes scattered on every continent and island. They were riddled with paganism coming from Nimrod, Semiramus and Tammuz!) The quotation continues, 'To the only land that had not fully yielded to the tempter's sway, Christ came to shed upon people, the light of heaven. Here, two rival powers claimed supremacy. Jesus was stretching out His arms of love inviting all who would, to find pardon and peace in Him. The hosts of darkness understood that if His mission should be successful, their rule was soon to end. Satan raged like a chained lion and defiantly exhibited his power over the bodies as well as the souls of men.'

Doesn't this speak to us today as we approach the next major climax in His Story when our Rescuer comes the second time. The situation now is similar to that in the first century AD, but is far, far worse. Isn't there idolatry in every single continent, nation and island on earth? In those days there was only a minority, a remnant of believers left in a tiny area on the planet. But praise God, because of Christ's sacrifice on the Cross, His gospel, good news, spread out to the gentiles. Consequently today, there is still a minority, a remnant, not just in one tiny place, but scattered all over the globe. These players, you and I, are the ones left to continue spreading the gospel.

The Future of Simon Magus

What is the future of Simon Magus, all the antichrists after him, and all their followers? Jesus already knew about the workings of the sorcerer when He came. He told of the time at the end of the world, in the parable of the sower and the seed. He said that the weeds are the *'children of the wicked one.'* Simon Magus was just a wicked weed. The verse continues, *'The enemy that sowed them is the devil. The harvest is at the end of the world, and the reapers are the angels. As therefore the tares are gathered and burned in the fire, so shall it be in the end of the world. The Son of man shall send forth His angels, and they shall gather out of His kingdom, <u>all</u> things that offend, and <u>them</u> which do iniquity; and shall cast them into a furnace of fire. There shall be wailing and gnashing of teeth.'* Matthew 13:38-42

So, we can be assured that Simon Magus Peter will be among those in the lake of fire. It was <u>his</u> choice and foolish decision to make Satan his Chief General. He could have easily submitted to Jesus. He was there at the time Jesus came physically. He could have easily submitted to the teachings of the gospel by the disciples. But no, he abused his precious gift of free will and determined his own fate.

The Great Controversy page 516 describes similar people who <u>knowingly</u> choose that direction. It reads, 'Those possessed with devils are usually represented as being in a condition of great suffering; yet there were exceptions to this rule. For the sake of obtaining supernatural power, some welcomed the Satanic influence. These of course, have no conflict with the demons. Of this class were those who possessed the spirit of divination–Simon Magus...' and she mentions a couple of others.

How many millions today in the Satanic church welcome the devil's influence? How many young ones today have been deceived through entertainment, music, movies, sports and computer games, and are fascinated and seduced into wanting to know more about this wicked side of the supernatural sphere. They may not suffer right now because Satan makes sure they feel good and happy and excited. Singers and actors and other entertainers get rewarded materially with fame and wealth and possessions, if they go along with the ways of Jesuit and freemasonry theatre. To them life is all about Self, self-pleasures and the present. They may enjoy the comforts of life and not suffer physically now, but their time will come in the end Judgment. All because of deception, poor choices and misuse of the gift of free will.

Let's move on now and dig into Simon Magus' legacy of Gnosticism and find out what that word reveals.

Scene 13. Gnosticism

Meaning of Gnosticism: Just like the word counterfeit, Gnosticism is another war weapon found in Satan's tool box of tactics. What is Gnosticism and how does it use sophistry? Gnosis is the Greek word for knowledge, science and awareness. Gno means to know.

Gnosis is <u>es</u>oteric. In other words, it is only understood and taught by a small group of people. It is private, confidential information and is made deliberately difficult to understand. Being esoteric therefore means, secret, mysterious and only for the chosen elect. It is hidden behind an <u>ex</u>oteric front which gives limited knowledge/science to the general public.

Gnosis is supposed to be a superior type of knowledge about supernatural, spiritual matters, about the nature of human beings, and how we can be delivered from this world. It assumes that a higher intelligence and ability is needed to understand its complexities. It automatically divides society into two classes—the superior, educated sophisticates, and the inferior, less educated or uneducated. The first group uses its power to have higher authority in Satan's pyramid government, to become wealthy, and be a part of the Elite. It aims to make sure that the second group becomes lower, poorer, illiterate and more like animals. That is

Simon Magus' Death and Legacy of Gnosticism

the essence of Gnosticism–superiority and inferiority.

History and Background: A very brief history trip takes us back to the roots of Gnosticism. Ultimately, like sophism and the original, very first sin of Satan's rebellion, it all started with the Great War of Words in Heaven. Satan, then called Lucifer, began manipulating the angels through their minds with words. Heaven was his first practice ground, and his sophistry soon continued on the earth with Eve at the forbidden Tree of Knowledge of Good and Evil. Eve was unaware that Satan was emphasising gnosis or secret knowledge, when he told her these words. '...*God doth know that in the day ye eat thereof, then ye shall be as gods, knowing good and evil.*' Until this moment, Eve had only ever experienced good and knew nothing about evil. Satan tempted her, not just with fruit, but also with higher intelligence. He offered the secret higher spiritual knowledge of the divine spark of life. Thus, he lured her away from simple trust, faith, and obedience to God's Law of Great Love.

As a consequence, Adam was also tempted and deceived, and then, so was the rest of humanity to come. This cost countless human lives. Hosea 4:6 tells how God's '... *people are destroyed for lack of knowledge...*' They lack knowledge of God's truth because Satan replaced it with confusion and his lies. And haven't we seen this in the previous four talks as we've travelled through the millenniums of our basic timeline and seen Satan's deception, destruction, mental torment, and murder of mankind!

Today scientists and technocrats focus largely on understanding how the world works in nature and discovering more about outer space. It's a seemingly good goal to bring people out of so-called barbarism and create a better, healthier, happier world than this one. But man's knowledge and goals are so limited compared with the Creator's. God's ultimate goal for us is to come back into right relationship with Him and live for eternity in perfection. His knowledge includes much more than science can reveal today. It is far, far greater than what we will ever learn on this planet. And God has exceedingly more for us in Heaven.

Exodus 35:31 describes a man called Bezaleel who was selected to work on building the tabernacle because of his vast knowledge and skills.

Bezaleel had six key things in order to have the same knowledge that God wants for us. Firstly, he was *'filled with the Holy Spirit.'* Secondly, he had *'wisdom,'* ie a sense of morality and what is right or wrong in God's eyes. The next two things he had were *'understanding* and *knowledge.'* So, he must have had good brains and been highly intelligent and educated. Fifthly, he also possessed *'all manner of workmanship'*, ie he was very skilful in different types of crafts. Sixthly, he must have also had 'a heart for God' wanting to do His divine will.

Satan does not want humans to have these six things and leads people away into his counterfeits of every one of them. He tempts his human prey with a fake Holy Spirit of himself and demons working in their mysterious ways. He tempts people to rely on man's judgement and wisdom which usually leads to immorality. Wrong becomes right, and good becomes bad. Man's understanding and knowledge are limited according to what scientific theories prove as true or not. Man prides himself at his human cleverness in all kinds of man-made inventions. Lastly, Satan tempts human hearts far away from God, so God's divine will is not carried out. Such is human knowledge/science/wisdom compared with God's. All this fake, false science so-called, is bound up in the deep, secret roots of Gnosticism.

What is that divine spark we mentioned earlier? It is the breath of life breathed into Adam and mankind which only the Creator can do. Satan targeted this very life because he knows he can never create life. Gnostic followers praise him for disguising himself in the Garden of Eden as a serpent, and promising Eve she would have gnosis ie knowledge of both good and evil. Gnostics believe this world is a prison bound by God's laws which are too hard to keep.

Satan was basically telling Eve she would be freed from this prison by having secret supernatural knowledge, and that she would become divine like a god knowing good and evil. And Satan knew all about evil because he is the father of it. In other words, he was implying she was not made in the image of God, and that it was better to be like himself. For a short time, Adam and Eve became actors, acting in the image of the Chief General and unknowingly carrying out his dirty work to overthrow their Father-Creator God. Praise God for His mercy and forgiveness, when He showed them the plan of salvation. Praise God, they left Satan's army. They switched from actors to players in the show.

Sadly however, sin had already entered the earth through sophistry and Gnosticism. Everyone ever since knows evil as well as good. Sin means breaking God's Law. In Heaven, Satan broke God's Law by rebelling and he has spent the last 6000 years still attacking the Ten Commandments in an attempt to destroy them. God's Law is the very foundation of His theocratic government. Satan, as Lucifer, was once a covering cherub standing beside the seat and gazing down on the Commandments. He knew them so well, but now, he hates them with a vengeance.

After Adam and Eve, the Great War in heaven continued when Cain chose Satan's army and went astray. The secret knowledge of Gnosticism continued through over one and a half millenniums right through to Noah's great grandson Nimrod. Nimrod took Gnosticism to the extremes. His tower of Babel was the centre of astrology, magic and Cabala and is the key to all occultism. Occultism spread around the globe in the great continental split and has flourished ever since.

Masses of tiny little ant-like humans have been scurrying around on earth, refusing to accept the truth of God. They have chosen not to accept the same wonderful words of wisdom and teachings which Adam and Eve received before the Fall. Instead, with the help of Satan and his demons influencing thoughts, these tiny little people have invented fiction stories about the sun, moon planets and stars to try and find some meaning in life. In this way Satan has continued to deceive and control the world's population.

The Gnostic Babylonian mysteries are the basis of paganism, nature worship, pantheism and all the counterfeit belief systems of the past 4000 years. The secret knowledge of Gnosticism has been a major part of the heathen religions of Assyria, Egypt, Persia, Greece, India, the Orient and the Americas. The pyramids, ziggurats and obelisks all over the world are variations of the Tower of Babel. They are like defiant fingers pointing to up to God heaven with the message, 'I will do things MY way, not Yours.' They are also phallic symbols attacking, mocking and ridiculing the very part of the body where God planted seeds to create human life.

The Greatest War Ever

Consequently, heathen nations developed all over the planet with their counterfeit religions. All are figments of the imagination and inventiveness found in Gnosticism and sophistry. Moving along in the timeline: in the sixth century BC, the Jews were influenced even further by magic when they were exiled in Babylon. Some brought back pagan beliefs and customs to Jerusalem. Satan especially attacked God's chosen people with his gnostic, secret, fascinating knowledge. Today, he still especially attacks all those who profess to be Christians and has led countless people away from God.

Words, words everywhere; the War of Words went on. The mental battle for minds and souls continued. Herein lies the roots of Gnosticism—the use of words. Words, words, words; weird, wacky and wicked. Sophistry and Gnosticism go hand in hand. Gnosticism is the secret knowledge, and sophistry is the twisted words to express it. So many things we have talked about in the previous four talks all come together in Gnosticism. Where do hear today, sermons about sophistry and Gnosticism? We don't. And we don't hear about Simon Magus, the father of Gnosticism. Yet, these are the essence of the Great War of Words, the Great Controversy.

Incidentally, what is a controversy? It means a state of prolonged public dispute or debate over matters of conflicting points of view. It comes from the Latin, 'turned in an opposite direction.' Surely, this sums us the last 6000 years of life on earth. The controversy over good and evil has been very prolonged. Praise God it is about to come to an end. And in Heaven, there will be no sophism and Gnosticism.

Two Types of Science
Meaning of Science—Let's look deeper into the word, science. The word simply means knowledge. Science and knowledge are exactly the same thing. Strong's Concordance tells us that knowledge means to be aware, to acknowledge, to perceive, to know and understand. This is found in H1847 and H3045. (H1847 doa'th cunning, know, aware;) The Greek G1108 is gnosis which means knowledge, science; G1197 ginosko means to feel, to know, perceive, understand, be sure. The Collins dictionary says science means knowing, familiarity by experience, information, understanding.

Simon Magus' Death and Legacy of Gnosticism

The Bible only mentions the word science twice. One is positive and the other is negative. The first is in Daniel 1:4 describing, '*Children in whom was no blemish, but well-favoured and skilful in all wisdom and cunning in <u>knowledge</u> and understanding <u>science</u>....*' Daniel was one of those and was chosen with a group of others to serve in the king's palace because of their intelligence. This was an example of God's <u>true</u> original version of science/knowledge. The second verse is in 1 Timothy 6:20 when Paul advised Timothy to avoid, '*profane and vain babblings, and <u>oppositions of science falsely so called</u>.*' The science/knowledge of his day, ie the Gnosticism of the first century AD, was riddled with opposition from lies and deception just like the present time.

Satan would have us believe that science is for the scientists, the so-called experts, and that we should put our trust in them and their experiments and research, and not in man's common sense, or inner heart knowledge ie science of God and His wisdom. Oh, can we see this happening all over the world right now with COVID. Politicians say, 'Trust the science.' 'This is what the experts say.' And people copy them as they justify why they have the jabs. The phrase gets repeated so often that it is believed.

But so many of these scientists, supposedly highly intelligent, knowledgeable people, are mere puppets. Their strings are pulled and moved around by the puppeteers above them. Financial rewards and pressures are given to push experiments through drug trials as fast as possible. Then, these highly intelligent minds bias and alter their results and statistics to deliberately deceive multitudes. I wonder how many scientists actually realise they are soldiers in Satan's army. I'm sure some truly believe they are doing the right thing by humanity, but even so, many are still having their consciences pricked by the Holy Spirit. They intuitively know things are not right and the handling of this COVID situation is catastrophic.

Praise God, there are some scientists using common sense, God-given wisdom, true understanding and awareness, plus heaps of scientific evidence to prove that things are deadly in the COVID crisis. Many are realising this is a man-made crisis invented in order to gain power and control over the population. Let's not get side-tracked. Back to the word, science.

Trust in God or Man: There are two types of science. One is the science of <u>faith in God</u> with access to His knowledge, understanding, wisdom. The other is the science of putting <u>trust in man</u>. The second meaning is the most common one where trust is placed in theories, hypotheses, and doing experiments to investigate and test what works or doesn't, and what is true or not.

Of course, Satan has to have his counterfeit of the two types of science. In the fourth century BC, there was a Greek philosopher called Plato who wrote a book called 'The Statesman.' In it he wrote, '... divide all science into two parts calling the one practical, Gk praktikos, and the other purely intellectual, Gk gnostikos.' Note that this is the same as gnosis which we learned earlier. Gnostikos or gnosis is only understood and taught by a small intellectual group of people, the sophisticates. And we have learned that it is private, confidential information and deliberately difficult to understand. And it is esoteric therefore also means, secret, mysterious and only for the elect.

Plato also says, 'Let us assume that all science is one, and that these are its two forms.' ie praktikos and gnostikos. So, he is saying that there is basically only one type of science but with two parts. One is practical as in experiments, and the other is intellectual as in interpreting the results. These are both centred around human thinking.

Therefore, Plato's definition of science is humanistic and does not involve God and His science of faith. But Hebrews 11:1 tells us there is the 'science of faith.' It states, '*Now faith is the substance of things <u>hoped for</u>, the evidence of* things <u>not seen</u>.' An important part of science/knowledge is faith and checking the Bible to see what it says. It seems such a waste of time, effort and money to spend so many years coming up with theories, and following with experiment after experiment, when the blatant truth is already in the Bible. Much of humanist science is a successful tool of Satan to distract from God. But praise God, there are some scientists who have acknowledged Him in their work and proved He has been correct all along. There's a lovely book by Ann Lamont called '21 Great Scientists who Believe the Bible.' It tells about just a few of them. Back to Gnosticism or we will get side-tracked.

Simon Magus' Death and Legacy of Gnosticism

Gnostic Science/Knowledge: The Greek word, Gnosticism, came into common use in the first century AD. It was well known to describe Luciferian occultism just like we could use the term New Age today. Irenaeus, bishop of Lyons in the Waldensian church in Gaul/France wrote that Simon Magus is the 'Father of Gnosticism.' Irenaeus wrote furiously against the beliefs.

In the developing Roman Church in the second century, Clement of Alexandria wrote a classic definition of gnostic knowledge in his book called 'Excerpta Theodoto'. He said Gnosticism is, 'the knowledge of who we were, and what we have become, where we were, or into what we have been thrown, whither we hasten, from what we have been redeemed.'[6] This definition might sound plausible to some, but when you get into the details it is full of lies and mythology. It is centred around Self. Notice how many times the word, 'we' is used in the definition–six times. Also, notice the phrase, 'into what we have been thrown.' This implies humans have been dumped into a situation and are victims of circumstance. In other words, whatever bad happens, it's not our fault– we aren't responsible for our choices.

This is Satan's character showing up through and through because he always shifts the blame onto someone else and avoids responsibility. Satan was the one 'thrown' out of Heaven and cast down to Earth. He was the one punished with banishment and he wants us to feel the same. But–no! God did not create us to be banished and 'thrown down' and cast out like Satan. God cast his first two players, Adam and Eve onto the perfect stage of the Garden of Eden and had wonderful lives all planned out for them. God created us with the purpose to defend Him in the great court trial to prove Him as rightful Ruler of Earth and all Universe.

As Christianity was just beginning to develop in that first century AD, Satan's immediate reaction was to counterfeit the truth with Gnosticism. The great cosmic war, the great controversy raged big time and has never stopped. Simon Magus was the chief human agent of the day, when he started his school in Rome. Just like the apostles, he and his students or disciples travelled around Samaria, Palestine, Syria and Ana-

6 The Gnostics by Tobias Churton Pg 74 Underlinings are the writers emphasis.

tolia/Asia Minor. Sometimes the two groups came into confrontation with each other. Throughout the following centuries, there were various movements of Gnosticism. In the next section, we will look briefly at some of the ideas.

I think that is a long enough study of the meaning of the words–Gnosticism, science and knowledge. You have a pretty good idea of what they mean. Let's see how they work in practice in belief systems. What follows is a few examples.

Examples of Gnostic Beliefs

Humanism: One of the foundations of Gnosticism is humanism which puts man and self above the Creator God. The creation becomes more important than the Creator. The following quote is from a famous twentieth century American gnostic writer called Elaine Pagels. (Princeton Uni and Barnard College). She has many followers and wrote a book called 'The Gnostic Gospels.' In it, she said, '…Gnosis involves an intuitive process of knowing oneself. Yet to know oneself at the deepest level, is to know God; this is the secret of gnosis.' BUT - the opposite is true. To know God is to know oneself. He created humans, therefore to know ourselves, we must understand how He designed and formed us and what His purpose for us is.

Other gnostic writers besides Elaine Pagels, have their own descriptions and definitions of Gnosticism. They say that gnosis is based on cosmology, myth, study of human behaviour and cultures, and putting the ideas into practice. Notice that all these things depend on man's interpretation of the stars and planets, man's fiction and imagination. They are open to unlimited, personal variations. And they are also open to demonic influence. Every person on the planet can have their own idea of right and wrong. This leads to billions of philosophies. And everyone is right and has their own rights. And, oh, how they fight for their rights! No wonder there is so much war, rioting, and conflict today. The result is chaos - all because they have rejected God.

We can see how man's version of science is based on humanism, self, imagination and the minds are open to Satan and his demonic influences. How evident is this when we look at the pharmaceutical companies, the sorcerers of Revelation 18:23 It says, *'For by thy sorceries were all*

Simon Magus' Death and Legacy of Gnosticism

nations deceived.' We know that the word sorceries comes from the Greek farmakiah, the root of our word pharmacy.

Let's go down the gnostic path just a little further. There is a saying, 'Know thy enemy.' Our invisible supernatural enemy needs to be exposed as much as possible. Gnosticism is not understood by most people and just a little knowledge of it will help to recognise it in everyday life. Like sophistry, it is evident all around us once we are aware of it. As I describe some of the features, notice the counterfeits and snippets of truth slipped in among all the lies to cause confusion.

There have been many different gnostic groups with various teachings throughout the millenniums. One summary lists at least 90 sects today. But they all have the same basis to distort the truth and combine truth with fiction, facts, imagination, secrecy, mystery and magic. This jumbled mess is designed to mislead, cause confusion and, most importantly, to distract from the absolute truth of the existence of the Godhead–Father, Son and Holy Spirit. Here are just two examples about different gnostic sects. Brace yourself.

The Sethian Sect teaches a creation and salvation myth about a 'first thought' called Ennoia. We heard that name in the last talk when Simon Magus' mistress Helena was also called Ennoia. Ennoia, being a thought, was produced from the Father's mind in order to create angels. To start with, Ennoia was just a thought with no material, physical body. Hmmm. Didn't we hear this in the last talk about how Simon Magus' claim to have created Helena? He called her his 'first thought.' In this Sethian sect of Gnosticism, angels are said to have created the visible universe. After this happened, the thought of Ennoia turned into a jealous thought. Doesn't this sound like Satan himself becoming jealous of Jesus?

Consequently, because of jealousy, Ennoia was imprisoned and placed in a human body so she could not return to the Father. She, the jealous thought, was doomed to pass from body-to-body. Eventually this included Helena, the woman with Simon Magus. The story goes that, in order to redeem and save the first thought (Ennoia), the Father descended in human shape as none other than Simon Magus. Isn't this a counterfeit of God's Son Jesus? Simon Magus was supposedly the one who came and offered salvation to human beings - if they recognised him as their first god. What a toxic concoction of poison to twist the mind!

It just gets worse and more unbelievable. The Sethians believe that the mind of the Father (ie God), suffered a mental breakdown and lost its wisdom. This mind was then called Aeon Sophia. Hmmm. Wasn't Helena also called Sophia? Consequently, Sophia became a mixture of insanity and emotions which eventually created the material world. To cope with this, she fooled herself into thinking she was a human. To restore a sound mind, the humans had to reconnect with the soundness of the Father-God's mind. BUT—wasn't that mind supposed to have broken down! That's enough to give us a taste of the Sethians.

Let's look at the Valentinians.

Valentinius A well-known common gnostic belief system is named after Valentinius who lived about 100-160AD, just after Simon Magus. Valentinius founded a school in Rome and was even a candidate for bishop/pope. But when someone else was chosen, he started his own group of followers called Valentinians. Over the centuries, many variations of this sect were formed.

The basic beliefs go something like this. Listen for the tiny bits of truth mixed into a soup of lies. There is a Propator, ie a Supreme God. Note the spelling. Pro means 'for something.' Eg pro-life. Pator comes from Peter, PTR, meaning god which we learned about in the last talk. So Pro-Pator means 'for god.' Of course, that is a pagan god with a lower-case g.

This Valentinian Pro-Pator, or Supreme God, supposedly lives in a divine realm called Pleroma. He has 30 Aeons. One of these is called Sophia (wisdom). Sophia lives in a middle region just below Pleroma but still above heaven. So, can you see a pyramid hierarchy forming? At the top, there is supposed to be the realm of Pleroma where the Propator Supreme God lives. Then there is a middle area for Sophia-wisdom. Then there is Heaven. So, it seems that Satan is creating two levels above Heaven, the highest possible authority in God's real Universe. Hmmm, interesting that he is admitting there is a heaven. But he is putting himself as the Supreme God, at the very top even higher than the

Simon Magus' Death and Legacy of Gnosticism

Most High!

The story goes on that Sophia apparently had a daughter, called Achamoth who is 'lower wisdom.' Achamoth created three kinds of substances - a) spiritual, b) animal and c) material. One special animal creation was called Demiurge. Today, Gnostics see the Demiurge as the equivalent of our true Creator God. Back in ancient Greece, the philosopher, Plato, wrote that Demiurge took material out of chaos and created the world. Hmmm. Could this be the origin of the Big Bang theory? Maybe.

Let's go on. According to Valentinian Gnosticism, Demiurge is not THE Creator. He was just born and therefore a consequence of something else. He was created part animal and part-human. Hmmmm. Is this possibly the true origin of the theory of evolution? Maybe. Other sects say that Demiurge was not created but he just was. The Demiurge was a god even though he was still an inferior ruler of the animal and psychic world. Apparently, he also made the devil. Hmmm. Satan is admitting there is a devil.

Note, that Plato was born 427 BC and Demiurge was a god way back then. Therefore, these Gnostic ideas which are still believed today, go right back to the ancient Greek Empire before the Roman Empire. But the word demiurge goes back even further to the ancient Egyptians, long before the Greeks. The Egyptians imagined the world in a perfect state conceived by a solar demiurge. This has to be the sun-god, Nimrod.

Anyway, the Valentinian legend goes on. Demiurge was apparently surprised the world turned out so well out of this chaos, but it was not perfect. So, he sent a Saviour, a Messiah to redeem humans. Hmmm. Surely this is a counterfeit of Jesus, the true Saviour! Some sects say that Demiurge is malevolent ie spiteful, revengeful, bitter, grudging. Others say he is simply ignorant and misguided. What a degrading image of our Lord, Jesus Christ!

Today, the word demiurge is used in ordinary language, not often, but it is occasionally heard. It describes an individual or group who is chiefly responsible for a creative idea. 'Dem' is Latin meaning 'master of craftsmen,' or an artisan. So, demiurge describes an artistic, creative person.

An artist is sometimes described as a demiurge locking himself away in his studio to create his work of art.

What does the Valentinian belief system hold for the future of mankind? According to this way of thinking, the three types of substances (spiritual, animal and material) created by Achamoth (daughter of Sophia, wisdom), all have different endings. Firstly, the purely spiritual beings who receive gnosis (the secret knowledge) will be freed from the Demiurge, and the prison of this world with its laws which are supposedly too hard to keep. These spiritual beings will be separated from body and soul to go with their Saviour and with Achamoth to the Father, Propator Supreme God, in the divine Pleroma above heaven, and above the middle region where Sophia-wisdom lives.

Are you following? It gets complicated. The second substance of animal-humans will go with the Demiurge and enter a 'middle state' and have a lesser form of salvation, whatever that means. The third group of material physical men, the most animal-like ones, will return to the grossness of matter and be consumed by fire. Aha - Satan knows there will be a lake of fire! Can you see similarities today with the Elite, the middle class, and the sheeple-people? Those at the bottom level are regarded as nothing but a body to return to the ground. Their souls don't matter to the Elite.

Here is a quote from a gnostic believer called Tobias Churton. He wrote a book called "The Gnostics", published in 1987. Chapter Three is entitled 'Madness and Blasphemy.' It describes the Valentinian system. He said, 'Sophia forms (makes) a demiurge—a creator—to make something out of the mess that has come about. He organises heaven, earth and the creatures which live on it. Most importantly, we can see that this demiurge is a poor copy of the eternal archetypes and is identified with the god of the Old Testament (who is) a deficient being who seems unaware of his deficiency and is determined that his creatures shall remain unaware of their source.'

In other words, what he is saying is that Sophia created the Demiurge, our Father God, who merely organises heaven and earth and all the creatures including human beings. This Demiurge, our perfect ever-loving Father, is depicted as bad, and one of the ancient archetypes. This

Simon Magus' Death and Legacy of Gnosticism

Demiurge wants humans to be ignorant of where they come from.

So, as a result, Gnostics believe that humans are not saved from sin, but they are saved from ignorance–ignorance of not having the secret knowledge. Oh, how Satan wants us to be ignorant of God's truth that we need to be saved from sin, ie breaking the law. Oh, how he distracts mankind from the existence of God's Ten Commandments and he claims they are too hard to keep, just like he told the angels back in Heaven.

What a description of our merciful, forgiving Father-God of Great Love who describes Himself in His own love-letters in His Word, the Bible! What a terrible view the Valentinians have of human beings! In Exodus 20:11 it says God is the Creator. *'For in six days, the Lord made heaven and earth and the sea and all that in them is...'* Exodus 3:14 says God told Moses at the burning bush *'I AM THAT I AM.'* Exodus 34:6 says, *'The Lord God, merciful and gracious, long-suffering and abundant in goodness and truth.'* Genesis 1:26 says about humans, *'And God said, "Let us make man in our image, after our likeness..."'* We are not animals. Psalm 8:1. *'How excellent is Thy name in all the earth!'* God is not a poor copy of previous beings called archetypes. There was none before Him.

A very quick look through the history timeline of Gnosticism. We have looked at the roots. In the 1400-1500s, came the Hermetic philosophy of Gnosticism with further developments. Gnosticism seemed to go underground for a time. But it never died and still existed in the Rosicrucianists of the 1600s, and freemasons in the 1700s. It was still in some of the Jewish Kabbalah, occultism of Alistair Crowley in the 1800s and 1900s. Crowley's law states, 'Do what thou wilt.' This goes back to gnostic belief in self-awareness in order to know God. In the 1800s, Madame Helena Blavatsky developed theosophy, and Annie Besant promoted her writings. These are flourishing today in the New Age Movement all over the world. Occult traditions blend with Hinduism and Buddhism and other beliefs to form a global gnosis or secret knowledge/science.

On and on the variations go. Essentially, they are all secretive, elaborate, invented, imaginative lies filled with big words and ideas which boggle the mind and cause confusion very successfully. If you have got lost and not understood Gnosticism, then don't worry. You don't have to remember any of this to get to heaven. I only present it to expose Satan and his incredibly complicated sophistry and deception. His lying knowledge, science falsely so called, is not a salvation issue—unless you believe it. Gnosticism is pure esoteric because its knowledge/science is hidden so well inside mountains of words. Generally, the whole gnostic experience is seen as one which is ineffable. Words cannot express it. Obviously, this adds to the mystery and secrecy. Tragically, it allows those in the small elite circle of human beings near the top of Satan's pyramid, to have power and control over others.

Words fail me. I found it very challenging collecting this information and putting it together. Most of the books, I could not even read. It was like God was closing my eyes and saying, 'You don't need all these details. All that matters is My Word.' How true. But at least you have more of an idea when someone mentions the word, Gnosticism.

Dualism: There is just one more important point about Gnosticism. It is connected to dualism, that there are two gods—one good and one evil. Isn't this the basis of the storyline of this greatest show on earth! Goodies against baddies. Earth was never meant to be like this, knowing good and evil. In Heaven, we will not experience one smidgeon of evil, not one. The absolute truth is that we only have One true God, not two. Satan merely attempts to be the other. The story is a tragedy of the greatest kind possible.

In dualism, the material universe is supposed to be evil, and the non-material, spiritual world is good. Gnostic Christians consider the God of the Hebrews as the evil, false god and creator of only the material universe. To replace Him, they have a god called the Unknown God who created the spiritual world. Interestingly, they still recognise their Unknown God as being the father of Jesus. Hmmm.

Over the past two millenniums, Gnosticism has been preserved in various forms in many societies such as the 90 gnostic sects I mentioned earlier, in the Kabalah, Manichaeism, Knights Templar, Rosicrucianism, Freemasonry and the Illumanati. Gnosticism is present in the international bank system, Marxism, Theosophical societies, World Council of Churches, New Age Movement and countless secret societies. In Islam, the gnostic knowledge of Self and God is called Sufism.

Simon Magus' Death and Legacy of Gnosticism

Names, names, names; words, words words! Whatever the name, all the organisations are controlled by occultism from Satan and his demons. Remember that Gnosticism goes hand in hand with sophism, the twisting of words in order to manipulate masses of minds, bodies and souls. That's what the Great War of Words is all about.

Music is a part of this battle. It is a powerful medium in manipulating minds but we won't go down that long track except to make one point. Many musicians are gnostics and are deceived whether they know it or not. Here is just one example. Timothy Leary, a gnostic and occultist wrote, 'The Beatles are Divine Messiahs - the wisest, holiest, most effective avatars that the human race has produced.' Avatars are supposed to be divine, incarnate, agents of God. He goes on to say, '… I declare that John Lennon, George Harrison, Paul McCartney and Ringo Starr are mutants, prototypes of a new race of laughing freemen, evolutionary agents sent of God, endowed with a mysterious power to create a new species.'[7] John Lennon wrote, 'It seems to me that the only true Christians were the gnostics who believe in self-knowledge ie becoming Christ themselves, reaching the Christ within. (Skywriting by Word of Mouth, 1986). These blasphemous words are so powerful and have influenced millions upon millions of young ones.

Words fail me and I feel sick in the stomach. But—let's move on to the next scene. Brace yourselves for the next onslaught which originated in Simon Magus' legacy of Gnosticism.

Scene 14. Gnosticism And Today

Quotations About Gnosticism: In the last scene, we related many things to today because they were relevant at that point. What we have heard so far has been a mere scratching of the surface of Gnosticism, but you can get a feel of what it is about. We can see the Satanic influence through and through in counterfeit after counterfeit, twisting and distortion of the original storyline of God's Script, ie His Word and His Story. The Great War of Words rages and rages on relentlessly.

I am rushing through now because time is running out, but here are just a few quotations from another book called 'The Gnostic Empire Strikes

---

7 Pg 132 The Gnostics, Tobias Churton

Back.' It is by a Christian writer called Peter Jones. There are some quotations from gnostic books found in 1945 in a place called Nag Hammadi, Egypt. They are called the Nag Hammadi writings. These words express some key points very clearly. You will be even more shocked and amazed at the effects of Gnosticism today.

Peter Jones writes on page 21 'The ancient Gnostics understood very well that if their system was going to work, they would have to get rid of God and the Bible. This explains the extremist anti-creation and anti-Old Testament sentiment found in certain gnostic texts.'

Page 23, '... According to the newly found Nag Hammadi text, ... Dame Wisdom, (What a name! Same as Sophia) the heavenly Eve, enters the snake called the Instructor and teaches Adam and Eve the true way of salvation.' Another Nag Hammadi text is called 'On the Origin of the World.' It describes the serpent as the "one who is wiser than all of them." And this is a recurring theme in the Gnostic literature. The serpent is the redeemer. The God of Scripture is the evil usurper.'

Page 28 'The true God according to the Gnostic, is strictly unknowable, without personality, and untouched by the world.... Elaine Pagels in her book, The Gnostic Gospels, has a chapter on the gnostic idea of God entitled, "God the Father/God the Mother." She notes that, the God of Israel shared His power with no female deity. But that was not the case for the gods of the ancient Near East. In the Gnostic god, there is a dyad (ie two parts) of masculine and feminine elements, a dynamic relationship of opposites like the yin and yang.'

Can you see the two gods of dualism again? In the previous talk we mentioned pagan religions all have a male and a female. Earth is the only place in the Universe with male and female gods/goddesses.

Listen to this next quotation and apply it to today to all the gender bender issues in our society. This is from page 29 of the same book 'The Gnostic Empire Strikes Back.' It quotes from more writings found at Nag Hammadi. One book is called, 'The "Apocalypse of Adam.'

It tells of a feminine power that became androgynous or lesbian. In another book, we read where a divine feminine revealer cries, 'I am an-

Simon Magus' Death and Legacy of Gnosticism

drogynous. (I am both Mother and Father) since I copulate with myself and with those who love me, and it is through me alone that the All (ie all of creation) stands firm. I am the Womb that gives shape to the All by giving birth to the Light that shines in splendour. I am the Aeon to come. I am the fulfillment of All, ie, the glory of the Mother.' Surely this is another revived version of Semiramus as well as a disgusting counterfeit of our Creator God and the basis of Mother Mary in Roman Catholicism.

Peter Jones' book goes on further to describe how Gnosticism has perverted sexuality today. I'm not going into all the gory details except to say how we see here the physical body is degraded. Page 32 tells about the Gnostic Gospel of Saint Thomas. It reads, 'Simon Peter said to them, "Let Mary go away from us, for women are not worthy of life." Jesus said, "Lo, I shall lead her so that I may make her a male, that she too may become a living spirit resembling you males. For every woman who makes herself a male will enter the kingdom of heaven."[8] Can you see the effects of this today on the youth?

Peter Jones also describes how the worshipers of the serpent were against the Genesis account of God creating male and female. These worshippers claim that the original Adam was a hermaphrodite. They even use Galatians 3:28 which says, '... _**there is neither male nor female for ye are all one in Christ Jesus**_.' Gnostics twist the words to mean 'In Christ, believers are physically both male and female.' And this is evidence that the new creature in Christ is a hermaphrodite! Can you believe this! This is pure blasphemous Gnostic sophistry.

No wonder Paul wrote in 2 Timothy 6:20-21, '_avoiding profane and vain (futile, useless) babblings, and oppositions of science falsely so-called (ie gnosis) which some professing have erred concerning the faith._' In other words, we must at all costs, avoid futile, useless rubbish words, fake knowledge and misinformation which is wrongly called science.

These are just some of the consequences of Gnosticism. I do want to go into five more. Bear with me.

Five Consequences Of Gnosticism These Are Just A Few Of Many.

---

8 St Thomas' Gospel, Last logion No. 114.

1. Effects on the Youth: Oh, the lies which are being taught in schools today to our precious young ones as they are just maturing and learning about their developing bodies. There is a toxic potion of miseducation and *'science falsely so called.'* Inject the COVID poisons into these fresh new bodies to destroy the way God designed them to function so they can't reproduce. At the same time, hormones are naturally being released, emotions are hard to control and the passions flow into immoral sexuality. Add in the blasting noise of music which destroys the tiny hairs in the cochlea, excites the emotions and hypnotises the minds. Pour in some addictive alcohol, drugs and cigarette nicotine. And top it up with the entertainment of movies, computer games and sports. And put these young impressionable fertile minds into a dumbed down education system.

It's no wonder the world is in the state it is in now. All because of Simon Magus, Nimrod, Semiramus and all of Satan's other agents we haven't got time to meet in this series. Phew!! And things will not get any better as humanism and Gnosticism run rampant. Praise God, He sees and know every tiny detail of this battlefield and very, very soon our Chief Commander and Saviour is coming to rescue us.

2. Effects on Eve and Humanity: Let's briefly revisit the Garden of Eden. The key to today's sad state is that Gnosticism is based on secret knowledge. It is a reflection of the character of its inventor, Satan and how He used his secret supernatural knowledge. This is how the serpent tempted Eve in the Garden of Eden when he told her what would happen if she ate from the forbidden Tree of Knowledge of Good and Evil. With all sophistry and rhetoric, (techniques of persuasion) with flattery, smiles, sly looks, smooth tone of voice, he appealed to her intelligence and said, *'Ye shall not surely die, for God doth know that in the day ye eat thereof, then your eyes shall be opened, and ye shall be as gods knowing good and evil.'* Genesis 3:5

Just these few words contained a whole big bag of lies. *'Ye shall not surely die'* led to the belief in reincarnation and lies about the state of the dead. *'.. your eyes shall be opened'* led to a sense of false enlightenment opening the eyes, mind and heart to endless counterfeits. *'... ye shall be as gods.'* Note the plural in god<u>s</u>. This led to dualism of two gods, the contrast between good and evil. It would go even further into polytheism, thousands and thousands of gods in different cultures and the millions of idols of all types today.

3. Education and the Three Degrees of Knowledge: Gnosticism says there are degrees of knowledge which are the three initiation rites. a) The first one is 360 degrees and refers to a complete cipher of knowledge ie steps to follow in order to become educated. b) The second initiation rite is the school of 360 degrees started in Egypt where some of its mysteries were used in secret societies. And these lead to the third level. c) The system of 33 degrees used by secret societies like freemasons, Illuminati, Rosicrucians and Theosophists. The 33 degrees are unbelievably complicated using fear, force and fascination of the supernatural. Entry to the levels is by invitation only.

Contrast all this with what our Father God's education is and what He wants us to know. He wants us be spiritually born again into His family. That means to be freed from the evil spiritualism of Satan. He wants us to be infinitely blessed by his Great Love. He wants us to have a close relationship with Him and live forever in perfect bliss with no sophism but all pure simple language filled with truth and honesty. He wants us to learn from His own Nature's Lesson Book and experience the gloriousness of His galaxies, planets and other inhabitants in the Universe. God's basic education is so simple and open with no secrecy and hidden agenda, no force or fear, no levels of hierarchy in a tyrannical pyramid government.

We could say that His three degrees of knowledge are these - a) believe in Jesus as the Son of God and our Mediator, b) apologise and turn away from sin. And c) Obey the commandments and keep the faith of Jesus. That's about it in a nutshell.

4. The Roman Catholic Church: The Roman Catholic Church claims to be connected by a secret tradition laid down in mystic writings. The hidden, mysterious knowledge is not accessible to those on the outside ie it is esoteric. They say it comes from early Christianity, the Saviour himself and his disciples. However, it really comes from Gnosticism. This religion of antiquity boasts of mystic revelation and deep wisdom and is filled with holy rites and rituals, acts of initiation, dedication and consecration. It is a religion of sacraments and mysteries. There are sacred formulae with names, numbers and symbols which have extreme importance in the gnostic sects. And human priests are the mediators, especially the counterfeit high priest, the Pope.

The foundations were set very early for the development of the Roman Catholic Church. The idea of salvation of individuals was vital because it was the very reason Jesus came to earth and died for mankind. But Gnosticism/Catholicism uses and involves Jesus for its own agenda. It uses the very Son of God to target individual souls with the goal of saving them, not from sin, but from the prison of this world which they are supposedly slaves to God in, and being forced to obey His Laws. Gnosticism/Catholicism does not say Jesus does not exist, but it uses Him for its own purpose.

Through the human agent popes, Satan has the arrogance and gall to claim that the Roman Catholic Church is the one and only true church, the universal one, and the pope replaces Jesus as the Vicar of Christ. And Satan uses this incredible religious system as the earthly basis for his government. It is a tyrannical, tight controlling, fear-mongering organisation with the goal of power and control, leading to destruction and death of mankind to prevent us from entering God's kingdom. His counterfeit Biblical teachings, the counterfeit language of names, numbers and symbols are very effective ways of achieving this. Many millions of minds and souls have tragically succumbed to it.

5. COVID Plandemic: There are countless consequences of Gnosticism, but we'll finish off with the latest stunt of Satan - the COVID plandemic. Gnostic believers see themselves as separate to the world - isolated, free, enlightened and above the lesser material humans, the so-called degraded matters of animal-humans, the 'cattle.'

Unfortunately, we do have to admit that COVID, the so-called virus, is a genius strategic battle tactic in the Great War of Words. Sophistry and techniques of persuasion have been monumental, an all-time high, in the propaganda machine. Satan is at his sophisticated global best so far in the storyline of the show. The virus has never been proved to exist in humans. It has not been isolated. However, it has been so cleverly planted in people's imaginations that they believe it is real. And the so-called vaccinations are the only way out because people are told over and over that they are 'safe and effective, safe and effective. Trust the science.' All the pictures of people having syringes thrust into their arms make the masses feel it's OK to have the jab. They think that everything will be all right. And they are free to do as they want.

Meanwhile, hidden away are the super Elite high up in Satan's pyramid, constantly pulling the puppet strings of those in middle levels - the pharmaceutical companies, the scientists, technocrats, politicians, those in the medical and education systems, those in the entertainment and sports industries. All these puppets in turn, become their own puppeteers pulling their strings of the bottom layer of puppets, the ordinary animal-people.

A three-tiered society has formed. Near the top, is the minority of un-jabbed Elite who know not to have the poison. Then there are the middle level ones in between, doing all the dirty deeds and being rewarded financially and materially. And then, at the bottom, there are the masses of the jabbed.

This disastrous three-tiered society fits in perfectly with Gnostic beliefs. COVID was just one tactic in the process leading to the control of multitudes. The Gnostic secret goals known to the Elite, are to implant devices in human bodies like branding a cow, and to harm or kill as many as possible in the process in order to quickly reduce the population. Another secret goal is to be able to trace and contact individuals from a technological control tower somewhere on the planet.

Climate Change is another tactic looming on the horizon. And before we know it, Sunday Law will be upon us. Already, the seeds have been planted around the world with groups of people desiring a day of rest from work, a day for families, one day of the week to reduce carbon emissions. Satan thinks that the world will worship and glorifying him by not keeping the seventh day Sabbath as the true day of rest. He thinks he will stop us developing further our relationship with God,

But - the great news is that Sunday Law will be the final major war weapon Satan uses. This time when Satan has total control over the whole planet, will be very short and his defeat will take place very soon after.

Jesus is coming again. The end of the Great War is almost over. Christ is already the Victor, but most of mankind just doesn't realise it yet.

Conclusion: Thank you for bearing with me this long. We're nearly there. There is so much more to say but the greatest show on earth must come to a close for now. What a script it has been! The storyline only gets worse as Satan's imagination and plot gets deeper, thicker and more and more sinister. Praise God for His truly amazing love for His precious human children. Praise God for His true and faithful remnant all through the millenniums. Praise Him for the Waldenses, the goodies, who were a glimmer of hope in the Dark Ages. These were the ones who preserved the original Script all through the time when the baddies were rising up in the monster beast of the Roman Empire and papacy. Only because of that small ongoing remnant, the Waldensian minority, can we read God's Word today. If it weren't for them continuing to fight the good fight and defend the Godhead, we would not be here now.

Right now, a tiny minority or remnant still battles on just like the Waldenses, as the Great War intensifies on a global scale as never before. We <u>must</u> keep battling on in the good fight. We <u>must</u> hold on to those cords of faith, always remembering Who is at the other end! We <u>must</u> keep wide awake and alert and - **Beware The Sophistry! Beware The Sophistry!**

Prayer Let's pray to our ever-loving Father in Heaven Who has not given up on us and is here for us. If God is for us, who can be against us? No-one can.

Our dear heavenly Father, we praise your holy name and give you all the glory and honour for Who you are, and what You are still doing for us with Jesus as our Mediator and High Priest in Your heavenly Temple. We are forever grateful that our Chief Commander, has already won the Great War and will be returning in the very near future to take us to our true home with You. We thank You for these few moments together where we can learn more about the deceptions of Satan and see how different his Gnostic beliefs, are so totally different to Your ways. Thank you for giving us intelligence and good brains to understand what sophism means, and how it is everywhere around us. We thank You in advance for being with us throughout the coming week, and we know that

Simon Magus' Death and Legacy of Gnosticism

you will have your angels encamped around us to guide and protect us in our daily battles. Thank You for your mercies and patience with us when we fall and You are always there to pick us up when we go astray. In Jesus' name we pray. Amen.

The curtains have closed but they will open again in one week's time, March 5, at 2.30.

In the next episode, we will focus on the script of the storyline again and break down some important words to discover their backgrounds. I know you will be very surprised at what they reveal and how they expose even more of Satan's evil character. One of my goals in this series besides wanting to encourage us, is to expose our enemy so we can know how to fight back. In the second half of the next talk, we will focus specifically on one particular word, blasphemy. What exactly is blasphemy? What makes a word blasphemous? How is it related to every single part of our being? And how does blasphemy attack the very heart of God? You will be amazed.

May God bless you all abundantly during the coming week until we meet again.

Part 6 - Act 6:
Word Examples Of Sophistry

Introduction And Review

Here we are again, sitting in our celestial seats in the outer space audience. We have joined the angels, the inhabitants of other worlds plus Enoch, Moses, and the hundreds of the human first fruits who Jesus took to Heaven after His resurrection. Once again, we have the privilege of God's Word to teach us and help us leave the earthly battlefield, the one black spot in the universe, and have some respite and breathing space. We are about to watch the next scene of this series on The Greatest War Ever.

I'm sure by now you are developing a deeper understanding of sophism and Gnosticism and can see clearly why and how the world has become the way it is. Yes, it's all about words in the greatest controversy of all time, the Great War of Words which began in Heaven with Satan's rebellion and the very first original sin.

By now, you will have realised that this greatest show on Earth is <u>not</u> entertainment. It's the real reality show of earthly life as it has been for 6000 years. I'm now just going to give a short review of what we have covered so far.

This series is founded on the script of Earth being a planet-stage with God the Producer, and His Co-Author Son Christ, who is also the Director and Chief Commander of His army of holy angels. The Holy Spirit is the Prompter behind the scenes whispering God's Word in the hearts of the performers. Human beings are the performers divided into two groups. There are the actors, acting out the character of their Chief General Satan, and the players playing the roles they were originally created for. The players are to reflect the character of Christ and use their God-given gift of free will, to live according to the Law of Great Love. Our ever-loving and amazing Father-God has willingly put Himself on trial. He desires for His human children to prove to the rest of those

Word Examples Of Sophistry

in His kingdom of Universe, that His theocratic government with its Ten Commandments, is the best and only way to rule any kingdom. All the details we have delved into in the previous five talks, fit into this theatrical drama and spiritual court case.

We have focused on geographical platforms of the ancient Greek and Roman empires. In the last talk we learned about Simon Magus. In Part Two we drew up a very basic timeline which I hope and pray is settling into your memories. Now, as we continue, the timeline in your mind will appear to have mental blotches, ink spots, splattered across the line, if you can picture that!

Today, words, ideas and beliefs will be linked up, and the blotches will be on the line of the last 2000 years since Jesus came and Simon Magus became the father of Gnosticism and the first bishop/pope. Words will be tied together like threads interwoven through the grand tapestry of the Big Picture of life on Earth. You might see the threads as a giant global ball of tight knots because that's what they are. It is a messy picture. No matter which viewpoint we might choose, from ground level on the battlefield, or from outer space in the audience, it still looks a mess, the one blotch in the glittering Universe. That's exactly what pagan beliefs have turned this planet into.

So, today, we will attempt to untangle just a few knots and make some threads straight with the help of our Triple O, our Outside, Objective Observer - God, His Son and the Holy Spirit. Of course, we will use the original Script, God's Word to show the contrast between truth and lies.

In the previous talk I said we would also look at the word blasphemy today. I apologise that this has to be postponed to the next talk. Sorry about that but you will soon understand why. As I delved into particular words, I became more and more fascinated and had to go deeper and deeper.

In today's talk, we will focus on six particular words to see how the Triple S, ie the Secret Subjective Satan, also the Super Sophist Satan, has twisted word meanings. Remember the simple definition of sophistry - to twist words and deliberately confuse, cause doubt and distract in order to get one's own way. Today, we will expose this invisible enemy even more. But before we begin, let's pray and ask for God's help in understanding the message.

Our dear Father God in Heaven, we come before you once again and ask for Your light and understanding and wisdom in today's talk. Help me to expose a little more of the enemy's tactics and to be an encouragement to the listeners. Please forgive us all our sins and cleanse out hearts and minds. Clothe our hearts in Your robes of righteousness so we can always be in right relationship with You. Thank You again for your Great Love, compassion, mercies and grace towards us. In Jesus' name we pray, Amen.

Scene 15. Six Word Examples of Sophistry

What's in a word? I find words and their origins fascinating. Often over time, their meanings change and we need to go back to the roots to find out the truth. Language is absolutely amazing and only God could have created it. Language is one of the things which make humans different to animals, plants and rocks. After the Tower of Babel, God created thousands of new different languages. And, soon to come, the language of Heaven will be a new one for us to speak. Wow! Isn't that something to look forward to? There will be no sophistry in Heaven, only pure simple truth and honesty. Yes, God is the Creator of language and can do anything He wants with words! However, unfortunately on planet Earth, Satan just has to interfere and twist meanings into tight knots.

Let's dig deeper. Let's look closely at six important words out of billions which the super-sophist has tampered with. These words are–1. Antichrist 2. Universal 3. University 4. Basilica 5. Allegories, and 6. Numbers and Signs.

1. Antichrist: The word antichrist was not in the Old Testament because the word Christ had not been used during those 4000 years. It's only since Jesus came to earth that He has been called the Christ because He was the anointed one chosen by God to come and show the true way to Heaven and eternal life. In the New Testament, God foretold us about the Antichrist.

Word Examples Of Sophistry

We need to understand there are two meanings of this word. It comes from the Greek, antichristos. One meaning is 'against,' and the other is 'instead of, ie to take the place of.' So, in the first meaning, antichrist refers to someone who opposes Christ and is an enemy, a foe. Many verses in the Bible tell us that antichrist means someone who is a deceiver and a liar. He lies about who Christ is and denies Jesus' existence.

Throughout the last 2000 years of His Story, ie God's Story, there have been, and still are, many antichrists. The Bible tells us that they were around even in the very first century AD. John was a mighty warrior for the Lord and an excellent player in the grand theatrical show. He wrote, '... as ye have heard that antichrist shall come, even now there are many antichrists...' 1 John 2:18. In verse 22, he says, 'Who is a liar but he who denieth that Jesus is the Christ? He is an antichrist that denieth the Father and the Son.'

In 1 John 4:3 he wrote, 'And every spirit that confesseth not that Jesus Christ is come in the flesh, is not of God; and this is that spirit of antichrist whereof ye have heard that it should come. And even now already is it in the world.' Finally, in 2 John verse 7, John also wrote, 'For many deceivers are entered into the world who confess not, that Jesus Christ is come of the flesh. This is a deceiver and an antichrist.'

It's no wonder that Satan was livid about Christ the Chief Commander, showing up visibly on the battlefield. Satan was still invisible but very 'anti,' in the first sense of being 'against' Jesus. The cosmic war reached a climax at the time of the Cross and was major turning point in the storyline. By taking on human form, divine Jesus became a man and proved Himself to be real, extremely real, because people could see and hear and touch and live with Him for years. Some even grew up with him during childhood, youth and early adulthood. When Christ's ministry started at the age of thirty, God's Word became more powerful and was heard audibly through their very ears. And after His death and resurrection, Jesus again proved Himself to doubting Thomas who touched Him. Yes, Christ was real without a doubt. It immediately became apparent to Satan, that merely opposing Christ was not a powerful enough war weapon to deny the Messiah's existence.

Then, after Christ returned to Heaven to stay there, the second meaning of 'anti' developed. Satan used his tactic of counterfeit once again and found a way of 'taking His place,' ie replacing Christ with a human being. This is where the system of bishops and the papacy came in—hence the title, Vicar of Christ, God on Earth. What arrogance and gall! Sophistry and Gnosticism began to reach new heights—or rather, they plunged into greater depths of deception!

Highly skilful sophistry had to be used to pull off this spectacular stunt. Satan used words and rhetoric, ie techniques of persuasion. Satan's evil character was acted out by the first bishop/pope of Rome, Simon Magus. Through this human agent, the father of lies began fresh new philosophies of secret, mysterious, superior, esoteric, gnostic knowledge which we learned about in the previous talk. Over the following twenty centuries, Satan developed his deception further by combining all these things with displays of wealth in grand cathedrals, elaborate costumes, pomp and ceremony, rites and rituals.

For the last 2000 years these tactics have successfully worked to deceive millions upon millions. The hidden agenda has always been for the hunter of souls to stop the human prey finding out the truth of the Godhead. The goal has always been to prevent people from entering heaven and perfect eternal life in God's Great Love. After Christ's resurrection, Satan knew he was doomed and would miss out on these things. He had sour grapes. If he could not have eternal life and all the glory, honour and worship, then he would drag down as many as possible with him.

What a tragedy! Can't we see his revenge happening on a ginormous global scale right now!

Back to the word antichrist. Since the first century AD, there have been many antichrists in both meanings of the word—to be 'against' Christ, and to 'take his place' as God on Earth. The number of popes since the first one, varies from 250-266 according to what one reads. That's a lot of antichrists. And it's interesting how they keep dying. Surely, if they really were God on Earth, they would not die!

600 years before Jesus came to earth, Daniel spoke of the antichrist without actually using that word. In great detail he described the most

terrible beast representing the Roman Empire. The beast image had a little horn which rose up and became extremely powerful. From our point at the end of the timeline of the story, we now recognise this horn as being the Papacy because Daniel so perfectly described it as one who *'..shall speak great words against the Most High and shall wear out the saints of the Most High, and think to change times and laws...'* Daniel 7:25

The head of the Papacy, the pope, is the one who blasphemes by claiming to be God on earth and able to forgive. He also claims to be infallible ie he cannot be wrong in anything, not one thing. We learned in a previous talk how the pope supposedly holds the two keys to the gates of Heaven. He carries out the whole complicated counterfeit plan of salvation through the massive system of gate 'hinges,' ie the cardinals and priests who anyone can go to and ask for forgiveness. This is the Roman monster beast of Daniel's vision with its horns and the little horn, the Papacy.

Obviously, the original Antichrist is Satan himself as he puts into practice both meanings the word 'anti.' He has always been against and opposed Christ since the start of the Great War in Heaven. And he still assumes to take the Lord's place as King and Ruler of this earth. He uses his human agent, the pope, as the tip of his human hierarchical pyramid government.

In the grand production of the greatest show on Earth, Satan has cleverly sabotaged and assumed the roles of counterfeit Producer and counterfeit Director of the theatre-stage. He has also assumed to be a counterfeit Prompter/Holy Spirit by operating in invisible, secret, mysterious ways with his army of demons. He has also assumed to take over God's Script and have another agenda in his counterfeit script using sophistry and gnostic beliefs. He has unrightfully assumed to have power and control over the whole globe, which really belongs to the Chief Commander, Jesus Christ, the true King. But the Bible sees straight through him and only calls him the *'prince of this world,'*–not the king.

All along, Satan's genius sophistry has continued to distract people away from who the Antichrist really is. This is another incredible fascinating stunt he has pulled off in order to draw attention away from himself.

He does not deny there is an antichrist, just like he does not deny there is a Christ. But he cleverly altered the timeline of when the antichrist will arrive on the planet. We have just proved the original Antichrist is Satan, and that he has already used many other human antichrists. And we know that one of them is here right now with us this very day–in plain sight for all to see, dressed in white like Lucifer the Light Bearer, the original angel of light. His name is Pope Francis. And there are the three other popes, black grey and red. Oh, if only more would open their eyes and hearts and minds to the truth staring them in the face!

How has Satan changed the timeline about antichrist? Four human agents in particular, were used to act out his scheming, wicked character. They lived in the sixteenth and seventeenth centuries, the 15-1600s. Notice that this was during the time of the Reformation, the time of Luther, Calvin and the reformers rebelling against the Roman Catholic Church.

The Church, in retaliation, started a Counter-Reformation. It pretended to begin reforming itself to make it look as if it was changing for the good. In reality, the papacy system just got more sophisticated, subtle and more devious. A new satanic actor-agent called Ignatius Loyola arrived onstage. Loyola formed the Society of Jesus and its members were blasphemously called Jesuits. What a deceptive name that is–to use the Lord's very name and make millions believe this is a good, Godly, Christ-based organisation! Clever sophistry once again.

The second man at the time of the Counter-Reformation and Society of Jesus, was a Jesuit from Spain called Luis del Alcazar. He lived 1544-1613. He wrote that the Antichrist had already come in the far distant past and was a Greek ruler. Alcazar is known as the father of preterism. Pre means before, so the Antichrist has supposedly already come and therefore there is no need to fear him now.

The third man was Francesco de Ribera, another Spanish Jesuit who lived 1537-1591. The fourth was an Italian Jesuit called Cardinal Robert Bellarmine 1542-1621. Ribera and Bellermine both developed the idea of futurism, ie that the Antichrist is yet to come in the far distant future, therefore, we don't have to fear him just now. Both preterism and futurism distract from the present day and the fact that the Antichrist is with

Word Examples Of Sophistry

us this very moment controlling world events. How clever is our invisible enemy!

In the late 1700s, just over a hundred years after the Counter Reformation began, there was another Spanish Jesuit who was actually on the right track. This was Manuel Lacunza 1731-1791. He is mentioned briefly in The Great Controversy page 363 as one, 'who found his way to the Scriptures and thus received the truth of Christ's speedy return.' Even though Lacunza had a few errors, he was not intending to deceive like the other three Jesuits. In 1816, his book was banned by the Spanish Inquisition. In 1824, the pope knew the book spoke truth and had it listed in the Index for Forbidden Books.

During the Reformation and following years, Martin Luther and many reformers like John Wesley knew full well the pope was the Antichrist. Many today believe this, but most are still fooled because some so-called Protestant denominations teach preterism, and others teach futurism. I say 'so-called Protestants' because they aren't protesting against the Roman Catholic Church anymore. Oh, how times have changed since the Reformation began over 500 years ago! All the while, millions continued to flock to see the white public pope, the tip of the little horn of Daniel's Roman monster-beast. With great admiration, adoration and worship, they acknowledge him as the most influential person on earth, a person with good morals and wisdom. As John prophesied in Revelation 13:3, '*all the world wondered after the beast.*' This means nations on every continent on the globe.

Today, the deceived protestant denominations have willingly walked into the fold of the Roman Catholic Church. They do not realise how they have been manipulated and lied to with smooth words, and so-called love for humanity and the common good. And the whole deception has been done through sophistry in the Great War of Words, the Great Controversy between Satan and Christ. Words, words everywhere; what a war!

Satan must be laughing with hideous glee and gloating over a seeming victory. But it won't last for long. Praise God for His Word which tells us the truth that Jesus, the real, true original Christ, is coming very, very soon. The original Antichrist will finally be defeated for everyone to see, and he will get his well-deserved punishment. There will be a happy ending for the true believers who stay strong in their faith and obedience to Gods Laws, especially the fourth one about the seventh day Sabbath.

So, that was just a little study on the word, antichrist.

2. Universal: Let's look at the second word on my list and uncover some more sinister roots. This word is 'universal.' I chose this word because it is part of the title of the Roman Catholic Church. Catholic, means universal or whole. It covers the general, overall big picture of the whole globe of earth. Universal obviously comes from the word, universe. So—what is the meaning of universe? This proved to be a most interesting study. Universe is broken down into two syllables—'uni' and 'verse.' Uni means one, as in unicycle (bike with one wheel); unite (to join as one); union (one group of people).

The second part of universe is 'verse' which means a poetic, metrical line or a rhythmic phrase from a poem. We have verses in the poetry of hymns. Words are mixed with rhythm to flow in phrases. Put the two syllables together and we see how uni-verse means '<u>one</u> rhythmic <u>word</u> or phrase.' This is to do with speaking or singing words and therefore also involves sound.

Is something beginning to click in your brain as it did in mine when I started looking into this word? How did God's kingdom of Universe, get its name? The name came through sound, God's Word, singular, meaning there is only one absolute truth, and that is in God's Word. God spoke one verse, a uni-verse, and all the parts of His vast kingdom (Universe), including Earth, came into existence at the appointed time. This ultimate, almighty power of speech of God's Word, created all the nebulae, galaxies, suns, moons, planets and inhabitants of other worlds in this immeasurable kingdom called Uni-Verse. And this includes us mere little human beings! WOOOW!

Genesis Chapter One tells us what happened. Which one, single word was used fourteen times in the days of Creation? It's a tiny little three-letter word - the word 'LET.' Three times it is linked with the phrase, 'Let there be...' meaning 'Let there exist' or 'Let there be life.' I did a concordance search for the word 'let' and was shocked. You know how there is

Word Examples Of Sophistry

a column of numbers which leads to the Hebrew or Greek explanation. Well, in the column of numbers, beside the word let, there is nothing, no number for the word. In the lines for Genesis Chapter One the number column is absolutely blank. I could not check the Hebrew origins of LET! In almost all the hundreds of times the word 'let' is used in the Old Testament, the column is blank.

So, I checked the Merriam-Webster dictionary online and that told me more. It says 'let' means to cause, to make, to permit, to free (release) as in 'letting out a cry or a shout.' That gives us some idea of what 'let' means. Our amazing Creator God let out a cry, a shout and caused His creations to come into existence. Life can only come from life. So, it's no wonder God's infinite kingdom is called Uni-verse. No wonder God's Word is called the 'living Word.' BIG WOOOW! And it's no wonder that Satan is full of jealousy and rage about this ability to create life, and he's doing everything he can to destroy it, not just in humans but animals and plants too!

What has this all got to do with the Roman Catholic Church? Everything. This Babylonian Church is Satan's governing body of evil and destruction. Names are chosen for a reason and the Roman <u>Catholic</u> Church is no exception. True, it is Roman. True, it is a church or an ecclesia, a gathering or fellowship of people worshipping together. BUT—it is definitely NOT catholic ie universal.

It is merely global—one tiny little planet in the vast, vast, true kingdom, the universe God has created. This planet belongs to God the Creator, because He was the One who said, LET' and spoke it into existence. Satan leads millions to believe he himself is ruler over <u>all</u> the universe. Incredibly, through the Roman Empire and Simon Magus, he had the absolute arrogance to start calling this new religion 'universal' when it should be called global.

There are two points to consider. Firstly, neither Satan nor Simon Magus spoke the earth into existence, let alone the whole universe! Secondly, their 'universe' or territory is a mere speck of fine dust compared with the whole of Universe. Satan had been cast down from Heaven, the seat of government of Universe, to this tiny planet earth. This global clod of dirt is the only kingdom or territory God allowed him to have power over.

Again, surely, this is the sheer height of arrogance, gall, assumption, haughtiness, self-importance and superiority of Satan to presume that he is the true king and ruler over the earth and all its people. Oh, how he has fooled billions into believing that he, through the counterfeit Pope, is the Most High. Simon Magus, the first of hundreds of popes, used sheer sophistry to achieve his and Satan's purpose. By the way, the word pope originates from the word papa. It is a counterfeit of Abba, Father God.

After Jesus left the planet stage, Satan began a whole new counterfeit language as a basis for the rising new counterfeit religion. Instead of the original word universal, the word catholic was selected because it also meant general or overall. So, therefore, the whole earth could be claimed under the authority of the new church/ecclesia. Over time, this new global religion became known as firstly Roman (true), secondly Catholic (lie) and Church (true). Two lies and one truth. As always, in sophistry and Gnostic sects, many lies would be mixed with a little truth in order to confuse. You can understand now why I will call the Roman Catholic Church, the Roman Church.

It's no wonder the Roman Church was not happy with the astronomer Galileo in 1583, when he published his discovery that the earth moves around the sun and not vice versa. Galileo proved the sun was the centre of the solar system and not earth. All through the Middle Ages or Dark Ages, people were lied to and believed that the earth was flat and the sun and planets revolved around it. With Galileo's proven discovery, the Church had a big problem. This knowledge might lead to the idea that the Earth was not the centre of all the galaxies and stars. Humans may not be the 'measure of all things' after all, as the ancient Greek philosopher Protagoras had said. Through centuries and centuries of misinformation, people were taught to believe the earth was the centre of the universe. Oh, the incredible sophistry and deceit!

But Satan has known all along the vastness of the real Universe because he used to be able to fly around in it! To him, the tiny planet Earth is just a ball to play games with, to toss words back and forth in an attempt to win and defeat his opponent, Jesus Christ. It's a nasty, vicious, deathly,

Word Examples Of Sophistry 151

word game of war.

Back to Galileo. The Church inquisition called him a heretic, ie someone who opposes the Roman Church. They sentenced him to house arrest until his death in 1642. Incidentally, this all happened in God's timing during the Reformation and Counter-Reformation, the same time as the beginning of the Jesuits' antichrist lies, of preterism and futurism. The Roman Church had major problems with the likes of Galileo, Luther, Calvin, the Waldenses etc.

Just a small, but very relevant issue currently related to the word 'universal.' One of the most recent variations of the word universe which has entered into language today, is Metaverse. Mark Zuckerberg recently changed the name of Facebook to Metaverse. Why would Satan cause this to happen? The word Metaverse is yet another superb example of genius sophistry because it is fooling billions of minds.

What does Metaverse mean? We have learned that verse means word, especially God's Word. Meta means super or above, beyond, transcending. Therefore, Meta-verse means 'above God's Word.' Is this a coincidence? I don't think so. The Australian newspaper, the Financial Review Weekend 29 Dec 2021, pages 40-42, had a long article describing life in an imaginary place called Metaverse.

You can google the meaning of metaverse and learn a lot about its roots. The letters M-E-T-A have been used to mean **M**ost **E**ffective **T**actics **A**vailable. How true! Satan is pulling out all stops now at the end of the Great War. He is using the **M**ost **E**ffective **T**actics **A**vailable right now through technology and the temptation of fascination into an alternative, invisible world.

Metaverse is Satan's current most efficient strategy to trap minds. It is a virtual reality, an invention of a complete counterfeit Universe. In the newspaper article, Zuckerberg says we will express ourselves, 'in a new, joyful, immersive way.' Oh, how minds are being immersed, submerged, drowning in virtual reality games. The article says that Zuckerberg's goal is to build a virtual environment where people can meet friends, go to work, shop and use virtual reality headsets, phones and computers to feel, 'truly present with another person.' In Metaverse, you can go into

The Greatest War Ever

a place called Decentraland which is short for 'Decentralised land.' You can mix with virtual people. And using cryptocurrency, you can actually buy virtual clothes, artworks, land, buildings, businesses, shares, and gamble in a casino. You can attend concerts, shows and even church services. Metaverse is a virtual, digital future world happening right now.

And there are many companies taking part in Metaverse eg Epic Games, Somnium Space, Ember Sword, Roblox, Minecraft. These companies are already worth billions of dollars. I've seen young children playing Minecraft where they create virtual cities, countries, buildings, people, animals and nature scenes. The game is supposed to be educational and is used in schools. But it's just another addiction to computer games and technology, and a distraction from God.

By the way, what does the word virtual mean? It means 'almost.' All the things in a virtual world are merely almost real, but not quite. Having virtual relationships with virtual characters, is a mighty entertaining distraction from feeling truly present and having a real relationship with our Father-God! The very word 'virtual' is just like 'artificial' as in Artificial Intelligence. Both words are oxymorons, contradictions in one word. Both actually admit there is an original and that the virtual, artificial things are fakes, the counterfeits. Virtual and artificial both imply pure imagination and fiction, not reality.

So, what is imagination? It is the opposite of creativity. The concordance H2803 tells us the Hebrew origin of imagination. It means to plot, contrive, cunning, devise, invented, to be like. Therefore, Metaverse and all the computer games are definitely not creative in the true sense of God's creativity and originality. They reveal Satan's character in full force. What does the Author of the story tell us through his mighty warrior Paul? In 2 Corinthians 10:5, Paul wrote, *'Casting down imaginations and every high thing that exalteth itself against the knowledge of God, and bringing into captivity every thought to the obedience of Christ.'* What powerful words these are!

Now, the word metaverse is being shortened to META only. The second part, verse ie God's Word, has been removed. What a sophisticated, loaded word those four letters are! Zuckerberg and all those involved have extremely intelligent God-given brains, but they are using lan-

Word Examples Of Sophistry

guage for evil and not for good. Whether they know it or not, they are serving Chief General Satan and not the Chief Commander Christ. So, next time you hear the word Meta or Metaverse, **Beware the Sophistry.** Remember META means '**M**ost **E**ffective **T**actics **A**vailable.'

Words fail me to describe the horrific and most evil effects on the minds of the young ones today. I'm sure you know what I mean so I don't have to go down that track.

By the way, isn't this War of Words also called The Great Controversy? Just a few days ago someone corrected me on how to pronounce Controversy. I and many people I know say contr<u>o</u>versy emphasising the second O. How often do we hear someone say, 'The Great Controversy?' However, the correct pronunciation is contro-<u>ver</u>sy.

I was just writing about the word universal when I was corrected, and it immediately dawned on me why. Contra means against, and verse is word—contra-verse. Therefore, contro<u>vers</u>y is against the word, God's Word. Aren't words fascinating?

Let's move on from universal to the next word under scrutiny.

3. University: The word universal leads into a third word which is similar—university. After understanding more about universal we can now see why these learning institutions are called uni-<u>vers</u>ities. They are, at their very core, a counterfeit education system of God's true education in Nature's Lesson Book of the Earth and Universe. Universities are Satan's attempt to manipulate, control and mould the minds of young adults in their prime years, away from God and towards himself. Emphasis is on man's intellect and not God and His creation. Humanism is continuously promoted and yet again, Protagoras' old saying is reinforced—'Man is the measure of all things.'

The Roman Church founded the university system and deliberately chose this name because it wanted to teach its own version of life. This is Satan's education system with the goal of completely changing the Script of His Story, God's Story. The so-called universal church has its own counterfeit uni-verse, ie its own message of words and verses to brainwash human minds. What better way than to build an educational structure to create its own <u>version</u> of God's original education system.

Aha. Did you notice I just said the word version several times? What are the first four letters? "Vers." Is this a coincidence? A quick search into its origins revealed the following. We already know that verse means word or phrase. But by the Middle Ages the Latin ie Roman, meaning of the word version, is quite different. According to the Latin, version means a turning back, a translation, converting to something else, something which is a contrast, or <u>changed from an original</u>. So, when you have a version of something, it is a variant of an original.

Isn't this precisely what Satan is doing with his weapon of counterfeit? The university education system, indeed, all levels of education, are a <u>vers</u>ion, a variant, something contrasting and changed from God's original.

Universities were originally created in Europe by the Catholic monks. The first one was founded in Bologna in northern Italy in 1088, nearly a thousand years ago. Since then, universities have spread into all continents in order to dominate the world's education systems today. The lower levels of preschool, primary and secondary all feed into the tertiary levels. Universities give out certificates, awards and degrees to prove that their courses have been completed, passed and the graduate is highly educated, ie sophisticated and superior. In other words, the humanist brainwashing has been successful. It is so easy for graduates to become skilled with big words, to think with the highly critical, doubtful mind of higher criticism. It's easy to fall into thinking habits of sophistry and beliefs of Gnosticism, the secret knowledge/science.

When a student graduates from a university, he or she wears a similar cloak and cap as was worn in the Middle Ages. The traditional graduation ceremony is impressive with all its costumes and pompousness. It gives the illusion of high intelligence and superiority over others. By the way, Avondale College has changed its name to Avondale University. It looks like a ploy to upgrade its image and status to be like other institutions - just like the Israelites wanted a king to be like the other nations. It seems that God's ways are not good enough.

How many parents are so proud to see their child complete a university

Word Examples Of Sophistry

degree? In my family, I am the only one who went to university and my parents proudly attended the graduation ceremony. I have a Bachelor of Music. Later, I did a Diploma in Teaching. I have other letters after my name for different achievements. It was only in years to come, after I received Jesus as my Saviour, that I realised how useless all this humanist knowledge was if I wanted to do God's will and teach according to His way. I told the Lord I would stop teaching unless He showed me what to do. That's a long story and I won't get into now, but suffice it to say, the Lord did show me another far better method of teaching music.

But my main point is that my sister and two brothers who didn't get to tertiary levels, still have the same opportunity to get to Heaven as I do. I am in no way superior to them.

Universities issue degrees for theological as well as secular subjects, and they offer levels from bachelor, to masters and doctorates. The highest academic level is a PhD, a doctor of philosophy. Someone described a PhD as, 'Permanent Head Damage.' And this could be right unless the person uses their gift of free will to choose to accept the science/knowledge of God's truth. While they are alive, there is always hope for repentance. Romans 12:2 tells us, '*And be not conformed to this world, but be ye <u>transformed by the renewing of your mind</u>, that ye may prove what is that good and acceptable, perfect will of God.*' What a sad state of things that intelligent God-designed minds have been brainwashed to turn away from their Creator, and they must be transformed and renewed, back to the original condition.

All the while since the first university in 1088, these institutions have developed more sophisticated, higher, critical thinking deliberately designed to distract and create doubt in God's existence and absolute truth. Over the last two to three hundred years, Jesuit mind-manipulation and brain-washing, so-called education, have infiltrated to every age group from kindergarten to adults. Even the elderly can do a university course if they want. To Satan, all ages are merely more minds and souls to prey on. The basic system of Roman education with its levels upon levels, is just like the Roman pyramid government. This basic structure is also seen in non-Catholic, private, public and so-called protestant schools.

In contrast to this hierarchical system. God's plans for education were originally in the home with parents as the teachers. Proverbs 22:6 has a message for parents to, *'Train up a child in the way he should go, and when he is old, he will not depart from it.'* Yet again, Satan has sabotaged the minds by removing little ones from the training responsibility of the parents. Day Care centres, kindergartens, primary and secondary schools, colleges and universities have all replaced God's design of education. Babies, toddlers, children, youth and adults are taught a different message, a different verse or variation to God's Word. Home schooling is looked down on and even banned in some places.

Roman roots of education have spread out slowly and insidiously through the body of humanity just like a cancer. Cancers can be in a human body for ten or more years before being detected. The influence of Roman education has been spreading around humanity throughout generations for nearly a thousand years since universities began. The ancient Roman Empire which began over 2000 years ago lives on this very day. Such is the legacy of Simon Magus.

The majority of today's population has no idea of the damage this Roman education foundation is doing to produce sick souls and wayward minds. This humanist system supposedly leads to greater intelligence but, at the same time, it dumbs down information for masses of school children. Today, students can go through twelve years of school and still not read and write properly. And this is called, 'progress,' and man is supposed to be evolving into a 'better species.'

Let's see what Wikipedia says about the word university. It derives from the Latin 'universitas magistrorum et scholarium' which roughly means 'community of teachers and scholars.' But from our little study of universe, we know it means much more than that. A common overly complicated Jesuit language has developed. It is essentially gnostic with its sophistications, hidden meanings and coded language.

The super-sophist Satan has so cleverly trained his human agents and graduates from the tertiary institutions, to form extremely complicated languages in whatever area with long words and lengthy sentences— just like lawyers do. Well, lawyers have been through the system and are well-trained, aren't they? So do doctors and scientists. Just look

Word Examples Of Sophistry

at their language. People are often considered experts if they have a string of letters after their names. But the sophisticated language of this apparently superior group is basically the same old Jesuit language of sophistry and Gnosticism.

The poor common, everyday person is left behind trying to fathom out what the big words mean. Usually, they can't and blindly place their trust in these higher educated sophisticates. Society is divided into the educated and the struggling uneducated, and those somewhere in between. And it's all about words, words, words.

But even the most illiterate person can still have an inner heart understanding that there must be a Creator God. God must feel so appreciated when he sees someone looking at a beautiful flower and acknowledges Him as the One who made it and gave it life. Every flower is an expression of His love. Just having trust and belief, the science/knowledge of faith, that God is with us and angels are around us, must make God so happy and pleased. Romans 1:20 tells us, '*For the invisible things of Him from the creation of the world are clearly seen, being understood by the things that are made, even His eternal power and Godhead, so that they are without excuse.*' Yes, just by observing nature, there is no excuse whatsoever not to believe in our Creator. What a magnificent verse that one is!

Let's look at a couple of so-called experts, two of the puppeteers in Satan's hierarchical pyramid-shaped government, who have been trained in his hierarchical pyramid-shaped education system. These elite puppeteers are pulling the strings of the puppets all through every education organisation. Even Christian schools are affected because many of them rely on funding from governments. The Elite are subtly training and selecting higher educated, superior ones to do all their dirty work in every area of life to reshape society in the Great Reset—political, medical, educational, recreational, every aspect they can get their power-hungry hands on.

Let's take Klaus Schwab as our first example of a skilful puppeteer. Schwab is the founder and head of the WEF, World Economic Forum. In 1992, he established the school for 'Global Leaders of Tomorrow,' and in 2004 the name was changed to 'Young Global Leaders.' In 2012,

Schwab and the WEF started the 'Global Shapers Community' to bring together leaders around the world under the age of 30. At least he's not calling the schools 'universal,' but by their correct word, global. These institutions train their graduates to infiltrate every nation and government in order to gain power and control over the whole world population.

In an earlier talk, we saw some examples of graduates of Schwab's schools—Angela Merkel ex-chancellor of Germany, Tony Blair Prime Minister of England, Jacinda Ardern of New Zealand, Emmanuel Macron of France, Justin Trudeau of Canada. And graduates are not just politicians. Those in technology and entertainment industries, and any group which influences people, can attend Schwab's schools. Bill Gates, Jeff Bezos, Richard Branson and Chelsea Clinton, famous singers and musicians have been there.

Those in the Elite like Tony Fauci and Bill Gates, control the universities by funding them or withholding funds. Gates has funded 471 universities in 66 countries in the past ten years. He and Fauci control the science experiments for the COVID injections and they manipulate the statistics. And all this scheming and plotting is done through words, words, and more words in order for Satan to get his own way—a One World Order with him sitting invisibly as the Most High at the very tip of the pyramid.

Meanwhile, at the bottom grass roots level, the little sheeple-people and cattle are kept busy. They are made dependant on the upper levels through services and supplies and jobs. They are herded and shepherded wherever the powers that be, decide. They are kept busy in a cycle of work-stress-relaxation. Firstly, they have to <u>work</u> to get paid to feed their families and survive. Secondly, they get over-worked and <u>stressed</u>. Thirdly, they must work harder to pay for <u>relaxation</u> breaks, entertainment and holidays. Then they go back to work again and keep pushing the pedals of the cycle—work-stress-relaxation; work-stress-relaxation.

In January each year, Klaus Schwab holds a conference in Davos, Switzerland. Just this last week, I saw some clips from it. Schwab introduced the opening speaker as quote, 'His Excellency, Xi Jinping, President of the Peoples' Republic of China.' Xi Jinping is the highest ranking official

Word Examples Of Sophistry

and head of the Chinese Communist Party. What an interesting person to invite to open such a global conference! It just shows where the world is heading. In one interview, Schwab said, 'One of the features of this Fourth Industrial Revolution is that it doesn't change what we are doing, but it changes us.' Let's find out how.

I also watched Dr Yuval Noah Harari who is Top Advisor to Klaus Schwab and the WEF. He is an Israeli historian and professor at the Hebrew University in Jerusalem. He wrote the book 'Sapiens: A Brief History of Mankind,' and also 'Homo Deus: A Brief History of Tomorrow.' Dr Harari is also a transhumanist. I wonder how God feels about someone descended from the chosen people writing as if humans evolved from apes. What does He think about a Hebrew university being in the very city His one and only begotten Son was crucified in?

Just listen to what Dr Harari recently had to say. These are just a few unbelievable quotations. He says, -

'Soon, some at least, corporations and governments will be able to systematically hack all the people. We humans should get used to the idea that we are no longer mysterious souls. We are hackable animals.'... Later he says, 'Data might enable elites to do something even more radical than just build digital dictatorships. By hacking organisms, elites may gain the power to re-engineer the future of life itself. Because once you can hack something, you can usually also re-engineer it.' Harari goes on and on about the laws of evolution over five billion years, then continues, 'Science is replacing "evolution by natural selection," with "evolution by intelligent design." Not the intelligent design of some God above the clouds, but our intelligent design, and the intelligent design of our clouds, the IBM cloud, the Microsoft clouds. These are the new driving forces of evolution....'

Hmmm. Isn't that a clever use of sophistry and imagery with the word clouds? What an insult to God! As if God is floating high upon a cloud with all the Roman little fat angelic cherubs with wings playing harps and floating on their own little fluffy clouds all around Him. That's the way angels are perceived.

Harari goes on to say, 'At the same time, science may enable life to

The Greatest War Ever

break out into the inorganic realm...... We are entering the era of organic life shaped by <u>intelligent design</u>.' He also talked about, 'the whole idea that humans have this soul and free will, and nobody knows what's happening inside me. So, whatever I choose, whether in the election or in the supermarket–that's over.' Hmmm. In other worlds, humans don't have souls and free will anymore! He also said, 'We have today the technology to hack human beings on a massive scale.... In this time of crisis, you have to follow science....Vaccines will make things more manageable. ... People could look back in a hundred years and identify the coronavirus epidemic as the moment when a new regime of surveillance took over, especially surveillance under the skin, which I think is the most important development of the 21st century. (It) is this ability to hack human beings, to go under the skin, collect biometric data, analyse it and to know people better than themselves. This, I believe is the most important event of the 21st century.' End of Harari's quotations.

What a horrible word hack is. Hack means to cut, chop with repeated irregular, unskilful blows like a murderer. Harari used the word many times so it must be important to him.

Praise God that we still have our soul and free will, and know the most important event of the 21st century will be the Second Coming of Jesus. There will be no hundred years of the earth in this present condition with its ruling Elite. We know much, much more than Harari does, all glory to God and His Word.

Don't Harari's words reveal the true hidden agenda of the COVID Plandemic - that humans are only animals to be hacked and used as guinea pigs; that human life will be re-engineered by man's intelligent design, by those who have graduated from the counterfeit education system of universities. Harari is admitting in plain sight that COVID is the beginning of a new regime of surveillance under the skin.

Phew!! Satan is certainly doing his absolute utmost to bring out the war machinery. He's in panic mode knowing his days are numbered. He knows the reality of the One true God far, far above the clouds! If it wasn't for God's Word, we could become very frightened with this information.

Word Examples Of Sophistry

But, we know that God's perfect love casts out fear. How much more hopeful and reassured are we, to have our God who is <u>for</u> us. No-one can be against us, especially not the mere humans who think like their evil Chief General. They can only <u>think</u> they will have ultimate control over the very souls of humans. Revelation 18:13 talks about the merchants of the earth weeping and mourning because they will no longer be able to buy their merchandise of all types including the *'souls of men.'* Our almighty Father God told us this 2000 years ago and warned of these present days. We can trust His Word completely.

Just an interesting thought about God's amazing Great Love. Do you realise that Schwab and Harari still have the opportunity of being saved and going to Heaven? Yes, they are murderers. But so were King Manasseh and Paul. Schwab and Harari are still alive and breathing, therefore they have time to change and repent, and turn to Jesus. If they did, God would welcome them with open arms. What wonderful testimonies these two would have if only they would switch army sides and become players, not actors.

We have learned a lot about the words universal and university, as well as related words like universe, catholic, metaverse, controversy and version. But there's just one more short titbit to finish off this section while we are still on the subject of university. The University of Pennsylvania is very interesting. So many people put their trust in factcheck.org and don't know its roots in this university. Last year I wondered about the credibility of this website and a good way to find out is to see who funds it. So, I googled 'who funds factcheck.org?' I was most surprised.

It was started by a man called Walter H Annenburg. Annenburg founded the 'Annenburg School for Communication' at the University of Pennsylvania which is, not surprisingly, Jesuit-controlled. Note, it is a communications school - the perfect place for words, words, words and sophistry. Annenburg turns out to be a Papal Knight Commander of the Jesuit Order of St Gregory the Great. The University of Pennsylvania and all its surrounding land is owned by the Roman Church. Bill Gates gave a large donation to be used for all levels of education from kindergarten to the highest tertiary levels. What's more, factcheck.org holds over 1.8 billion dollars of stock in vaccine companies.

Many people put their trust in this site and ask questions expecting truth. But they are lied to with clever, scientific-looking explanations using Jesuit language which sound logical and plausible. Again, these are mere excellent examples of sophistry. You can try a test. Just google the following–'factcheck.org Do COVID vaccine injections have magnetic ingredients?' You will read extremely clever examples of sophistry.

As I was reading about the University of Pennsylvania, a link came up on the side about Annenburg so I clicked on it. Again, I was shocked as a bright red and black Luciferian website appeared with the word Lucifer across the top. Sure enough, further down in the article was Annenburg's name. So, there we have it - the founder of factcheck.org is a known Luciferian and actor-agent of Satan. This is just one small result and consequence of the Roman Church. Such is the roll-on, snow-balling effect of the clever use of just one simple word, catholic/universal in the title of the Church.

That's enough study on the word, university. Let move onto the next one. It's also related to the word universal. Isn't it fascinating how one thing leads to another?

4. Basilica: The next link in the word chain is basilica. How did Saint Peter's Basilica get its name? It's not by chance with a few letters just thrown together. Every name is chosen because of its meaning. Basilica also stems from the word universe. In the concordance, G932, the Greek word for universe is basileus. Basileus means kingdom of heaven, royalty, rule, realm, reign. So basileus represents God's kingdom of Universe.

But as usual Satan has his counterfeit kingdom here on earth and central to this is the building called Saint Peter's Basilica. Peter the apostle, was called a saint because the Roman Church used its counterfeit royal divine authority to claim to be able to do that. So, this is why the Basilica is given the name, Saint Peter. And now we understand that Basilica means universe ie uni-verse–the one word or message preached by the Roman Church. And this message is based on esoteric, secret, superior knowledge/science of Gnosticism, which we learned about in the previous talk. Saint Peter's Basilica contains the seat of government where the Pope sits and oversees his global kingdom.

Word Examples Of Sophistry

Every kingdom has a name, a title and a territory. The King of Universe's <u>name</u> is Lord God and He is the Law-Giver; His <u>title</u> is Creator, and His <u>territory</u> is Universe. Compare this with Satan. The three features are represented in his headquarters of Saint Peter's Basilica. Firstly, Satan uses the <u>name</u> of Saint Peter. Secondly, his human agents have the <u>title</u> of Pope with its variations - Black, Grey, White and Red. The white Pope has titles of Holy Father, Pontifex Maximus (greatest bridge-builder), Summus Pontifex (highest priest), Servant of the Servants, God on Earth, Vicar of Christ, Bishop of Rome, Primate of Italy, His Holiness, Holy Father etc. And thirdly, Satan's <u>territory</u> is only a small globe, the tiny little planet Earth.

What a pathetic counterfeit kingdom this little ball is. It is contained inside a thin layer of atmosphere as its boundary. Compare this mere dot with God's infinite kingdom stretching out with no boundaries! This comparison certainly puts things into perspective.

So - Saint Peter's Basilica is a counterfeit royal authority of a counterfeit god of a counterfeit universe. This modern-day Peter Temple or god-temple in Rome, is where Satan is orchestrating the Great Reset and planning his own New World Order, through his broad pyramid-shaped government. From here, he gives orders to the four popes who pull the strings of the next levels in the Roman Church including the Jesuits. Jesuits also become puppeteers pulling more strings in all directions to the lower levels of authorities of the *'kings and merchants of the earth'* (Revelation 18:3.) These world leaders in turn pull more strings of the multitudes in the bottom level of puppets.

I hope you are seeing more of the Big Picture and exactly what is going on in our world today. Through the Bible we can be certain that Satan's days are numbered and are rapidly reducing.

By the way, did you know there are actually four basilicas? They are called the major 'papal basilicas?' The oldest one is called the 'Archbasilica' and also has a typical Jesuit long name of 'The Cathedral of the Most Holy Saviour and of Saints John the Baptist and John the Evangelist in the Lateran.' What a name! Or for short, 'Archbasilica of Saint John Lateran.' Hmmm. Big names with more words. And, like the Society of Jesus using Christ's name, they also claim the two Johns as their own along with Peter.

This Archbasilica lies outside the Vatican City about four kilometers away to the northwest. The French President, Emmanuel Macron has the title of 'First and Only Honorary Canon' of the Archbasilica. So, Saint Peter's is just one of the four basilicas. It's not actually the true mother church of all Catholic churches as many believe. The real mother church is the Archbasilica of St John Lateran. Just an interesting titbit.

That's enough on the word, Basilica. It just gives more insight to the word universe, and exposes further the arrogance and gall of Satan to <u>think</u> he is the Most High. The saying goes, 'The higher one flies, the further he falls.' What a long way Satan will fall from attempting to be the Most High, to the depths of the lake of fiery sulphur.

5. Allegories: The last two words we'll look at are not words to be broken down and analysed. They are just two effective tools in Satan's toolbox of tactics, his ammunition in the Great War of Words. They have much shorter explanations, but need to be brought to attention in the big umbrella of sophistry which covers this whole series of talks.

The fifth word to look at is—allegories. An allegory is a symbolic fictional story where characters and events merely represent ideas about human life. The stories did not actually happen but are used to illustrate and describe a political or historical situation, or try to explain the purpose of human existence. This is why so many believe the Bible stories are mere myths and fables with a moral message but are not literally true. Allegories are another example of Satan's sophistry. In order to blend paganism with truth, allegories were used way back in the first few centuries AD to try and explain away and distract from the Old Testament writings and God.

6. Other Languages - Numbers and Signs: There are other types of languages than those just using words. The word, language, simply means to communicate, and this can involve tones of voice, gestures, body language, numbers, signs and symbols. Satan loves numbers because they can have codes and hidden meanings. Just one example is found in the number seven. Seven is known as God's perfect number and Satan attacks it with a vengeance. The number 7 relates to the sev-

Word Examples Of Sophistry

enth day Sabbath. Satan knew that the Jews kept the seventh day of the week as their sacred day of worshipping the true Creator, because it was and still is, the Fourth Commandment. But through many actor-agents, the number 7 was changed to number 1 and first day of the week was made the sacred.

In the Fourth Century, Emperor Constantine made it law that everyone must keep the first day of the week for worship. This day had the Roman name of Sunday named after the sun-god ie Nimrod and ultimately Satan himself. Satan made his mark, by claiming the first week day as his own day of worship. This is the mark of the monster beast of Daniel's vision and John's words in Revelation 13:16-17. Satan only thought to change God's Law by changing the appointed worship day, but he merely changed the day number from 7 to 1. Only a small minority question this today and stick with the seventh day.

I'm not going into all the details of numbers because it would be several talks. Suffice it to say that Revelation 13:18 tells how God has given Satan his own special number. *'Let him that hath understanding count the number of the beast. For it is the number of a man, and his number is six hundred, threescore and six.'* ie 666. We know God's perfect number is seven.

There is an old phrase sometimes used today, 'sixes and sevens.' If someone is 'at sixes and sevens,' it means they are confused, frazzled and disorganised. The phrase originates in the Great War of Words between the two invisible super-powers, the Chief General 666, and the Chief Commander. The Triple S or the Triple 6, is at odds against the Triple 0, (Outside Objective Observer), whose perfect number is 7. For Satan, numbers and signs are other exciting, fun war language games just like words.

Again, I'm not going into details of signs and symbols either as we mentioned some in a previous talk. These are the secret unspoken meanings of circles, circles within circles, triangles, pentagons, hand signs, body language, three wavy lines etc. And besides, other people have done excellent research and given plenty of examples. Walter Veith covers these extremely well in his presentations about freemasonry.

And I highly recommend you watch a YouTube video by an ex-rock musician who came out of freemasonry and is a Christian. It's amazing. I took eleven pages of notes and thought of doing a summary talk on this, but it's best to view the real thing and see all the pictures and evidence. Just google, 'Altiyan Childs Exposes Freemasonry." His parents are Croation and Serbian.

Altiyan's talk was presented on April 15 2021, and he knew he was risking his life and that his YouTube video could be taken down at any time. If it is still there, it is long, five hours, but well worth watching over a few days. I warn you, it's not appropriate to watch on a Sabbath Day. It goes into details of dozens of entertainers who are freemasons. It goes into the symbols, all the degrees of freemasonry, their emblems and initiation ceremonies. He even shows a chart listing names of demons in a hierarchy. Even Satan's army of demons has its own pyramid hierarchy. I really encourage you to watch it.

Conclusion In conclusion, we have looked at six important words—antichrist, universal, university, Basilica, allegories, and numbers and signs, plus a few associated ones. We have exposed more of our greatest enemy. This is just a taste of the countless changes and twisting of words, numbers and signs that Satan and his human actor-agents thrive on. But this is enough for now. You have probably guessed how I am passionately interested in words and their meanings. Each word has its own story. I could choose hundreds of thousands more words and never exhaust them all. This is the beauty and miracle of God-created language. God wants us to know His truth, the absolute truth and uses language to do this, especially His Word. Let's close in prayer.

Prayer Our almighty Father in Heaven, Creator of language, what a talk this has been! It has been my small attempt to use words in the Great War so I can expose the enemy more to the listeners, and they will be even more aware of his tricks and sophistry and be prepared in daily battles. We have learned a great deal, but still don't know the full depths of Satan's wickedness. We thank you Father that You do know the depths he has stooped to. Oh, You must be feeling the full brunt of these Satanic forces, much more than we do. Oh, what your Son must have gone through when He came to earth and died for us! We thank

Word Examples Of Sophistry

You again for Your Great Love, Your mercy and forgiveness towards us mere humans. Your Love is unfathomable. We know how you accept with welcome arms, anyone who sincerely comes to You—even people like Klaus Schwab and Yuval Harari and other world leaders in Satan's pyramid government. Lord, we uplift all those kings and merchants of the earth to you. They are alive and there is still hope for their salvation. It is not Your will that anyone should perish. May it be that the world leaders choose to switch sides from actors to players, and join the army of our Chief Commander and Saviour, our Messiah, Jesus Christ. We pray all this in His precious name. Amen.

Thank you for being here and listening once again. I look forward to meeting you when the curtains open in two weeks' time on March 19, at 2:30pm. In our next talk, we will look at one particular word—blasphemy. And I plan to also expose some techniques of persuasion used in the powerful propaganda machine operating in full force today.

As we leave our celestial seats to return to the planet-stage, please enjoy the journey because this is the journey we will be blessed with on the way to Heaven. On the way back to our temporary home, just marvel at the scenery, the sights and shapes of the glorious galaxies which surround us in deep space. Gaze at the brilliant scintillating colours of the stars as they flash by while we zoom along at angel speed. Enjoy the weightlessness of the freedom of flying, the absence of aching, tired, weary, burdensome bodies. Experience the electricity pulsating through our very being, and the sharpness of mind, and clarity of vision over vast distances. It's only a few short years till we leave in reality and experience these marvellous rewards of our labours. May God bless you all and give you peace and comfort amid the storm.

PART 7 – ACT SEVEN: Blasphemy and Techniques of Persuasion

Introduction and Review

Welcome back everyone! How time flies! We are one week closer to that great day when our Chief Commander Jesus Christ, comes back to take us to Heaven. We are now at Part Seven of the series called The Greatest War Ever. So far, our journey through the 6000-year timeline of the story of planet Earth has been an extremely rough rocky ride.

His Story, ie God's Story, has certainly been the most spectacular show ever on earth. Actors acting out Satan's wicked character have been attacking the players who try their hardest to play the roles they were designed for. Life on this earth is not just about knowing God and enjoying Him forever. We are pilgrims passing through this earthly way with a divine mission. Let's pray before we start.

Prayer: Our Lord and God, we thank you for bringing us this far in the series and for strengthening us on this most terrible battlefield. Oh Father, on our own we are weak and feeble and often stumble. We ask your forgiveness for all our sins, especially those in our minds and thoughts, because they are what determine our actions. We thank You for Your Word and claim Your promises when you say in 2 Chronicles 20:15, 17, 'Be not afraid, nor dismayed by reason of this great multitude, for the battle is not yours but God's. ... Ye shall not need to fight in this battle. Set yourselves. Stand ye still and see the salvation of the Lord with you.' And just as the psalmist wrote in Psalm 18:2 'The Lord is my Rock and my fortress and my deliverer, my God, my strength in whom I will trust; my buckler and the horn of my salvation, and my high tower.' Thank You Lord for all those promises. And we also ask for extra special doses of Your Great Love in our hearts so we can pray for our enemies when it's really hard and we feel the force of their attacks, especially our world leaders who are merely puppets of the puppeteers who are above them carrying out Satan's orders. Help us to live out your Law of Great Love

Blasphemy and Techniques of Persuasion

in a world filled with Satan's Law of Great Hate. We pray these things in the all-powerful name of Your Son, our High Priest, Jesus. Amen.

In previous talks, we have learned how the whole Great War of Words began in Heaven when Lucifer rebelled and became Chief General of his own army of a third of the angels. None of these fallen angels died in Heaven because the war was all about mind manipulation, not death. So, right now, these demons are still alive, fighting for Satan. This once glorious planet has been reduced to a 6000-year old battlefield and is the only black spot in the glittering Universe. The whole war has been a very lengthy debate or controversy lasting millenniums.

By now, you will have a very good understanding of the word sophism, ie twisting of words to cause doubt and confusion in order to get one's own way. And you will also know how Gnosticism is the secret, superior, science or knowledge. The words science and knowledge mean exactly the same thing. This sophisticated science/knowledge has become a belief system. It permeates the whole globe in every area of life through Satan's pyramid government full of hierarchies within the Roman Church. This pagan religion is Satan's counterfeit of true Christianity.

In the previous talks, we also met some baddies, Nimrod, Semiramus, Simon Magus and a few of the antichrists, just to name a few who served their Chief General Satan. We also met goodies like Solomon, Daniel, Peter, John, Luke and Paul who were mighty warriors for their Chief Commander. God spoke His Word through them, not just for those alive in their day, but for all who followed, including us. All the works of the Old and New Testament writers are simply God's love letters to humanity to encourage and comfort us, and to warn us so we can be prepared for the climax just around the corner in the Great War. How good is our ever-loving Father God who reveals truth when we need it in our present time.

There are the billions of other players who fought for the Lord and they remain nameless. They died as martyrs, defending their Father-King. They are the minority or remnant who battled on against the majority. Their role, purpose and mission has always been to prove to other humans, to the rest of the angels and inhabitants of other worlds, that theocracy with the Godhead, the Royal Ruling Trio, is the best and only

The Greatest War Ever

way to govern any kingdom. And today, there is still a tiny minority scattered around the globe still battling on, holding onto the cords of faith with Christ at the other end.

A thousand man-made movies could not completely cover all of this drama. But at the very end of the earth's time, we know that the most amazing panorama, the greatest movie ever, will pass before our very eyes. The real Authors of the storyline, the Producer-God, Director-Jesus and Prompter-Holy Spirit will present the drama and all will be revealed exactly as it happened. No lies, just the pure unadulterated truth for all to see. Baddies and goodies will be exposed in two groups in full sight so there is no doubt at all about the truth.

We have used different names for the Chief General Satan. He is a saboteur, the Triple 6, the Triple S standing for Secret Subjective Satan, or Super Sophist Satan. This supernatural enemy of the Chief Commander will be among those bowing down and confessing Jesus is Lord. We have also used different names for our Father-God, the Triple 0, ie Outside Objective Observer who we can call upon at any time. The Royal Rulers of the Godhead—Father, Son and Holy Spirit—were always in control of the storyline, and they still are. Everything happens for good reason and at the appointed time according to their prophecies and their will.

In this talk we will cover two scenes. The first is called Blasphemy and the second covers Fifteen Techniques of Persuasion. You might like to have a pen and piece of paper handy to write the list. Both scenes reveal more about the relentless, massive monster beast, the ancient pagan Roman Empire which turned into the Roman Papacy. We know this is a fact because it is described so brilliantly in Daniel Chapter 7 and in Revelation Chapter 13. This beast is like a modern army tank slowly but surely lumbering on and rolling over everyone in its path.

We will see how the Great War of Words continues to rage furiously. What we see on earth is a reflection and manifestation of the extreme, intense anger and jealousy, racing around Satan's evil heart and mind. Words in sophism and Gnosticism are like an uncontrollable fire. Only the power of God's Word is able to quench it. The Lord's warrior Paul wrote a letter to the Ephesians describing how we are to '...*be strong*

Blasphemy and Techniques of Persuasion

in the Lord, and in the power of His might. Put on the whole armour of God that ye may be able to stand against the wiles of the devil. For we wrestle not against flesh and blood, but against principalities, against power, against the rulers of the darkness of this world, against spiritual wickedness in high places.' Ephesians 6:10-12 Paul goes on to describe the coat of armour and one part of it is '... the sword of the Spirit which is the Word of God.'

Two words from this last verse are fascinating. They are sword and words. If you take the 's' from the end of 'words' and put it at the start, you get a new word, sword. So, words becomes sword. Just think about how significant that is. Just by putting the last letter first, we can see how words become swords in the Great War of Words. We are about to see more of how Satan uses his own sophisticated complicated sword-words against God's Word in the weapon of blasphemy. We will also learn how he uses sword-words in techniques of persuasion to manipulate the global population. We will expose more of Satan's verbal magic tricks. There is an excellent quotation from Great Controversy 516 which says, 'There is nothing that the great deceiver fears so much as that we shall become acquainted with his devices.'

Let's remember in these talks, how we have phased off the planet-stage in our minds, to be part of the audience watching the spectacular show with great interest, along with the angels, the inhabitants of other worlds, as well as Enoch, Moses and those first fruits who Jesus took to Heaven after His resurrection. So, once again, brace yourselves in your celestial seats for the next language bombardment from the enemy.

Scene 16. Blasphemy

Biblical Examples: First, we'll start with some Biblical examples of blasphemy from the Bible. In Luke 5:21,24 we are told of the reaction of the scribes and pharisees, when Jesus forgave the man who was lowered down from the roof. They accused Jesus of blasphemy when they said, 'Who is this which speaketh blasphemies? Who can forgive sins but God alone?' And in Matthew 26:63-65, we read how the high priest asked Jesus if He was the Christ, the Son of God. Jesus replied by saying, "Hereafter shall ye see the Son of man sitting on the right hand of power and coming in the clouds of Heaven." Then the high priest rent *his clothes saying, "He hath spoken blasphemy..."*

So, there are two Biblical definitions of blasphemy. 1. claiming to be God and 2. having the power to forgive sins. These were seen as a crime with the penalty of death. The Papacy has always done both forms of blaspheming. No wonder God gave John the vision in Revelation Chapter 13:1. John saw, *'a beast rise up out of the seas, having seven heads and ten horns, and upon his horns, ten crowns and <u>upon his heads the name blasphemy</u>.'* What a monstrous beast! John goes on in verse 2 to describe how this beast of the Roman Empire, is a culmination of the three previous empires–Babylonian, Persia-Mede and Greek. The Roman Empire and the papacy contain pagan customs and characteristics of all the three previous empires put together. No words can adequately describe this monster beast machine.

Origin of the Word Blasphemy: There is much more to blasphemy than just those two Biblical definitions. As always, one thing leads to another. Satan's use and abuse of language in his distortion and twisting of the storyline of this earthly show, just gets more and more knotted as his imagination and plotting gets more and more wicked.

What else constitutes blasphemy? What is it precisely? Why are certain words called swearing? I grew up in a worldly environment where swearing is used in almost every single sentence. And I admit to also using them until becoming a Christian at the age of thirty. About three years ago, I decided to analyse blasphemy and get to the roots of it because certain words kept popping up in my thoughts. I thought about my childhood and pre-Christian life and analysed as many swear words as I knew. This scene is based on personal experience.

Swearing is such an ingrained habit that, most of the time, the utterers don't even know they are doing it. Blasphemy is everywhere every day and new words keep coming into language. Modern dictionaries now include many swear words and label them as colloquial terms to justify them as part of normal speech. Swearing is made acceptable. Peer pressure to conform and be accepted is a major part of the corrupted language. Some time ago, a teenage student told me that her school banned swearing, (sounds good) but there was a secret club of girls where you had to swear in order to be a member and friend. And even

Blasphemy and Techniques of Persuasion

pre-schoolers learn to swear at an early age by copying their parents.

Let's look at the origins of the word and glean some more of Satan's word weapons so we can be shielded and not use these words. The word, blasphemy comes under other names such as profanity, cursing and swearing. It originates from the Greek, blasphemia, meaning to speak impiously, revile, speak evil of, defame and vilify. The Miriam-Webster online dictionary goes further. It says, to attack a person's reputation with strong, abusive criticism, to malign, to make vile, to debase, degrade and disgrace. Phew! Blasphemy is a most destructive weapon in the War of Words.

Of course, the ultimate target of <u>all</u> blasphemy is the very Creator of language. We will soon see how each Person of the Godhead - Father, Son and Holy Spirit—is cursed. Language was originally designed to be a means of expressing their Great Love, and the way of communicating between them and their human children. However, much of it has been counterfeited or destroyed through unbelievable disrespect, contempt and hatred towards the Godhead, or the denial of its existence. This divine Trio, the true Royal Rulers of Universe is the ultimate target of Satan. As always, he uses human agents to carry out his dirty deeds and to attack whether they realise it or not.

How does blasphemy work? Let's briefly study the process of what happens in the mind when someone swears. After all, this Great War is a battle in the mind and for the mind.

The Process and Effects of Blasphemy: Blasphemy is a bit like a magic trick. Once we know how it's done, the trick loses its fascination and power over us. Likewise, if we understand what is going on inside our minds, we can expose the mystery, the fascination and addiction to foul language. Yes, it can be a habit and addiction. Blasphemers cannot utter one sentence without swearing and they aren't even aware of doing it.

So, let's firstly think about what happens before the words even come out of the mouth. The process essentially goes like this: the bad cursing idea starts in the heart, and proceeds to the feelings, then the mind and silent thoughts. These thought-words become spoken words which are consequently expressed along with body actions. From the heart can come negative feelings of irritation, annoyance, frustration and exasperation when things don't go one's way. Often there is a need to shift the blame from oneself to someone else. This is so Satan! He attacks our heart/spirit. Huffs, puffs and hurtful thoughts rise up into the mind. Then, if there is no self-control, no submitting the mind to Christ, the words burst out. More feelings can quickly flare up into stronger anger, fury and rage. An adult can behave just the same as a two-year-old throwing a temper tantrum, because he's not getting his way.

So, this is the process of blasphemy broken down from heart and feelings, to thoughts in the mind, to speech and behaviour.

At all levels there is negativity and countless number of disgusting words used to express feelings. The effects can be devastating. The toxic emotions, the shouts and name-calling are like poison-tipped arrows used to verbally abuse others. They pierce deep into the very heart. Effects can result in diseases as they build up and infect the body of the user as well as the listener. Proverbs 10:19 says, *'In the multitude of words, there wanteth not sin; but he that refraineth his lips is wise.'* Or, as the Clear Word Bible puts it, *'The more a person talks, the more likely he is to sin; but he who listens more than he talks, is wise.'* Proverbs 13:3 says, *'He that keepeth his mouth (ie closes it), keepeth his life; but he that openeth wide his lips shall have destruction.'*

Many times, silence is golden.

The process of blasphemy is pure cause and effect. The cause starts with beliefs in the heart, ie whether God is real or not. If someone believes He is not real, then God automatically gets the blame—even though He's not supposed to be real! What crazy logic is that! So, when something goes wrong, negative feelings follow, then swearing, cursing words. And even if the words don't come out of the mouth, the person is still cursing, because God knows our thoughts.

The result is a release of frustration which attempts to dump the anger onto someone else causing emotional hurt and sometimes physical harm. The receiver of blasphemy can be terribly crushed even to the point of suicide, as has been seen in bullying at schools or in the workplace. But, as terrible as this is, give a thought to the Creator of language. All the while, our ever-loving Father God and His Son Jesus,

Blasphemy and Techniques of Persuasion

must feel the effects far worse as they see billions upon billions of their beloved children suffering from word abuse. They know who is behind it all and how Satan attacks human minds in order to pierce their heart of Great Love.

Sadly, however, even believers can blaspheme without knowing, because many seemingly tame swear words have become such a normal part of everyday speech.

Words To Remove From Your Vocabulary: We will now look at some blasphemous words. Please note that as I say them, I am not blaspheming because part of swearing is an angry, hateful tone of voice, or lack of control. I am just stating some words as examples and am only selecting a few mild ones. Of course, just like sin and lies, there are no big or little ones. All of them break the third commandment of God, *'Thou shalt not take the name of the Lord thy God in vain, for the Lord will not hold him guiltless that taketh His name in vain.'* To take the Lord's name in vain means to make it worthless and of no value. Our Aussie language is filled with swear words and most people don't think twice about using them to colour their speech. The words only reveal how limited their vocabulary is.

Here are just a few samples and what they really mean. Notice that often the first letter of the swear word is the same as the word meaning. I'm just going alphabetically so there is order and control. Here we go!

'Crikey and Cripes' mean Christ. 'Damn, Dagnammit, Doggone and Darn' all mean damnation in the sense of putting a curse on someone or something. 'Drat' means God rot it. 'Golly and Gosh' substitute for God. 'Gee Willikers' stands for Jesus. 'Gorblimey' means God blind me. 'Good Grief, Goodness Gracious and My goodness' mean Good God, but in a negative way as if He is to blame for some mishap. 'Gee, Gee Whizz and Jeez' stand for Jesus. 'By George' or 'By gum' mean 'By God.' 'Heck' is Hell. 'Holy Cow' is Christ or Holy Spirit. 'By Jove' means By Jehovah. And with technology and texting, the carnal, sinful human mind continues to invent new words. There are new abbreviated swear words, the most common one being 'OMG' - Oh, My God. God gets the blame.

I've heard Christians use some of these words. The words mentioned have lost their affect to such a degree that they have blended with everyday speech. They flow out unnoticed and unchecked. Satan continues his sophistry through language abuse and verbal attacks. There are many, many more blasphemous words than these ones, but they are so foul and disgusting and are unutterable. To list them would only justify and reinforce them, and make our minds filthy. And we don't want that.

Related Features of Blasphemy: Such sacrilegious use of language has many facets and is connected with other means of communication such as 1. Tone of voice, 2. Humour, and 3. Body language. These all work together and are designed to hurt, crush and even kill the hearer. Let's look briefly at each one.

1. Tone of Voice changes a simple word into blasphemy. Can anyone swear using a sincere, kind, loving, gentle tone of voice? No. It's not possible because blasphemy is not a language of love, but of hate. The words don't have the same stinging, piercing effect if there is no angry, vicious, nasty tone.

2. Humour is a cloak which covers cursing and is found in jokes, teasing, mocking, cynicism, sarcasm and bullying. Word meanings are twisted and lies are spoken in another form of sophistry. Actually, to the swearer, they are heartfelt truth of what they believe and feel at the time. Whatever comes out of the mouth comes from the heart. The abuser is expressing what he or she believes to be right. The horrible, humorous blasphemy is disguised with smiles, laughter and feelings of fun and excitement. Gloating makes the speaker feel superior. This is a part of Gnosticism.

Sadly, the cruel humour only reveals a desire to puff up oneself because of possible feelings of low esteem and worthlessness. Or else, it reveals a desire to gain power and control. This sick humour is found in multitudes of filthy, blasphemous jokes which degrade and mock the human body and its Maker, as we shall soon see. The Godhead is grieved to see the abused children and adults suffer through these scorning word attacks. Again, Satan ultimately aims at the Creator of language by attacking and crushing their beloved children. But Galations 6:7 tells us, '*Be not deceived; God is not mocked, for whatsoever a man soweth, that shall he reap.*' Proverbs 3:34 says,

Blasphemy and Techniques of Persuasion

'Surely He scorneth the scorners, but He giveth grace unto the lowly.' Or as the Clear Word Bible puts it, *'The Lord is not pleased with scorners, but delights in giving grace to the humble.'*

3. Body Language also goes hand in hand with blasphemy. Facial grimaces, obscene gestures and aggressive, abusive physical movements naturally accompany blasphemy in times of extreme anger. And when combined with alcohol and drugs, the results are even more destructive. So, the blasphemer loses all self-control and thinks he feels good afterwards. All he has done is to release feelings of anger and frustration on someone else.

It's so, so horrible. How are you feeling? As sick as I am? Well, praise God, we have His Word full of wonderful words of love, praise, hope and positivity, to use and fight back against the enemy's bombardments. We will see how to do counteract the onslaught later in this talk. Our Chief Commander is always with us to help ride over the billowing waves of a rough ocean of warring words.

Toned-Down Blasphemy: Sometimes, other seemingly legitimate words have crept into the foul language which try to soften and tone-down the intent of the user. Anyone familiar with blasphemy will realise which swear words I am referring to. If you don't know, then treasure your ignorance because you don't need to know them. Sometimes, ignorance is bliss. I apologise for arousing any memories of such words and will attempt to be factual and explicit without actually saying the word. Understanding and exposing the origins of profane words may help prevent them ever being thought or uttered again.

When we know our enemy and his strategies, when we submit our mind to Christ, it becomes much easier to resist the devil. He must flee and stop bombarding his word war-weapons into our brains. By wearing our spiritual coat of armour with its shield of faith, we are protected from the word arrows.

For now, let's uncover the meanings of some more of Satan's verbal magic tricks. Let's break that power and mystery.

Some people, especially females, may think they are not really swearing when they water down words to try and make them socially acceptable. For example, the simple words, 'Sugar!' and 'Shoot!' often replace a swear word starting with the same sound. 'Far out' does the same. The speaker and hearer both know what is meant because the tone of voice, plus body language and a smile or giggle, expose the blasphemous intent of the heart. Even beautiful, blooming flowers which are an expression of God's love, can be transformed into blasphemy. The lovely word, blooming, can be changed by the tone of voice to 'bloomin' which substitutes for a swear word starting with the same first two letters.

This Great War of Words gets more and more intriguing and sinister and foul. We are now going to focus on specific targets of blasphemous language. You will be shocked—if you aren't already. Brace yourselves again and tighten those seatbelts. In any war, both sides try to discover secrets and strategies of the opposite side. This is what we are doing right now, so that swear words lose their power and effect on us. Satan and his army of demons plus all his human agents, attack four main targets.

Targets Of Blasphemy: The four targets of blasphemy are: 1. *Physical Body- internal and external; 2. Invisible Parts of Humans; 3. Procreation; 4. Relationships.* Remember that Satan is essentially jealous. With blasphemous words, he attacks things which only God can do and he can't, ie miracles. These four things are examples of God's miraculous creation of life. Man and Satan cannot create them, only destroy them. Let's look briefly at these areas.

1. Physical Body–Internal and External: Satan sends blasts of mocking words to degrade the visible, physical part of God's design of the human body. An example is found in the miraculous internal 'plumbing system' of the body. How many swear words and jokes are there about the way the body expels its solid, liquid and gas wastes!

Yet, when we lift the lid off the compost bin, do we start laughing and joking about waste rubbish from plants? No. What is it about human waste that is supposed to be so hilarious? Nothing - except that it is simply one way of mocking the divine human design and emphasising the repulsive, poisonous things which the body needs to reject. I don't have to give examples because I'm sure you know which words I am talking about.

Blasphemy and Techniques of Persuasion

The external shape or outward physical appearance of the human body is also often attacked. Oh, the verbal cruelty that pierces the heart of someone when they are laughed or jeered at because of how they look–a blemish or body deformity, the colour of their hair, how thin or fat they are, the way they dress. This can be devastating, but again, it is ultimately aimed at hurting the Creator.

Private body parts are also attacked by being ridiculed with degrading swear names. Does anyone laugh about their exposed arms or elbows or feet in the same way they snigger and scoff at the hidden, private parts? No.

Why is this? It's because the private parts are directly linked with reproduction of life which Satan cannot do. The phallus is blatantly seen in towering pillars, obelisks and columns all around the world but very few see the symbolic connection with human anatomy and life-giving power. The Collins dictionary describes the phallic symbol as representing 'generative power of nature in religious systems.' So, this symbol refers to sacred, life-giving power. This is why the phallus is a constant source of jest.

Female anatomy is also portrayed in most disgusting, derogatory ways. Private, life-giving body parts are meant to be covered and protected because of their precious sacred value. We are meant to dress modestly because of the shame of Adam and Eve at the Fall when sin entered the world. Our clothes are a reminder of the guilt of breaking God's Laws.

However, the fashion today is to expose as much of the body as possible, if not all of it as in nudist clubs. As a result, the flesh becomes more of a temptation for carnal lust. Sin becomes a desirable, positive thing and the body is degraded unbelievably at times, to the point of cruel abuse. Sexual lust is also part of the sacrifice ceremonies of children and young women. Over and over again, the very heart of our Father-God, the Designer and Creator is attacked.

The Blood: Another significant part of God's design of the human body which is assailed with word weapons, is the blood. Why is this? Blood is at the very core of our life and existence. Without blood we are dead. Leviticus 17:11 tells us, *'For the life of the flesh is in the blood; and*

I have given it to you upon the altar to make an atonement for your souls; for it is the blood that maketh atonement for the souls.' This is another miracle of God. Hence, one of the most common swear words in the Australian language blatantly derives from the word, blood. This vile, irreverent swear word is a direct attack on Jesus and how He sacrificed His own blood to save our souls. It aims at the very essence of life itself, the very thing Satan cannot create.

Other related words are 'bleedin' and bloomin'. The Roman Church even calls that word blasphemy by claiming it derived from, 'By our Lady.' How hypocritical is that! Satan also uses blood as blasphemy by having it portrayed as something scary, gory and evil in horror movies and murder mysteries. Children are often scared when they see themselves bleeding because they don't understand its purpose in the body. Blood is seen as something bad. The colour red, along with black, are Satan's favourite colours and are seen in all satanic things.

When the body is degraded in any way, the Holy Spirit is also blasphemed because, since Christ was the final atonement, our body has become the living temple of the Holy Spirit. 1 Corinthians 3:19 says, *'Know ye not that your body is the temple of the Holy Ghost which is in you, which ye have of God, and ye are not your own?'* Oh, how the Holy Spirit must grieve to see how far man has degenerated. He and the Father and Son know full well that we could have all been wearing glorious, glowing robes of righteousness which Adam and Eve once wore in the Garden of Eden.

If you think all this has been bad enough, then hold on to your seats for what is coming next. This next part is going to be hard to take, so I will go slowly and factually.

Remember that Satan is a predator. Peter described him when he wrote in 1 Peter 5:8, *'Be sober, be diligent, because your adversary the devil, as a roaring lion, walketh about, seeking whom he may devour.'* We need to see just how the mind of a predator lion works to understand even more of why Satan has such a passion for the death of human beings. His agents are literally human predators just like lions because they prey on other humans using similar hunting skills. They especially go for the little ones who are young and fresh and we are about to

Blasphemy and Techniques of Persuasion

find out why. Remember these predators are the actors acting out the character of their Chief General, Satan. They are carrying out his deadly deeds.

We have just been talking about the blood and how it represents life. Lions drink blood. Believe it or not, like lions, Satan's human predators also like to drink blood, the very essence of physical life. I used to wonder what precisely is it about the blood and sacrifice of children and young virgin women that makes it so desirable. Women represent motherhood and life-giving, so by sacrificing them, new babies cannot be born. That would make sense to Satan. But babies and children? Is their sacrifice to prevent them growing up and reproducing? Is it the thrill to kill and to have power over someone smaller? Maybe.

But recently, I discovered the main reason when I watched two YouTube videos of women who survived these sacrificial ceremonies. I couldn't watch anymore as the stories are so horrific. However, I will merely state some facts without going into the gory details.

It is the blood which is crucial to satisfy and appease Satan just as it was the blood that pagans in the Old Testament offered to appease Baal, Molech and all the other gods. Why the blood? It's because of something called adrenochrome.

Adrenochrome is a chemical produced in the body by adrenaline being oxidated. It accumulates in the blood in times of extreme fear and terror. This particular adrenalized type of blood is a drug which the Elite especially are addicted to. These addicts are actually psychopaths, the predator lions of human prey. They are found in royal families, the rich and mega-rich, and those in the upper levels of Satan's pyramid government. In freemasonry and secret societies, the members are trained to have such hardened hearts that they have no guilt whatsoever about killing a little one to drink its blood.

Babies and children produce what is called 'pure adrenochrome.' 'Child harvesting' is a term used to gather up children to satisfy the addiction. This is why hundreds of thousands of young ones go missing each year. In Australia 20,000 go missing. In India it is 96,000. Germany - 100,000; UK–112,000; USA - 460,000. This is an average for just one year. Most children are taken from third world countries. This addiction is one reason why politicians want borders open so the trafficking can continue.

Phew! That's probably more than enough about Satan's blasphemous attack of the external and internal physical body and the blood. You can google adrenochrome and find out more if you want. But I warn you, it's not for the faint-hearted, especially when you see well-known famous names and faces and hear the details from survivors.

The most important thing to understand about all this horror is that Christ's human blood was the last and ultimate sacrifice to pay for our sins. This is the only time that human blood should have ever been offered. Satan's fury knows no boundaries about Jesus' victory over death on the Cross, and the significance of the blood in the mighty plan of salvation. We can see how this most wicked enemy is all out to get revenge in the most deadly ways he possibly can.

2. Invisible Parts of Humans Satan's second major target of blasphemy besides the external and internal physical parts is the miraculous invisible part of the human being—the mind/intellect, feelings/emotions, and the soul/spirit. There are many ways a person can be crushed on the deep inside. They can bottle up the hurt and no-one else sees it. Those with learning difficulties are teased, ridiculed and called 'dumb.' Dumb actually means they are incapable of speaking at all, like a deaf person can't hear, or someone who is blind and can't see. As well, there are those who are at the other end of the scale and are extremely intelligent but are pulled down or chopped off in the 'tall poppy syndrome.' And then there are those who have very sensitive feelings who are called weak or sissy or other belittling names.

Through the mind and feelings, someone's spirit can be crushed and beaten down through hurtful words, harsh tones of voice, warped sense of humour and aggressive body language. The human soul is denigrated. Once again, the Godhead is deeply grieved to see human mental and emotional suffering. God wants us to be sensitive and compassionate. Oh, how He desires for us to have a heart of flesh and not of stone. He wants us to use our minds to think and exercise our intelligence, and to use the precious gift of free will wisely. Satan wants the exact opposite.

Blasphemy and Techniques of Persuasion

3. Procreation The third target, the very act of procreation of life, is bombarded most terribly because Satan cannot procreate. Only God, the Life-Giver, can give life. Satan hates humans with such a vengeance because we are the only beings in the universe which are made in the likeness of our Creator Godhead and can reproduce. Angels, Satan and his demons cannot reproduce.

Procreation is an extremely sore point and the evil enemy sends bombardments in full force in order to destroy new life. Why? Because generating life is conclusive evidence that the one who wants to be *'like the Most High,'* can never ever be a creator of life. The very act of human reproduction is a massive target to aim blasphemy at.

Do people make fun of trees, flowers, mountains, waterfalls, rocks or anything in nature? No. But animals can be made fun of. Because many animals mate in the same way as humans, they are often laughed at when they are seen mating. If people believe they are just another animal as evolution teaches, then it's carnal and natural to laugh to see a male and female animal coupled together. Parents either turn their children's heads away because they are embarrassed, or else they make jokes about it and laugh. Yet no-one laughs at watching plants germinating and reproducing seeds. Again, the human body is the goal of attack. Again, the Creators of the sacred act are targeted.

4. Relationships (Mother, Father and Children) Besides the visible and invisible parts of the human body, and the act of procreation, another divine miracle is besieged. This is relationships. The whole design of family relationships is under fire. Why? Because it also directly attacks the relationship between the Godhead and their beloved children in the huge global family. Satan was cast out from the heavenly family, and cut off from his once-perfect relationship with the Godhead. Consequently, he is deeply envious of God's family to the point of hating it. As always, he uses language and sophistry as his weapons. Let's look briefly at each member of the family he attacks—father, mother and children.

Firstly, <u>the father</u>: The protective, comforting word, father, is mutilated. The Roman Church counterfeits it. Its members go to one of a large number of human so-called 'fathers' in the system, to confess their sins and receive forgiveness. The very word, pope, means papa or father.

No human being is to take the place of Jesus or Father-God. This is pure blasphemy because Jesus said in Matthew 23:9, *'And call no man your Father upon the earth; for One is your Father, which is in heaven.'* Therefore, we are to go only to God who is in the Most Holy Place in the Temple in Heaven, not on earth. We are to ask forgiveness from the Abba Father, through Jesus, the Son, our High Priest and Mediator. In John 14:6 Jesus said, *'.. no man cometh unto the Father, but by Me.'* The role of a father as the head of the family is second only to the heavenly Father, not a human priest.

Human fathers are dragged down through blasphemy. Humorous words in comedy shows degrade fathers' rightful positions in the family. This is also an indirect attack aimed at dethroning God the Father from his position as the Most High. Young men growing up soon learn through the works of the feminist movement, that they are weaklings and not very important. They lose their God-given sense of purpose as males and are robbed of their roles as head of the family. The ways of the world with its feminist assertiveness and aggression sadly overrides them. That's enough about the word father. I know you understand what I mean.

Secondly <u>mother</u>: The beautiful, loving word, 'Mother' has been changed to one of the foulest of foul curse words which has come into the English language. With certain tones of voice, it becomes short for another disgusting swear word too horrible to utter. You may be able to guess from what I say next. Just think about it, analyse it and work out what it really says and Who it attacks. The mother referred to is Mary, mother of Jesus, who was a virgin. In a divine, supernatural, miraculous act of procreation, the Holy Spirit came upon her and she became pregnant. The Holy Spirit replaced a human male. The Holy Spirit is the one directly attacked in this most blasphemous word. It was He who breathed the breath of life into Adam's nostrils and into all subsequent humans. How many of us realised that this precious word, mother, could be used in the most blasphemous way of all!

When this mother swear word is spoken, the Godhead is grossly degraded and disrespected. It's miracle of giving life is discarded. The Holy Spirit is so deeply grieved and cannot seal people who continue to use it, and allow them, to be taken to heaven. Ephesians 4:30 says,

Blasphemy and Techniques of Persuasion

'*And grieve not the Holy Spirit of God, <u>whereby ye are sealed</u> unto the day of redemption.*' The Holy Spirit is the One who does the sealing in the foreheads. He cannot allow any blasphemous words to enter and exist in heaven, the perfect place of perfect love and respect for the Godhead.

And thirdly, there are the <u>children</u>: The last members of the family besides father and mother, are the precious darling children. These young ones are especially targeted by Satan from babies to young adults with the most tragic, devastating consequences which can last the rest of their lives. Little ones hear and see blasphemy all around as they grow up, and they think it's normal. They get attacked by many kinds of verbal abuse—belittling, teasing, ridiculing and sarcasm. For example, let's look at a couple of words describing children. Let's see what's in a name?

How many of us realise that when we call children, kids, we are blaspheming? Analyse it. What is a kid? It's a baby goat. What did Jesus come to do? He came to separate the goats from the sheep. Matthew 25:32-33 says, '*... and He (Son of Man) shall separate them one from another as a shepherd divideth His sheep from the goats. And He shall set the sheep on His right hand and the goats on the left.*' This includes the little kids. The scapegoat of the Old Testament ceremony on the Day of Atonement, represents Satan.

But Jesus is the shepherd, the sheepherder caring for His little lambs, the goodies in the grand story. And He will take them to Heaven. Jesus is not a goatherder. Goats, the baddies, will not be saved. So, when we call our little darlings 'kids', we are basically cursing them and saying they belong in the paddock with the goats, and are doomed. And if we try to tone it down with an endearing tone of voice and call them 'dear little kiddies,' it doesn't change anything. Isn't super sophist Satan so clever! Every single day, people say 'kids.' Surely, we should call our children 'little lambs' or little darlings. The word darling is actually in the Bible and means precious one.

Also, parents can be heard saying their mischievous child is a 'cheeky little monkey.' The parent has a smile on his or her face and a bit of a giggle as if to say 'It's OK. Just let it go.' But they are trying to tone down the fact that the child is a rebellious naughty brat who needs discipline.

They treat the behaviour light-heartedly and are looking for an excuse to avoid the responsibility of taking disciplinary action. And at the same time, they are promoting the theory of evolution by saying the human child is a monkey or ape.

And what's more—children are blatantly labelled as 'little devils' when they are naughty. And, like 'little monkeys,' the words are usually said with a chuckle as if this is normal child behaviour. Again, the parents want to avoid their responsibility. Parents feel incapable and feel they can't do anything to change it. Consequently, the bad behaviour is justified and accepted, all through humorous blasphemy. It's interesting that the parent must instinctively know that devils exist if they use this term. Oh, how clever and cunning is Satan through a little light, seemingly harmless humour!

Our heavenly Father fully understands what it means to be a parent, especially a parent whose children have rejected, and abandoned them. How would human parents feel if their child denied their existence, yet used their names in angry, harsh and grievous tones of voice, and blamed them for all their problems? How would parents feel if their child scoffed, mocked and cursed them, even if the child said they didn't exist?

Interestingly, even atheists use swear words against the Godhead even though they believe there is no God. But by using the curse words, they are actually admitting there is a Father-God, Jesus and the Holy Spirit. Why would they use their names if they don't exist?

Tragically, many human parents do experience total rejection from the young ones they raised up. God feels this rejection billions of times over from the billions of His beloved children He created, who disown Him. All over the world, most of His children use blasphemy against Him in countless ways they don't realise. Yes, blasphemy destroys relationships, the very foundation that was created so humans can remain connected with their Father-God.

Blasphemy is like a light switch that Satan flicks off. He sabotages to stop the flow of the current of God's light and His Great Love which flows around the whole of His kingdom of Universe. If that current of

Blasphemy and Techniques of Persuasion

Great Love in relationships is cut off, only darkness remains. This is why planet Earth has been called the 'one black spot' of the universe. But praise God there are still a few flickering lights in the hearts of those in the tiny remnant who remain connected to the Father and Son through the power of the Holy Spirit. There is still a trickle of current of Great Love dotted around the globe.

Satan and Blasphemy: Not surprisingly, we never hear Satan's own name used in a blasphemous way. Never are the words, Satan, Lucifer, devil or demon used in angry tones of voices, or with aggressive body language, or mockery. Satan's name is not spoken disrespectfully, and he is not defamed, vilified, reviled or spoken evil of. Why? Because one of Satan's greatest lies is that he is not real. He wants to maintain the mystery of his existence. The Holy Spirit is a mystery which we will never understand fully. So, Satan wants to counterfeit Him by taking His place as the third Person in the Godhead and also working in mysterious, unseen ways. If Satan's name was used blasphemously, the user would be admitting that Satan and his demons are real. This would be the same as those unbelievers who use sacred, holy names and unknowingly admit the existence of the Godhead.

Interestingly, at the same time, Satan is very happy with imagination and science fiction. He doesn't care if he is portrayed in horror stories, movies, literature and artworks as a hideous monster, vampire, good witch, bad witch, magician, wizard, fairy, elf or whatever. The temptations of fascination, curiosity and entertainment only serve to distract from the divine truth of the Godhead. Incredibly, when confronted with Satan's existence, people are happy to unknowingly defend him by saying, 'He's all in the imagination. He's only fantasy and not real. We are just being creative.' The hideous ghastly words and images become accepted and impressed in the minds. Before we know it, ugly has become beautiful.

Through imagination, Satan is very happy to manipulate the minds of the young and old away from the truth. The lies, fantasy and fiction possibly started with fairy tales back in the 1600s. It probably goes back much further. Fairy tales were based on European folklore which originated in pagan beliefs which ultimately go right back to the first Babylonian Empire. When I was little girl, Mum let me join the Brownies Club.

The Greatest War Ever

I was put into a group called the Fairies. Another group was named Elves. Fairies were seen as good imaginary pretty little creatures with wings and made me feel happy. But these seemingly tame names were pure imagination.

We know from a previous talk that imagination means contriving, plotting and devious. It is the opposite of creativity. Today, imagination has got totally out of control and is even encouraged under the false name of creativity.

In the 1800s, the Grimms brothers and Hans Christian Anderson did much to boost the popularity of fairy tales. Thousands of stories were written and were still very popular in the 1900s. Many are still around today with modern interpretations. At some point the term, science fiction, took over. Science fiction, or Sci-fie, is now a very common theme of movies and literature. We know that science simply means knowledge. Therefore, science fiction is knowledge not based on fact, but is imaginary, contrived plotting and devious. It is just another satanic counterfeit of the true Bible stories.

Today, Satan is happy for audiences and readers to think that the Earth is about to be invaded by alien monsters. He has been working at this mind preparation for decades and decades through Hollywood and children's literature. Dr Who and Harry Potter just gave the movement more impetus, and countless other stories have followed suit using the same theme. At one time, the hideous monsters were baddies and seen as being scary. Children, including myself, were very frightened of them. But by now, they are just creatures to befriend and communicate with.

There is an excellent quote from Great Controversy 516, describing Satan's tactics, which says, 'The better to disguise his real character and purposes, he has caused himself to be so represented as to excite no stronger emotion that ridicule or contempt. He is pleased to be painted as ludicrous, misshapen, half animal and half human. He is pleased to hear his name used in sport and mockery by those who think themselves intelligent and well-informed. It is because he has masked himself with consummate skill, that the question is so widely asked, "Does such a being really exist?" .... And it is because Satan can most readily control the minds of those who are unconscious of his influence, that

Blasphemy and Techniques of Persuasion

the Word of God gives us so many examples of his malignant work, unveiling before us his secret forces, and thus placing us on our guard against his assaults.' [9]

All I can say is that Satan must know that Jesus is coming extremely soon because he's increasing the intensity of his deception. He is directing attention towards the supernatural aliens ie demons, and not Christ and His host of holy angels. Oh, how does our Father-God feel about this Great War of Words? Yes, He has feelings like we do, but they are far greater and more intense. He has the greatest love possible. And He also has the greatest wrath possible. He hates sin. The showdown between Satan and Christ is just about to happen. God will pour out His wrath upon Satan and this one black spot in His kingdom.

Revelation 14:10 tells us how Satan and all those in his army, *'shall drink of the wine of the wrath of God, which is poured out without mixture into the cup of His indignation....'* In other words, these ones will experience the full forces of God's judgment which will not be diluted or watered down and weakened. No mercy whatsoever. God's anger is called a righteous indignation because, as we have seen evidence in the previous six talks, He has every right to be angry. Yes, God will have the final Word in this War of Words.

How Can We Combat Blasphemy?
Our Goal, Mission and Weapons: We need three things: 1. to understand the enemy's goal and his strategies so we can form our goal; 2. Remember what our mission is. 3. Know what our weapons are.

1. Our Goal Satan's ultimate goal is to bring down the Most High, along with the theocratic government, and then set himself up as counterfeit Most High. We have learned his main strategies are using words through sophistry and Gnosticism and these include blasphemy.

2. Our Mission We need to remember what our mission and purpose are on this earth. These are to defend the kingdom of our Father God and to prove His way of government of Great Love using the gift of free will, is the only way to rule. Christians are often seen as being namby-pamby, ie weak, indecisive, lacking in strength and moral character.

9 Great Controversy p. 516

But no! We are soldiers fighting the good fight for our Chief Commander Jesus. And remember we are in the Lord's army along with two-thirds of the holy angels. We cannot lose.

3. Our Weapons Know what our weapons are: We need to fight back with words which stem from our hearts, minds and thoughts, and the fundamental belief that our Godhead is real. Paul said in 1 Timothy 6:12 *'Fight the good fight of faith, <u>lay hold on eternal life</u>, where unto thou art also called* (ie the mission we are called to), *and hast <u>professed a good profession</u> before many witnesses.'* 'Professing a good profession' involves speech. Eternal life is also mentioned in this verse and we must hold onto that. Consequently, our salvation and eternal life depend on our thoughts and words! Blasphemy becomes a salvation issue.

Therefore, the way we respond to verbal abuses and threats is crucial. The blows will be crushed by using self-control, one of the fruits of the Holy Spirit. Calm, controlled, objective, logical analysing will divert the direction of Satan's word-arrows. Psalm 91:5,7 promises us that, *'Thou shalt not be afraid for the terror by night, nor for the arrow that flieth by noonday....A thousand shall fall at thy side and ten thousand at thy right hand, but it shall not come nigh thee.'*

So, what is our actual ammunition? It is found in God's Word, the Bible, as represented in the sword of the spiritual coat of armour. Bible words are our swords. With the almighty power of God's Word on our side, nothing is impossible. We can fight back with word weapons of God's love by selecting certain scriptures, claiming the promises, memorising them and living them out in our daily lives. Just one example is found in Matthew 4:10-11. These are Jesus' own words when Satan attacked Him with the temptation of offering all the world's kingdoms if Jesus bowed down and worshipped him. And this is what Satan wants us to do—bow down and worship him.

Jesus response was to say, *'Get thee hence, Satan, for it is written that thou shalt worship the Lord, thy God, and Him only shalt thou serve.'* What happened next? Verse eleven tells us that, by merely resisting with words, *'... the devil left Him and, behold, angels came and ministered unto Him.'* How easy are those two verses to memorise and fire back

Blasphemy and Techniques of Persuasion

when blasphemous words pop into our minds!

James 4:7 tells us to, *'Submit yourselves therefore to God. Resist the devil and he will flee from you.'* Swearing and cursing <u>can</u> be prevented from crushing us, and also be stopped from coming out of our own mouths. Remember that, if we blaspheme, we reveal whose army side we are on in the great spiritual war–Christ's or Satan's.

In Desire of Ages page 490, we read, 'The omnipotent power (ie the unlimited power) of the Holy Spirit is the defence of every contrite soul. Not one that has impenitence and faith, and has claimed His protection, will Christ permit to pass under the enemy's power. The Saviour is by the side of His tempted and tried ones. With Him, there can be no such thing as failure, loss, impossibility or defeat. We can do all things through Him who strengthens us. When temptations and trials come, do not wait to adjust all the difficulties, but look to Jesus, your Helper.' DA 490 1898

There is another excellent quote from the Review and Herald April 10, 1888. It says, 'Build a wall of scriptures around you, and you will see that the world cannot break it down. Commit the Scriptures to memory, and then throw right back upon Satan when he comes with temptations—"It is written." This is the way that the Lord met temptations of Satan, and resisted them.'

What a war of words this is! I sometimes wonder what the original War in Heaven was like. Words must have been flying everywhere as Satan practised on the angels. By now he is a genius and an expert. Someone once defined an expert as 'a drip under pressure.' And Satan is certainly under pressure right now. His blasphemous words are numbered just like his days are numbered. Praise God for His reminders of His Word weapons from millenniums past. Countless times he has sent wise reminders through the prophets and writers of the Bible books.

God's Instructions and Reminders: Oh, how wise is our Father God when He told Moses 3500 years ago to teach the simple Third Commandment which we read earlier. God expected everyone to trust and obey with a simple, easy childlike obedience! Blasphemy is a sin because it breaks this Commandment. And I repeat that blasphemy is a salvation issue because the Holy Spirit is the One who seals the souls for the day when Jesus returns to take His people home to heaven.

How good is our God when, over 400 years after Moses, He inspired Solomon to write many proverbs reinforcing His words of wisdom instructing us not to blaspheme! Just one example is Proverbs 18:21. *'Death and life are in the power of the tongue; and they that love it shall eat the fruit thereof.'* How patient was our ever-loving God 1000 years after Solomon, when He inspired Paul to write in Ephesians 4:29, *'Let no corrupt communication proceed out of your mouth, but that which is good to the use of edifying, that it may minister grace unto the hearers.'*

And now, 2000 years have passed since Paul's time. Divine patience is coming to an end. God has His perfect standards and we must do our part by controlling our thoughts and tongues and avoiding all blasphemy. Our eternal future is at stake. Satan knows his universe is confined to this small planet earth and that is why he doesn't want anyone to know the truth about every Bible teaching. He wants to hide the truths about the Godhead, Heaven, the original Sanctuary, and other worlds with their inhabitants living in perfection. He does not want people to know about the plan of salvation, the true state of the sleeping dead, 1844, the cleansing of the Sanctuary, and how Jesus is now working in the Most Holy Place in the Investigative Judgement. Satan does not want anyone to know about the health message, the seventh day Sabbath, Christ's imminent second coming, and the true timing of the millennium.

It is our mission as soldiers for Christ to fight back with words of love sharing with others about all these topics. And when you think about it, all we are doing is telling stories of truth to replace all those fairy tales and science fiction stories. All we have to do is tell His Story, God's story of the truth. Bible stories are the very best stories, the true information, not misinformation, not conspiracy theories, imagination, myths or fables. Bible stories are literal and absolute truths, vital truth for the present time. They need to be told with the same enthusiasm and life as a parent or grandparent reads a bedtime story to the little children. Bible stories need to make us want to hear more, to be in awe and have great reverence and love towards God. One of my favourite quotations

Blasphemy and Techniques of Persuasion

is from Desire of Ages 826. 'The gospel is to be presented not as a lifeless theory, but as a living force to change a life.'

The Bible, the gospel, the good news, God's Story, His Story, are all the same thing. These stories are the present truth which humanity needs right now before it is too late to choose which army to enlist in. All these stories belong in the message of the first angel which John wrote about in his vision. Revelation 14:6 says, 'And I saw another angel fly in the midst of heaven, having the <u>everlasting gospel</u> to preach unto them that dwell on the earth, and to every nation, and kindred and tongue and people; saying with a loud voice, "Fear God, and give glory to Him, for the hour of His judgement is come. And worship Him that made Heaven and earth, and the sea, and the fountains of waters.' What a monumental verse that is! We can do this by simply telling stories.

No wonder Satan is doing his utmost in entertainment, literature and blasphemy to destroy all that is good and created by God. As the hymn goes,

> 'Onward Christian soldiers marching as to war!
> With the Cross of Jesus going on before!
> Christ the royal Master leads against the foe;
> forward into battle. See his banner go!'

May we all stay in the army of our almighty Lord and Chief Commander who is already the Victor.

I really should finish this talk right now. I know I have given you overwhelming information. But I don't want to carry the following short section into the next talk. Next time, you will find out why. That talk will be very different and a special surprise. We have been learning about word weapons to use. In a few moments, I want to give you some army training to help you identify fifteen of Satan's key strategies.

Scene 17. Fifteen Techniques of Persuasion

In this brief session of army training, we will cover some strategies of Satan so we can be aware and forearmed when we go back onto the battlefield. The following list contains fifteen techniques of persuasion used to cunningly manipulate minds. The list comes under the great umbrella of sophistry and Gnosticism.

This global COVID crisis of the past two years has been brought about through sheer word weaponry and manipulation of minds. It did not happen suddenly and unexpectedly. For decades this was planned behind the scenes before it was put into public practise in 2020. COVID has been a superb example of complicated contriving and sophistry by those higher up in the pyramid government. Just look at the propaganda about the virus, the twisting of statistics and deaths and cases, the way the media reports events. The reporters are all actors repeating the scripts from higher authorities. We are about to find how words specifically have been used to bluff billions around the world?

As we go through the list, notice how the techniques are combined with other tactics as well. All the body senses are bombarded with heaps of information. The ears hear endless words which are sometimes combined with the power of music. The eyes see thousands of images connecting ideas and lies. Body language uses smiling, happy, kind looking faces to reassure that all will be OK. The taste buds are tempted by bribing people to have the jabs with lolly pops, ice-creams, donuts and free beers. Greed is also appealed to with bribes of money in lotteries.

Let's now list fifteen ways this assault on humanity has and is still being carried out. They are not in order of importance, although I will start with a biggie and finish with another biggie. So, hang in there. There's a bit of a rough rocky ride coming up. The techniques listed are briefly explained by just a few examples of words and phrases used. The first one is NLP and probably covers all other fourteen in one way or another.

1. NLP: This stands for Neuro Linguistic Programming. Neuro means neurons ie brain cells and nerves. Linguistic means language, so therefore, words are involved. Programming means putting in behavioural patterns through experience. Therefore, NLP means using language to put in behavioural patterns into the brain. One word sums it up– brainwashing. We can immediately see how NLP is highly applicable to the Great War of Words. In true secretive, gnostic form and Jesuit language, Neuro Linguistic Programming is sophisticated, complicated and manipulative.

Blasphemy and Techniques of Persuasion

According to Wikipedia, NLP is 'a pseudoscientific approach to communication, to personal development and psychotherapy.' Hmmm. Interesting. Pseudo, means fake, counterfeit, and sham. And we already know that science just means knowledge. So, this 'pseudoscientific approach' of NLP is widely recognised as a counterfeit knowledge. NLP has been adopted by hypnotherapists, and government agencies, businesses and companies running seminars for leadership training. They learn different skills on how to get their message across, ie manipulate minds.

Incredibly, even some church pastors are now using NLP. This is just one example. I've heard this happen several times in church and wondered about it, but could not pinpoint what was wrong. Sometimes, a preacher quotes scripture but changes one word to alter the meaning to the exact opposite. He wants to see if the congregation is awake and listening. This is deception because the listener starts to doubt and question. Then the preacher smiles and everyone chuckles, reassured that they heard correctly. It was only a humorous test and they had been tricked but they were reassured they knew what he really meant. This is a ploy of Satan. In reality the preacher is lying and he breaks the ninth commandment. And we know if he breaks one, then he breaks the lot. This is just one example of NLP.

2. A sense of belonging: This is peer pressure to make people feel accepted and united. Eg 'We're all in this together.'

3. Elitism: People are made to feel part of a superior group. Eg 'If you are vaxxed, you can enjoy the freedoms of travel, entertainment and dining out. If you are not jabbed, then you are a lesser person and will be shunned.'

4. Emotive words: Certain words and phrases cause favourable or unfavourable reactions. Eg home and family are positive words, but irresponsible and thoughtless are negative words. Eg 'If you have the jab, you can cross the border and go back home from your holiday to your family; You can go visit Grandma again; Think of others; Think of your neighbour; Don't be selfish; Think of the common good; Don't be irresponsible.'

5. Exaggeration: Reports use extreme words and phrases making something sound better and more important than it is, but they are not supported by facts. How often have we heard that the injections are 'safe and effective, safe and effective' with no evidence. We hear, 'case-loads are soaring; cases surge.' How often did we hear, 'There is no alternative but to get the jab!' Also, the word 'misinformation' is everywhere, but according to who. It's only misinformation if it goes against the hidden agenda and the one narrative being pushed. It's like the Roman Church and the word heretic. Someone is only a heretic if they speak against the Church.

Here are a few examples from a COVID update which The Age newspaper emailed me a few days ago. Notice how they want to keep up the level of fear. Phrases include the following—'there are concerns; waning immunity is in the 1000s; rising infection numbers; hospitals under stress; the virus is sweeping through school staff.' At the end of the article, a false hope is given by saying, 'Moderna is researching a combined COVID-flu vaccine.' These examples are just from one short article.

6. Facts and Figures: Statistics, charts and graphs are manipulated to support the agenda. They sound objective to prove evidence, but many people don't even understand them. For two years, every daily TV news report had numbers and more numbers of deaths and hospitalisations with colourful complicated charts and graphs to impress and look accurate and true. But you can go on youtube and see how people can manipulate the information to suit themselves.

7. Big names of famous people: Popular rock musicians, actors, celebrities, royalty, anyone with a wide reputation has been used to advertise and promote the injections. Music concerts were held for only those who were jabbed to make them feel privileged, and for others to feel as if they were missing out.

8. Preying on hidden fears: The fear of suffering and death has spread around the world. Pictures of mass graves were often showed. Injections are seen as protection against the virus but, there is still a hidden fear that, if you do get it, the symptoms are reduced, so you will still be OK.

9. Magic ingredients: In the early days of COVID, pictures of pink spiked balls were everywhere. Explanations were given about how the

Blasphemy and Techniques of Persuasion

spikes are used to make the so-called vaccinations. But the other ingredients were not revealed. Thankfully, some doctors and scientists have worked extremely hard to expose what poisons are in these injections.

10. Name-calling: Names for the un-jabbed sprang up everywhere. Politicians who are brave enough to speak out truth are called rogue politicians. Protesters are called extreme right wingers, fascists or Nazi supporters.

11. Newness: It didn't take long for new companies and new types of so-called vaccines to appear. To start with, we were only offered Astra-Zeneca and Pfizer. Many new confusing medical names keep popping up. This is a quote from the Australian Financial Review newspaper article entitled 'Everything you need to know before Borders Reopen on Monday.' It lists ten different options. You will soon get the gist of the language. It is a superb example of sophisticated medical Jesuit jargon designed to cause confusion and make one feel ignorant. It reads, 'For those not vaccinated in Australia, the TGA (Therapeutic Goods Association) recognises the following vaccines: Coronavac (made by Sinovac); Covishield (by AstraZeneca Serum Institute of India); BBIBP-CorV for people under 60 years of age on arrival in Australia (made by Sinopharm China); Covaxin (by Bharat Biotech); and Sputnik V (by Gamaleya Research Institute.)' The quotation goes on–'This is in addition to all vaccines approved for use in Australia: Comirnaty (by Pfizer); Vaxzevria (by AstraZeneca); Spikevax or Takeda (by Moderna); COVID-19 Vaccine (by Janssen); and Nuvxovic (by Bioelect on behalf of Novavax).'

What a smorgasbord of deadly toxins to choose from! The list is so confusing and it's much easier to just leave it all up to the experts, and let them decide which one is best for you. Mind you, there is no mention or option given for God's natural ways of building up the immune system.

12. Focusing on ordinary people: The masses are appealed to including all ages—babies to the elderly as if the injections are suitable for everyone. It's interesting how they started with those over 70 and gradually worked their way down bit by bit to primary school children. It's all been done very gradually because those powers that be, know the population would not accept if everyone was to be jabbed at the same time. There's only one more age group to go. Right now, the government is awaiting TGA approval for four-month year old babies to six-year-olds to have the poison. They are so cleverly manipulative.

13. Patriotism: The patriotic song–'We are one. We are Australia,' brings such warm fuzzy feelings of oneness and togetherness and strength. But it is all emotional, giving a false peace and safety which the Bible warns us of.

14. Testimonies: Famous people and ordinary commoners are interviewed to relate their positive experiences with the injections. Some give emotional stories about those who survived or died from COVID because they did or didn't have the jab. All interviews are selected and presented in ways to agree with the hidden agenda.

15. Repetition: Finally, we come to a real biggie—repetition. This is used in nearly all the above techniques and is an extremely effective way of brainwashing. The same words, phrases and pictures are used over and over again. How many times have we heard the word COVID? How many times have we seen pictures of pink round balls with spikes sticking out, needles being thrust into arms, and swabs being pushed up noses and twisted around? People cringe but they go ahead and still get the jab and the tests. Repetition of lies is possibly the most effective technique of persuasion used.

To conclude this section on Techniques of Persuasion, I want to quote from a few places. In the book, Mein Kampf supposedly written by Hitler, it says the following, '... in the big lie there is always a certain force of credibility, because the broad masses of a nation are always more easily corrupted in the deeper strata of their emotional nature, than consciously or voluntarily. In other words, he works on the subconscious. And thus, in the primitive simplicity of their minds, they more readily fall victims to the big lie than the small lie, since they themselves often tell small lies in little matters, but would be ashamed to resort to large-scale falsehoods. It would never come into their heads to fabricate colossal untruths, and they would not believe that others could have the impudence to distort the truth so infamously.'

Phew!! How perceptive this is! Yes, people can be gullible and are happy to tell small fibs, not big ones. They disbelieve the big lies because

Blasphemy and Techniques of Persuasion

they trust the authorities. This is how Satan, operates on weaknesses. But, praise God, there are many who are not fooled. These ones actually listen to the quiet promptings of the Holy Spirit and have a sense of morality, of right and wrong.

In 1941, Goebbels wrote an article about the English people called 'Churchill's Lie Factory.' In it, he said, 'The English follow the principle that when one lies, one should lie big, and stick to it. They keep up their lies even at the risk of looking ridiculous.' Today this could be said about nearly every nation on the planet. How ridiculous do many current world leaders look! I won't give examples because I'm sure you already know some.

The final quotation is from a psychological profile of Hitler by the OSS. Eight of Hitler's rules are listed. As I read them, apply it to world leaders and politicians today in Russia, China, America, Britain, Europe, Canada, Australia and the pharmaceutical industry, the WEF and all the controlling organisations. The quotation reads, 'His (Hitlers) primary rules were:

1. Never allow the public to cool off;
2. Never admit a fault or wrong;
3. Never concede that there may be some good in your enemy;
4. Never leave room for alternatives;
5. Never accept blame;
6. Concentrate on one enemy at a time and blame him for everything that goes wrong;
7. People will believe a big lie sooner than a little one;
8. If you repeat it frequently enough, people will sooner or later believe it.'

As the saying goes, history repeats itself. As Solomon said, *'There is nothing new under the sun.'*

A part of any deception is often not what is said, but what is left out. Just look at the news reports today. There are millions of words spoken by TV reporters and written in newspaper articles. The same ideas are repeated endlessly, and all are expressed in an infinite variety of ways. But the most important truths are deliberately left out. There were a few short reports about the worldwide truckie Freedom Protests. There are reports of how popular our premier is here in Victoria because there is an election coming up. But the truth of what is really going on behind the scenes is left out or glossed over. Right now, as the Russian-Ukrainian conflict dominates news reports, even more true information is being left out. Fear levels of nuclear war increase. Fear, fear, fear. Walter Veith's What's Up Prof Number 106 covers this Russian-Ukrainian war issue very well and puts it into Biblical perspective. It's well worth watching. As Walter says, 'The propaganda machine is running at full capacity globally.'

Conclusion

So, there we have it. That's a summary of fifteen techniques of persuasion to keep in the back of your minds—fifteen weapons which will be fired at us when we return to the earthly battlefield.

Again I say, **Beware the sophistry! Beware the sophistry!**

Just before we return to the battlefield, let's finish off our army training session by putting on the six garments in the whole armour of God. We have to be ready for the coming onslaughts from the invisible enemy. There are many more troublesome times to come. Paul tells us what the six garments are in Ephesians 6:13-15. He says, *'Stand therefore, having your <u>loins girt about with truth</u>; and having on the <u>breastplate of righteousness</u>; and your <u>feet shod with the preparation of the gospel of peace</u>. Above all, taking the <u>shield of faith</u> wherewith ye shall be able to quench all the fiery darts of the wicked. And take the <u>helmet of salvation</u>, and the <u>sword of the Spirit</u> which is God's Word.'*

Let's pray to close.

Prayer: Our dear Father in Heaven, all glory and honour and praise go to You. Thank You for all the listeners who have heard these talks. My prayer is that we will all be greatly encouraged in our daily battles, no matter how big or small. Thank you, Lord, for Your Word, the ammunition You freely provide for us to use. Thank You for Your Son, Jesus our Chief Commander and for what He did for us by dying on the Cross so we too can be victorious over temptation and death. And Father, we

Blasphemy and Techniques of Persuasion

also uplift all our enemies to You to deal with as You see fit. You don't want anyone to perish and while they are still alive, there is hope of eternal life for them. Thank You for never leaving nor forsaking us. We pray in the glorious name of Jesus Christ, our Saviour. Amen.

So, that's it for now folks. There are no clues about the next and final talk except that it will be a Grand Finale appropriate for this series. Be there. Don't miss it! See you in the same place, same seats, same time, in one week, Mar 26, 2:30. God bless you all.

Part 8
A Glimpse of the Future: Hanok's Story

Introduction and Review

Here we are, at talk Number Eight in the series. Thank you for listening to these talks entitled The Greatest War Ever. What a roller coaster ride it's been!

We started off the series setting up the planet as a stage for the greatest show ever on Earth to be performed on. The grand show is all about stories and more stories because life is all about stories. We know Who is always in control of the earth's storyline and the script. Our Father-God gives us the Script in His Word, the Bible, His collection of love-letters full of stories as examples for us to learn from. All the Bible stories make up His Story, not manstory by humanist philosophers. There is so much packed in the Bible books and letters—lessons and prophecies and role models. The good and the bad, warts and all are exposed. God's Word even gives us actual phrases and sentences to use as word-weapons, ie word swords to fight with against the sophistry and Gnosticism of the enemy.

We have learned how God is the Producer of the show and His Son Jesus is Co-Author, as well as Chief Commander in the Great War of Words. The Holy Spirit is the Prompter quietly speaking in the hearts of the performers. There are two types of performers—the actors acting out the character of their Chief General Satan, and the players playing the roles reflecting the character of their Chief Commander. The Great War of the battle for the minds, the greatest controversy, has been raging on the planet for 6000 years between the two superpowers of Christ and Satan.

By now you will be much more aware of Satan's main weapons of attack in sophistry–ie twisting of words to cause doubt and confusion in order

A Glimpse of the Future: Hanok's Story

to get one's own way. We have seen how Satan also uses counterfeit, blasphemy and many techniques of persuasion to brainwash the minds of his human prey. His goal is to cleverly force people to worship him and not God. But God has permitted Satan to <u>only</u> be a prince of the planet, not the king. We know the number of the enemy's days is small. He knows time is running out and is pulling out all stops to do his worst.

Along the way during this series, we have met some key actors and players, goodies and baddies, in this long, drawn-out saga. We met the Terrible Trio of Nimrod, Semiramus and Tammuz who founded the Babylonian Empire and began the legacy of Babylon which has lasted right up to this very day. We also met Simon Magus, father of Gnosticism with all its secrecy, lies and superiority. We discovered Simon Magus was the first bishop-pope of Rome and how the Roman Empire is the monster-beast of Daniel's vision. This beast developed into the Papacy and the Roman Church which has extended its power over the whole world today. We also met some of the heroes who wrote down God's Word—Daniel, John, Paul, Luke, and the Waldenses who preserved the Word so we can read it now.

All through the talks, we have related everything in the past to current situations today. The world has become what it is now, because of simple cause and effect. Everything in the past is connected with the present.

In this final talk, I want to present something totally different to the previous ones. It will not focus on the negative side of the Great War of Words, but on the Grand Finale of the greatest show ever on planet Earth. It will take us into events which will happen after the end of the show. It will be about the Great Hope, and our future in eternal Heaven with the Godhead, the holy angels, and those created beings from other worlds who have been in the audience with us. Eternal life and restoration to perfection is our goal, and has always been God's original plan for us human beings.

Maybe you have been overwhelmed with all the information presented so far. Now, it's time for a break–an intermission in the 6000-year-old theatre drama of life on Earth. All through the series, we have been picturing ourselves being off the planet, in outer space with the audience, observing the story from an outside objective viewpoint. But right now, we are going to have a treat and meet someone very special to find out his side of the story. As I've said before, life is all about stories. Some are true and some are not. This one is based on truth. Just before we get into it, I want to pray and share a very brief testimony as to how this story came about.

Let's pray. Our dear Father in Heaven, thank You for everything you have done for us to bring us this far in Your story of the Earth and humanity. Oh Lord, we are so tiny and helpless without You in our hearts. Please continue to help us all to stay strong in faith and obedience, and to be courageous soldiers in our Chief Commander's army in these most perilous end days. And please help me now as I present this final talk. Help me to glorify You in all my words and please let the listeners be blessed and encouraged by what they are about to hear. In Jesus' name we pray. Amen.

Testimony: I want to share a very quick background about how this story came to be written. Six years ago, I started a project about His Story, ie God's Story, to try and present an objective view from outside the planet. It morphed into a much bigger project than planned. The book is based on the idea of Earth being like a theatre stage and aims to takes the reader through the whole Bible. What you have heard in the last eight talks is based on tiny snippets from this. Now the project is into its second volume with almost 600 pages written and I'm only up to halfway through Chronicles and Kings. There is still has a long way to go. But I feel such an urgency that time is running out with the anticipation of Jesus coming very, very soon. I may not get it finished, so it's appropriate that I start sharing some parts now.

The urgency to write was also brought on by a sharp wake-up call seven years ago when I was diagnosed with breast cancer and did not know how much of my life was left. I became even more dependent on God and am very grateful for still being here today with no signs of cancer. Life on this planet is so precious and short. I have always wanted to do something significant for God in sharing His Great Love to others. I had already written books about music from a biblical perspective. But, during the cancer years, I started writing more strongly for God.

A Glimpse of the Future: Hanok's Story

I discovered a new natural therapy called writing therapy. Expressing myself in words helped focus my mind on the real important things of life. I found so much freedom in the world of words. Heaven was heavy on my mind. I pondered much on what it will be like to see our Father-God and Jesus physically, face to face, and to live in perfect bliss and harmony of the current of Great Love forever and ever.

One of the many things I look forward to is flying, and being rid of this frail, weak cumbersome body. For over forty years this human form has been hindered by Rheumatoid Arthritis. I've discovered some reasons why God allowed this to happen and am OK with my lot. But, to me, my body is getting past its use-by date and I'm ready for a new one, if and when God sees fit. By His mercy and grace and sustenance, I am still here to tell the tale. I believe that my mission in the Great War of Words is to write to share God's Great Love, and be an encouragement to others.

Anyway, that's enough about me and how these writings and talks came to be. In this next section, I hope and pray you will be blessed by what you hear, just as I have been blessed by preparing the series. This next story is a condensed version taken from the first volume of my book. I call my style of writing <u>crea</u>factivity. Creafactivity is based on many facts but with some creativity thrown in from my own expression. I'll let you decide what is creativity and what is fact. Creafactivity is a style which I hope and pray will reach the ordinary person who knows nothing about God. But I also want it to bring fresh interest to believers of all ages, youth and adults, who know a lot but want their faith strengthened.

So, here we go. We will now return to the past in order to get a glimpse of the future. Snuggle up in your celestial seats and be blessed. No rocky rides this time. No need for seatbelts. No sophistry. No Gnosticsm. Let's turn our seats around with our backs to the planet-stage. Let's turn our attention far away from the earthly battlefield towards Heaven. Heaven is a very serious topic and we need to always keep our eyes upward. Heaven is our goal. Let's hear the story of someone who has been here in the audience with us all along. He has been in Heaven for 5000 years, so he is even older than that. This person has a wealth of wisdom and information to share with us. His name is Enoch. Let's learn what we can from Enoch and get just a taste of eternity.

Please note that, in the story, I have used Hebrew names from the concordance, but I think you will quickly realise who is who. Enoch is called Hanok. The Godhead, is called the <u>Theo</u>tes Family. Theo means God and this is where we get the word <u>theo</u>cracy. Heaven is called Ouranos, the Greek word for home of God. Pagans have used this name in their counterfeit worship of the planet Uranus, their own god of heaven. Planet Earth is called the Heart of Grace, because it was made from God's heart of Great Love. And the last 6000 years is known as the Kingdom of Grace.

Interestingly, the word heart and earth are connected. Just put the H from heart at the end of the word, and what do you get: earth. Amazing! Aren't words fascinating? In Part Six of these talks, we learned that basileus means universe, hence where Saint Peter's Basilica gets its name from. So, in this story, universe is called Basileus. Jesus is called Prince Yehosua, and angels are called angelos. It's all quite logical. Enoch/Hanok's story is broken down into six chapters called panoramas. They will be general, overall pictures of what Hanok has experienced.

And as we go through the story, I hope and pray your memories will be quickened as you might occasionally catch references to scripture and other Christian quotations. This story is a coded one with hidden truths for those who know the codes of scripture and other writings. Hopefully, it will plant seeds in those who aren't aware of the meanings.

So, sit back in your celestial chairs, facing the rest of the glorious, glittering galaxies and stars. The curtains have now temporarily closed on the planet-theatre, but all is wide open in God's kingdom of Basileus. If you were sitting in a movie theatre, it would be easy to watch a two-hour movie in one sitting. This story is a movie but with words only. Just let the pictures, the colours, the sights and sounds form in your mind. The title is Hanok's Story.

Hanok's Story
Prologue/Introduction

To start with, I would like to share four very short quotations from someone who has had visions of Heaven and been there. This renowned popular Christian author shares many wonderful vivid descriptions and these can be found in the final chapter of the book, 'Last Day Events'. I encourage you to read this chapter. Some of the quotations include the following. 'Oh, to be home at last where the wicked cease from troubling and the weary are at rest.'[10] 'Heaven is all health.'[11] 'Human language is inadequate to describe the reward of the righteous. It will be known only to those who behold it. No finite mind can comprehend the glory of the Paradise of God.'[12] In the book Early Writings page 19 it says, 'Oh, that I could talk in the language of Canaan, (ie Heaven) then could I tell a little of the glory of the better world. '

My feeble version of Hanok's Story is in no way an attempt to describe Heaven accurately. But may it still glorify God and be a blessing to you all.

Panorama 1 – Hanok's Background and the Journey

Overview Of Hanok's Life: Hanok had lived for 365 years on the earthly battlefield. He had been a mighty, mighty warrior for His Lord and Chief Commander. He never actually died but left the planet at the end of the first millennium after Creation, just after 3000 BC. Therefore, with the last 2000 years, he is now about five and a half millenniums old. Since joining the vast audience, he has watched the events in the grand earthly performance along with everyone else in outer space. He saw his son Methuselah fighting in the Great War. He saw the birth of his grandson, Lamech, his great grandson, Noah and the three sons. With grief and sadness, he watched the troublesome times at the end days of the old planet-stage. He saw the Flood, the destruction and rebuilding of the new global stage. Many times, he shook his head in dismay as he watched the Babylonian-Roman-pagan-Papacy-monster beast develop over millenniums. He watched as sin spread all over the planet.

---

10 Letter 113, 1889
11 Testimonies for the Church Vol. 3, p. 172, 1872
12 The Great Controveresy p. 675, 1911

The Greatest War Ever

But from living with the Royal Theotes family in Ouranos, Hanok has been able to see his war-torn old home with a whole new perspective. He had a panoramic view of how the tiny planet fitted into the Big Picture of the endless Kingdom of Basileus. He was now experiencing the rewards of centuries of fighting. Oh, they were far greater than he had ever dreamed of! All those battles were well, well worth it.

The Transformation: What had actually happened to Hanok when he left the stage so mysteriously? How could he not die? How did he get to Ouranos and end up in the audience? Only the Theotes Trio could do such a miracle as taking him straight to Ouranos.

When it happened, Hanok was in a quiet place away from everyone else. He often liked to retreat into the forests and nature to escape the war zones of the cities and spend time with his Lord and Chief Commander. At the time of his transformation, he was enjoying a few moments of silence and peace. There were no human witnesses but plenty of invisible ones. No person saw how his ageing, imperfect human body was instantly and completely transformed. In the twinkling of an eye, he was a brand-new creation. This was a Theotes miracle!

Hanok was most surprised at his new body. He looked down at himself and, to his sheer amazement, he was suddenly wearing new and very different clothes. They were made of a material he had never seen or touched before. It was pure white and shone brightly as it draped loosely and weightlessly from the shoulders to his feet. The old heavy garments had been made of fabric woven by human hands. Now they were replaced with light, pure white royal robes made by Theotes' hands. The old clothes had always got dirty, tattered, torn and they wore out. But these new ones would stay fresh and clean forever.

Hanok glowed and could hardly believe how clean and spotless he felt. It was as though he was wearing robes of dazzling radiant light. He was fully clothed inside—and out. On the inside, his heart wore invisible pure white robes of right relationship with the Theotes family. On the outside, he was cloaked with a visible pure white gown. What an amazing feeling! This was the way he was designed to be–the same way as his four-greats grandparents, Adam and Eve, when they were originally created in the Garden of Eden.

A Glimpse of the Future: Hanok's Story

Hanok looked down at himself again and thought, 'Who is this? Is it really me?' He touched himself all over–his arms, waist, hips, legs, feet, face and hair. Yes, he was all there but completely different. Every part of him was absolutely perfect. And the inside of his body had changed too. He felt so refreshed and healthy with not a trace of an ache, tiredness or sadness anywhere. He had far more energy than he could ever remember. New life oozed out of him as warm electrical currents flowed throughout his whole being. He felt like bursting and wanted to move somewhere real fast. He was all fired up and ready to go.

An Old Friend: After the amazement of his transformation, Hanok suddenly realised he wasn't alone. He was surrounded by a group of angelos who had been watching and smiling and chuckling with delight. Hanok was like a little wide-eyed child who had just been given the best present he had ever wanted. One particular angelo stretched out his hands and Hanok reached out to grasp them. Then they hugged as if they had known each other for years.

The angelo smiled and said tenderly, 'Welcome to your new life, Hanok. I am P-A, your Protector Angelo, who has been with you ever since you were born on the Heart of Grace. I have been with you all your life through good times and bad, and helped you when you weren't even aware. Many times, I saved you from dangers, in ways you did not know. I was in that dark city lane when a group wanted to attack and kill you, but I warded them off. Often, I gently guided you in safer directions to prevent you going into fatal danger zones. And at certain times, I even caused blockages and delays so you would avoid being involved in terrible accidents. At the time, you were a bit frustrated and not happy, but it was for your own good. I even gave you food sometimes when you had given all yours away to those who were starving. Now, my dear Hanok, I want you to meet my friends.'

There were so many new and unusual angelo names to remember, but Hanok found his brain had also changed in the transformation. His memory was phenomenal. After all the introductions were done, P-A said, 'It's time for us to take you on a long journey. We have come to personally escort you straight to Ouranos.'

Hanok was stunned. He began crying but managed to utter the words,

The Greatest War Ever

'Ooooh! Thank you. THANK YOU!' Then the two of them hugged another long hug, and more tears of joy flowed.

P-A held out his hand holding a white wafer which looked sort of like bread. Hanok said, 'What is it?' His friend replied, 'It's called manna. We have a long way to go and this will sustain you.' This was a brand-new food. He gave thanks for it, then placed it on his tongue and savoured the sweet delicious flavour. Then, he was ready to go.

The Flight: Once again, electrical currents surged through Hanok's new body. Flying came so easily and naturally. No lessons were needed. Before he knew it, he was high up in the sky with P-A and the other angelos. This had been his dream and now he was finally doing it. Higher and higher he soared in wondrous rapture and ecstasy, even further than the eagles flew. He turned his head and looked down. The trees, mountains and cities were tiny shrinking specks and he could not see his home or family.

The party zoomed on through all the various spheres from the troposphere, the stratosphere and right to the exosphere at the edge of outer space. In just minutes, they travelled about 480 kilometers (nearly 300 miles). This was unbelievable but true. They passed through a thick canopy of fresh cool water droplets which served as a protective layer around the globe from the strong harmful rays of the sun. On and on they zoomed till even his old home planet, the Heart of Grace, seemed to fade into a small dot. The happy travellers sped along at angelo speed, much, much faster than the speed of light.

Hanok suddenly realised he was in a place with no air, yet he was still alive. His new body did not seem to need oxygen. They zoomed past the moon and soon left the warmth of the sun behind. But he didn't feel cold. He had perfect body temperature. Planets and their moons glided gracefully in their orbits around the sun. The travellers weaved their way around some huge floating rocks which came closer and closer and then silently drifted away. Soon, there was clear flying through pure, empty deep outer space. And then the home solar system was no longer seen. It disappeared into a vast ocean of tiny twinkling stars.

The flight was smooth and tireless. So often Hanok had dreamed of

A Glimpse of the Future: Hanok's Story

flying, and now he was zooming along at incredible speeds. On and on the group of angelos sped bringing their one and only rescued human being closer to Ouranos. As Hanok gazed ahead, he saw a long, cloudy mass of something. But as he travelled further, he realised he was actually right inside it and in the depths of a vast mass of billions of stars just like his old sun. They looked very close together like a gloriously thick white milky cloud but as he travelled further inwards, great spaces opened up and the flyers had a clear path ahead of them. Multitudes of stars quickly flashed by as the group pushed on through the cloudy mass. Hanok had no idea which way was north, south, east or west.

In bewilderment, he asked P-A the simple question, 'Where am I?' P-A laughed and replied, 'You are not lost my friend. We do know where we are going and have travelled this path many times before. You are in just a tiny, tiny part of the endless Kingdom of Basileus. This section is called the Milky Way because it is so full of clouds of stars. Did you know our wonderful King has given a name to every single star in His kingdom? After all, He created each one and knows them individually–just like He knows the name of every single human on the Heart of Grace.' P-A pointed to a giant star glowing brighter than the others and said, 'Look over there! That one is called Alpha Centauri.'

He explained further. 'The Milky Way galaxy is only one of many, many others. They are all different and have their own names. There is the Whirlpool Galaxy, the Tadpole, the Sunflower and the Cartwheel. In the whole Kingdom of Basileus, there are hundreds of billions of these magnificent galaxies full of trillions of stars. And most of the stars have their own small families of planets orbiting around them. These include many other worlds with their own unique inhabitants different to those on the Heart of Grace. In my entire long life, I still have not been to all of them and met their occupants. I wonder if I will ever get to visit them all. Probably not.' He grinned.

Hanok's face was expressionless. He was overawed. No wonder he didn't know where he was. This was all a completely new and overwhelming experience. He was stunned, lost for words and all he could do was stare in amazement. He thought about all the people back on his old planet and how their feet were always touching the ground or were close to it. The force of gravity always pulled them down. But now he was far away from that relentless tug. He had total trust in his cosmic tour-guides and it was good to have some names of stars and galaxies, and know where he fitted into the vast scheme of things. Oh, he was so miniscule, yet His Father-King still cared for little ol' him. With tears in his eyes, he burst into a new song.

> 'O, King of Basileus, how excellent is your name!
> When I consider the works of your hands
> and all the stars, galaxies and lands,
> Who am I that you still think of me?
> Who am I that You take me to be with Thee?
> O, King of Basileus, how excellent is Your name!

The angelos all copied his song and blended in with beautiful harmonies. Their voices rose higher and higher as they sang it over and over, praising the Theotes Creators.

Kesil-Orian: The journey continued and the party passed through more and more great constellations of stars. Faster and faster they sped. Further and further they flew. Time was left behind. Time meant nothing here because all was eternity. Hanok had entered into foreverland. Along the way, P-A pointed to certain bright stars and told Hanok their names. He explained a little about them. 'See that very bright star over to your left?' Hanok nodded and answered, 'Yes, its enormous and looks so much bigger than my old sun!' P-A continued, 'Some call that star Betelgeuse. It is 950 times bigger than your old sun. Look just below Betelgeuse, and you'll see three other bright stars in a row.'

Hanok laughed at such a funny name. He quickly found the three stars and noticed a fuzzy patch just below them. 'What's that fuzzy spot underneath?' he asked. 'Aha!' exclaimed P-A. 'Good question! That is precisely where we are headed for right now. That is another mighty cloud of more stars. It's a nebula called Kesil, but some call it Orian. Very soon we shall pass through it. Kesil-Orian is a sign we are now getting closer to Ouranos.

The vast nebula loomed up in front of them. It was most gloriously bright and looked like many gi-normous bulging, colourful, hazy clouds with

A Glimpse of the Future: Hanok's Story

no particular shape or form. Massive lumps seemed to swell out like burly bumps oozing out of a tree trunk. Hanok's eyes were wide-open trying to take it all in. It wasn't long before they entered and passed deep inside. Hanok saw it was simply another humungous cluster of more countless stars. The travellers glided through a long deep canyon of starry clouds and P-A went into great detail.

'My dear friend, you have travelled an extremely long way from your old home. Let me tell you just how far you've come. You are now nearly fifteen trillion kilometres (about 9 trillion miles) away from the Heart of Grace. Kesil-Orian is nearly 145 trillion kilometres across (90 trillion miles). So we still have some way to go before we reach our destination.'

Hanok was dumbfounded and looked behind him. Of course, the Heart of Grace was nowhere to be seen. All around him was a whole new world he could never have pictured in his mind. There were an infinite number of worlds. Words failed him. How amazingly awesome were the Theotes Creators!

The angelos were so delighted to hear Hanok's gasps and see his face and eyes light up on this incredible journey. P-A had been watching him deep in thought and said, 'Welcome again to your new life, dear friend. All you see around you now, is just a small part of the rest of Basileus. Our great Theotes family has spread all these stars and planets throughout space and there is no end to them. We are still only in the same Milky Way galaxy as the Heart of Grace. And there are countless more galaxies out there inside great super clusters of galaxies. On and on they go. This whole miraculous Kingdom was all created by our beloved Theotes Royal Rulers. And they govern all the worlds in it, according to their Law of Great Love.'

Hanok was intensely curious about these other new worlds. He had known they were there somewhere outside his old planet, but had no idea how many. He looked forward immensely to exploring Basileus and discovering much, much more than any humans knew about. Even the scientists and technocrats and the most brainy and intelligent had never observed close up what he was seeing right now.

P-A went on, 'One day, my dear companion, you can come back and

The Greatest War Ever

visit these worlds and meet their inhabitants. I and my friends will bring you here and you can spend long times in these places. And you can explore other galaxies and meet their occupants. There is plenty of time ahead of you. In fact, there is eternity and you can come back again and again. Welcome to Basileus!'

It had only been a few days that the group of travellers had whizzed through space at breathtaking speed and seen dazzling sights. Hanok was homeward bound and not turning back. Along the way, when he wasn't absorbed in the amazing cosmic scenery, he had time to talk with P-A and share about past experiences. He realised how much he had left behind - and did not miss it at all. All the discussions were filled with wonderful words of love, admiration, curiosity and endless questions.

Gone were the word attacks of wicked war weapons of the clever twisted sophistry and manipulative mind games. Gone were the mocking, jeering, sarcastic tones of voices. Gone were the fiery arrows tipped with poisonous crushing words. Gone were the bombardments of temptations and bad thoughts. Gone were a multitude of unpleasant negative feelings he had to control. And gone were the tedious times of packing and preparing for mission trips into the city battlefields. All pressures, all problems and worries were left behind. Gone! Gone! Gone!

Superman: As the days of the cosmic journey flew by, Hanok noticed it did not take much time for memories of the Heart of Grace to fade. A full rich new life beckoned him. His earlier life seemed more and more irrelevant. During the trip, Hanok had time to notice many more changes within him. His brain was being filled with so much new information, but his mind just seemed to expand to fit it all in. It felt as if a thick murky fog had cleared from his old fuzzy, forgetful brain. He even understood immediately the heavenly language of the angelos, and could speak it without having lessons.

Hanok had also become super-sensitive. His eyes seemed to have a veil removed from them and he had far greater vision than with his old eyes. He could gaze into the distance and see things so brightly and clearly. His ears heard new sounds. Back on the old planet, he had thought outer space was full of silence, but now it seemed as if the very stars were singing. Beautiful tones, vibrations and harmonies resonated all around.

A Glimpse of the Future: Hanok's Story

As the party kept flying, he heard the angelos singing the most glorious songs of praise to the Godhead. Their music was even more magnificent than he had ever heard before, completely different to the loud noisy thumping sounds back on the Heart of Grace. Now, he could hear far higher and lower than he could with the old human ears. And his voice box had changed too. He found himself joining his companions singing in the new language, his voice sounding louder and stronger and in perfect tune as never before.

How did Hanok feel? Human language had no words to describe the happiness, the joy, bliss and calm he felt. It was the deepest peace which passed all understanding and had to be experienced to be felt. Theotes Great Love flooded into every cell in his new body and washed away the emotions of sadness, sickness, anxiousness, fear and any other awful, dreadful feeling possible. The release and relief from the pressure of built-up, hurtful negativity from his old world were indescribable.

The new Hanok was one hundred percent positivity and totally liberated in the fullest sense of freedom from sin. He was far healthier than any human being still on the Heart of Grace and was in the perfect form all humans were designed to be. He was a super human–a real superman. And he could now fly without the help of flying machines! This journey alone was worth everything he had suffered and fought for in the Great War. Unbeknown to Hanok, there was much, much more to come! Oh yes! Ouranos was cheap enough! The trip had cost him no money, only his earthly life.

Seven days whizzed by. The group had not stopped to rest and had no sleep, but no-one was tired at all. And then—Hanok saw 'IT.' Yes, it was Ouranos, that great city he so strongly yearned to be in. He was almost there. Brighter and brighter shone its glorious light as they came closer. His heart beat faster with anticipation. He was truly coming home where he belonged forever and ever. His years as a pilgrim and a stranger on the Heart of Grace were over. He had always been seeking a better country and now he was almost there. Yes, he <u>was</u> still wide awake and not dreaming. He was <u>not</u> in the deep sleep of death knowing nothing! This was soooo real!

He shouted out from his new loud voice box, 'I'M HOMEWARD BOUND!

OURANOS–HERE I COOOME!!!'

This is the end of the first panorama.

Panorama 2 – The Homecoming Welcome

The Sea Of Glass: Hanok's thrilling week-long expedition from the Heart of Grace to Ouranos was sadly over. But a new never-ending adventure was just beginning. The glowing city of Ouranos appeared bigger and bigger as they got closer. It was the most impressive metropolis he had ever seen. It made all those cities back on the Heart of Grace look small, insignificant and ugly. At last, he had arrived in his new home.

The party approached the landing platform in front of the city. It was a huge square which looked like a sea of transparent golden glass. Light from the city streamed out onto the square so it shimmered and gleamed like a mass of fire. The group of travellers descended and, as their feet gently touched the bottom of the square, they were engulfed by the fiery light. It was like being in flames but perfectly safe.

Meeting the Prince: Standing in the middle of the vast square and waiting to welcome His mighty warrior home, was none other than the beloved Chief Commander, Prince Yehosua Himself and a large group of angelos. The Prince's majestic frame was larger and taller than Hanok and the angelos. He looked exceedingly lovely and noble and regal. His face shone brighter than the old sun and His eyes were as flames of fire. The pure white robe covering His body was whiter than the whitest white. His hair was also white with curls which lay neatly on His shoulders. Fire seemed to cover His feet, and on His head were layers of glorious crowns. Straight away, Hanok knew who He was.

The Prince-Commander looked down at his loyal soldier with a beaming, smiling face and said, 'Welcome! Well done, my good and faithful servant. You have been faithful over a few things. I will make you ruler over many things. Enter now into the joy of your Lord. You have fought the good fight exceptionally well and have come through with clean hands and a pure heart. Everything you have done to help each poor sorrowful person, you have done for Me. Now is the time for you to come into our Presence. It's time to be rewarded for staying loyal, faithful and trusting, and for spreading the good news of our Great Love to

A Glimpse of the Future: Hanok's Story

our beloved human children.'

Prince Yehosua had the sweetest melodious voice. It was kinder than any voice ever heard by human ears. The sounds were the purest language of love, tones unheard of on the Heart of Grace. They were pure exquisite music to Hanok's ears. A massive surge of the Great Love filled his whole being again, and he was overcome with emotion. The feeling of the utmost joy of finally being home with his beloved Chief Commander, Prince Yehosua, was overwhelming. In this most wonderful place, deep personal feelings did not have to be controlled, suppressed and hidden. The word embarrassment did not exist in Ouranos. Hanok uttered the words, 'My Lord!' He fell down in adoration, crying tears of sheer relief and thankfulness.

Whatever sadness and grief, hurt and anger that was left from the old life, drained away completely. The long, hard pilgrimage of wandering around that distant, battered planet was definitely over. He had never felt that he really belonged there anyway, and now he understood why. He had been sent to the Heart of Grace as a soldier in the Prince's army with a mission pre-planned by his Theotes family. Using their precious gift of free will, he had fortunately made wise decisions to choose the narrow way of The Good and not The Bad of sin. He had carried out his mission in the Great War according to Theotes desires and instructions. And now, at long last, he was in his true home. For him, the Great War was over. He had come through as victor, a conqueror and an overcomer. Mission accomplished.

Finally, Hanok's sobbing stopped and the tears no longer flowed. The Prince's eyes looked down ever so kindly deep into the heart of His humbled child. He bent down, gently and lovingly lifted up Hanok's head, and wiped away the tears. There would be no more death, neither sorrow, nor crying. Neither would there be any more pain, for the former things had passed away. Then the Prince helped Hanok to stand up on the fiery glass.

The Royal Garments – The Crown; The Harp; The Palm Branch; Music and Hanok's Song:

The Crown: To Hanok's surprise, an angelo handed the Prince a most glorious golden crown. It shone even brighter than the old sun did. The crown was studded with many colourful sparkling gemstones. The Prince gently placed it on Hanok's head. It was exactly the right size. Like the pure white robes, it was a crown of right relationship because of his trusting obedience to the Royal Family. The crown was also engraved with his new name, as well as the words, 'PURE AND PERFECT IS THE LORD.'

The Prince explained that each gemstone was for every human Hanok had helped to switch sides into His army. The crown glittered with many stones. Hanok did not realise he had helped so many people. Now, he was a truly honoured and highly respected member and close friend of the royal Theotes Family.

The Harp: Next, another angelo handed the Prince a shining golden harp which was passed into Hanok's arms and invited him to play. Hanok held it lovingly. As his fingers touched the strings, he instinctively knew how to play it immediately. Lovely melodies flowed out and he strummed a few chords. Oh, he marvelled, 'I don't even have to practise. I'm going to really enjoy playing this instrument and making up new songs for the glory of my wonderful Royal Family.'

The Palm Branch: Then, Prince Yehosua placed a perfect unblemished palm branch upon Hanok's arm. On each leaf was written the word, VICTORY. The branch represented his efforts in overcoming the dangers and battles in the Great War. More importantly, it told of how it was actually the power of his Prince-Chief Commander which had ultimately given him the victory by turning his weaknesses into strengths.

Oh, what a stunning sight Hanok looked in his white robes, wearing a golden gem-studded crown on his head, a palm branch on his arm and holding onto a gold harp. Theotes Great Love radiated from inside to the outside. Hanok's eyes sparkled and he had the biggest ever grinning smile on his face. Never before had he looked and felt <u>sooo</u> good. In fact, he was better than good—he was perfectly perfect! He looked at

A Glimpse of the Future: Hanok's Story

his reflection in the Sea of Glass beneath him and could scarcely believe his eyes. He did not recognise himself. The old had certainly gone and the new had come. He liked what he saw.

Music and Hanok's Song: But wait, there's more! A nearby angelo sounded a musical note. Hanok looked around to see some angelos holding up their own harps. Their hands skilfully swept across the strings with triumphant, welcoming music. Other angelos were playing silver horns and blasting out a triumphant fanfare. A massed choir sang magnificently and Hanok's fingers flew across the strings of his harp along with the orchestra. His voice sang high, loud and in beautiful harmony with the rest. Indescribable rapturous thrills filled his whole body as songs of praise flowed out of his mouth. He was completely filled with deep heartfelt gratitude to the Royal Family for all they had done for him. The perfect music, rich in melody and harmony resounded all through Ouranos and out into Basileus. Inhabitants of the other worlds heard it and also rejoiced in welcoming the first human being into Ouranos.

Hanok's whole being was electrified with superb musical soundwaves. The choir and other musicians stopped to let him burst out with a solo song. It was a new song he had never sung before. The words just flowed.

> 'I will sing to my Lord for You have been good to me.
> Through fierce fires and deep waters of life, You have led me.
> From across the starry sea of space,
> You rescued and brought me to my true home place.
> Your guidance and protection were with me from the start.
> You have clothed me in white robes and cleansed my heart.
> You are my strength, my song and my Rescuer,
> You had already pre-planned my present and future.
> Who is like You, Oh my Lord?
> You have kept Your promises and Your Word.
> No-one is so wonderful, so mighty and giving.
> No-one is so gracious, so merciful and forgiving.
> From now on, we shall be together.
> and You shall reign forever and ever!'

The Greatest War Ever

Prince Yehosua beamed another great grin and His eyes pierced lovingly into Hanok's eyes. The current of Great love flowed abundantly between them both. The Prince was delighted at the home-coming of His precious human child. His own powerful voice sang along in a final song with the royal choir and orchestra. Sounds of victory blasted all around. At last, one human individual of all the billions had made it to Ouranos. The Prince-Chief Commander and His army of holy angelos would still continue to fight against the enemy Satan, and bring many, many more home. Nearly a thousand years earlier, a vow had been made to Adam and Eve that the Lord would be the Promised Seed and come to rescue more precious children. The Theotes Rulers never ever broke their promises.

What a welcoming ceremony this was! It was far, far grander than any counterfeit royal human ceremony in any palace or stadium. On the fiery Square of Glass, the retired war warrior was rewarded for all his efforts of over three hundred years on the battlefield on the one black spot in Basileus. And this welcome was just the beginning. The Theotes family had countless more surprises in store for their beloved child. This was the type work which gave the Mystery Holy Spirit the greatest pleasure of all, ie to give good surprises. Carrying out the process of cause and effect was unpleasant when sin occurred, because the wages of sin is death. But for those who love their King and Lord, for those who answer the calling and carry out the mission given to them—all things work together for good.

This is the end of Panorama 2.

Panorama 3 – The Royal Tour Through Ouranos

The City: *The Walls; The Gates of Pearl; Gold Streets and Buildings; Nature.*

The Walls: From the middle of the flaming Sea of Glass, Prince Yehosua turned and pointed towards the mighty city of Ouranos which towered high up into the distance. He said to Hanok, 'Come, beloved of My Father. Enter in and receive the rewards which have been waiting for you ever since the beginning of the Heart of Grace. For so long I have wanted for you to come and be with Me. Come, let me show you My

A Glimpse of the Future: Hanok's Story

home, which is now also your home.'

Hanok was again filled with adoration and gratitude for his beloved Prince. Yes, Theotes surprises never ended. There were so many new things to see. With his new body and sharper vision, Hanok's eyes were wide-opened to everything around him. He could see close up, intricate details ever so clearly, as well as into very long distances. He did not have to squint at the incredibly glorious light surrounding him. How much light could there be? Back on the Heart of Grace, light from the sun was too strong for human eyes to look at. But here in Ouranos, everything shone and glowed splendidly. There were so many varieties of bright light, easy to look at, but impossible to describe.

The grand procession led by the Prince and new royal member Hanok, moved gracefully across the fiery, glassy sea and closer towards the towering metropolis. From where he stood, Hanok could only see one side of four great walls which surrounded the city. He paused a few seconds to take it all in. Later, he would learn the exact measurements of this ginormous place. To be precise, each of the four sides was 603 kilometers long (375 miles). The total circumference was 2414 kilometers (1500 miles). The height of the walls was the same as the length - 603 kilometers high (375 miles). At the start of his journey to Ouranos, Hanok had flown through the atmosphere around the Heart of Grace. That distance had been about 480 kilometers (298 miles). Therefore, the height of Ouranos was greater than the old atmosphere! This was SOME city.

Hanok stared in wonderment at the giant wall. With his new perfect eyes, he could see colours in layers of gemstones. The twelve levels of the bottom foundation stretched up higher and higher. First there was a layer of multi-coloured jasper with its streaks of beautiful red, brown, white, yellow and green running through. It shone brilliantly as it transferred light from inside of the city to the outside. Then came layers of blue sapphire, glittering chalcedony, a type of quartz. On top of these were layers of green emerald, sardonyx, reddish sardius, yellowish chrysolite, green beryl, yellow topaz, light green chrysoprasus, purple jacinth and violet amethyst. What a stunning sight!

The Gates of Pearl: On the side that Hanok was standing, he saw a massive gate in front of him which was made of one spectacular creamy, shimmery pearl. It was exceedingly majestic and beautiful. In the distance to the right was a second pearl gate, and far off to the left was a third. In each side of the city walls were three giant pearl gates.

Prince Yehosua gestured to Hanok to move on. When they reached the pearl gate, the Prince raised His strong glorious right arm and, with mighty power, swung it open on its glittering hinges. He looked at Hanok and said in His lovely, melodious voice, 'You have served Me well in My army and stayed loyal to Me. You have kept the good faith, obeyed my commands and fought the good fight. You have stood firmly for My truth. Now–please enter in.'

Hanok stepped into the entrance. Then, the Prince led the way through a wide, high, tunnel in the bottom layer of gemstone. Long orderly lines of angelos followed in procession. They were all surrounded by a solid, deep wall of gorgeous coloured jasper. It was transparent and Hanok could see light shining from the Sea of Glass outside. Light from the city inside also filtered through and illuminated it further. There was no need of man-made artificial light here. Hanok later learned that this huge corridor measured 65 meters long (216 feet). The bright white light of the city glowed at the other end and invited him to come closer. What was awaiting him there?

Gold Streets and Buildings: When Hanok stepped out of the entrance, he was met with another awesome sight. His eyes opened wider and wider as his head moved from side to side trying to take it all in. Never had he seen so much gold. Here, the gold was the purest, refined, shining, transparent, perfect gold possible. The very street he walked along was paved with it.

The Prince told him that gold was extremely valuable and important, because it represented keeping the faith and trust in the Royal Family. It symbolised how characters were constantly tested, cleansed, refined and purified to a state of perfection. Yes, Hanok had certainly kept this faith of gold and was most worthy to walk along these streets.

Back on the Heart of Grace, a sign of the purest gold was that your re-

A Glimpse of the Future: Hanok's Story

flection could be seen in it. Hanok looked down at his own magnificent image. Yes, this street <u>was</u> made of perfect pure gold. Again, he was surprised at what he saw. He did not see his old human self. Instead, there was the picture of the new creation of his own tested, cleansed, refined, purified and perfected being which reflected the Prince's own character. Hanok had never been a wealthy man, but now he exceeded all the riches of the wealthiest, most powerful elite human beings put together. Billionaires did not come close to this wealth. Hanok thought he did not deserve all these rewards being showered upon him. But, at the same time, he felt he had every right to be here and felt so much at home. He was in the right place at the right time.

Once again, human words could not adequately describe the sight before Hanok's eyes as he looked up and around. The metropolis was so vast with so many new things to comprehend. There were countless gigantic buildings of all sizes, shapes and architectural designs Hanok had never seen before. Many towered far, far taller than any man-made skyscrapers on the old planet. Some reached kilometres into the sky. Countless steps and staircases lead around corners and upwards. Angelos walked around streets, up the steps or simply flew through the air. Hanok wondered where they were all going and what they were doing.

As the royal tour continued, the accompanying angelos gradually left their two leaders and went to their own homes. Hanok saw some of them enter, remove their crowns and lay them on the shelves inside their open front doors. Prince Yehosua led Hanok higher and higher through the city streets, up more steps and into magnificent gardens. Fountains shot upwards and waterfalls cascaded down over giant boulders. All the boulders and rocks were beautifully smooth and rounded in all shapes and sizes. Narrow creeks twisted around, streaming out from wider rivers which flowed down from nearby rolling hills. The hills merged into mountain ranges leading to even higher mountains spreading for hundreds of kilometres. Along the way, the Prince pointed to certain objects of interest and explained about them. As the royal pair climbed higher and higher, the scenery and views became more and more breathtaking.

Nature: The Prince loved taking Hanok on this special tour and watched his companion's face light up in awe. As the adventure continued, every corner they turned revealed incredible new scenes. Fabulous gardens spread out between buildings. There were stunning flowers of colours and fragrances Hanok had never seen or smelt before. He breathed in deeply and took in the exquisite perfumes. He also breathed in the fresh city air, something he could not do on the old planet with its pollution from man-made machines.

Large shrubs and bushes of all shapes and sizes were scattered around. Gardens were lined with rows of huge oaks, willows, maples, firs, pines and many trees Hanok had no name for. They all waved their branches to welcome him. Fruit and nut trees of all types were in abundance and readily available for anyone to pick and eat at any time. There were the biggest fruits and nuts Hanok had ever seen—almonds, walnuts, cashews, peaches, pears, apples, grapes and nameless others.

After a while, they came to some woods with a creek winding its way through. Bears splashed in clear blue water filled with colourful fish which had no fear of being eaten. Animals roamed around in open patches. Hanok recognised a few but there were also other new, unusual creatures. Foxes and rabbits played together and rolled in lush, silvery-green grassy fields.

Further along, a large lion lay on the grass with a cute little sheep snuggled up next to it. The lion looked up and noticed the Prince and the new human creature. It gracefully stood up, stretched its back legs to reveal its huge size, much bigger than lions back on the Heart of Grace. Then, it wandered over to Hanok and rubbed its nose against his shoulder. Hanok realised he wasn't frightened of this once-feared beast. He rubbed noses with it, put both arms around the thick neck, and lovingly combed the beautiful bushy mane with his fingers. He had never done this before. The lion closed its eyes, purred loudly and smooched up for more. The thought occurred to Hanok that these beautiful animals in Ouranos would never hunt, or kill and eat each other. They too had eternal life and never died. Oh, he wondered if he could have a lion as a pet.

The Prince watched the pair and smiled. Then he patted the lion on its

A Glimpse of the Future: Hanok's Story

back and sent it off to its waiting sheep. The pair moved on.

Mount Siyon–The River of Life; The Tree of Life: At the very centre of the great city, the loftiest mountains arose. There were seven highest mountain peaks which stood out, and of these, the mightiest one towered even higher. This was Mount Siyon. On its summit sat the magnificent glowing Temple of Miqqedas, the heart and home of the Royal Theotes family, and the seat of government of all Basileus. The Prince explained that Miqqedas meant holy place set apart, consecrated, a sanctuary and the sacred temple. Here was the ultimate Source of all the light, energy and the electrical circuit of the Great Love which kept the city in continuous daytime. This is why there was so much light. This is where the Father-King lived with his Son.

Oh, how Hanok wanted to be way up there and see more closely! How he wanted to meet his mighty Father-King he had heard so much about and talked with, but never actually seen. He began to feel a little impatient and had so many questions to ask the Prince, but didn't know where to start. He just couldn't wait to be up on the top of Mount Siyon.

But suddenly, he realised, 'What's the hurry? This is life in eternity. I have infinite time ahead of me and it doesn't matter if my questions get answered now or later. There are millions upon billions upon trillions and zillions of years ahead of me!' He relaxed and more of the great peace swept through him. Oh, there was so much to do, and so, so much time! Yes, he could wait. The word, impatient, did not belong here. Hanok sighed a huge breath of contentment. Yes, he was very content in Ouranos.

The River of Life: The Prince had read Hanok's mind and knew his heart's desire. They began the climb up Mount Siyon, even flying some of the way. The happy pair landed beside a wide and mighty river which looked like flowing, liquid crystal with diamonds of light bouncing and sparkling off it. Prince Yehosua said, 'This river starts at the Temple of Miqqedas and flows down through brooks and creeks to the city. You may drink from this water anytime and it will give you life forever. It's called the River of Life. Anyone who comes to Me can drink freely of this water. Are you thirsty? Please - try our water.'

The Greatest War Ever

Hanok nodded thankfully to say, 'Yes.' He knelt down and scooped some of the cool, clear water into his hands and drank. He took in more mouthfuls. This water was the freshest, purest, most delicious water he had ever tasted. He scooped up more and splashed it over his face. New surges of energy filled his body as he took in the most life-giving drink possible.

Prince Yehosua then escorted his friend up through the final stage of the royal tour. As they walked beside the great river to the top of Mount Siyon, they passed more giant trees which surrounded and beautified the great Temple of Miqqedas. There was the box, the pine, the fir and the myrtle. Branches of pomegranate and fig trees were heavily laden with the weight of their fruit, and almost touched the ground. Huge bulrushes lined the edges of its water. Further along, lilies, roses and many vivid coloured, fragrant flowers also lined the banks.

The Tree of Life: The Prince walked over to a tree with a huge trunk of pure transparent gold. It was laden with an amazing type of silvery-gold fruit. He picked two pieces and offered one to Hanok. They both sat down on the lush shiny green grass dotted with little white daisies and blue forget-me-nots. Hanok studied the perfection of this shiny piece of fruit which had no bruises, spots or holes bored into it by pests. On its stem was a leaf still attached. The leaf was a dark shiny green, perfectly shaped, again with no blemishes.

Hanok smiled and thanked the Prince before biting hungrily into the crunchy, juicy fruit. Once again, words could not describe the taste of how scrumptious it was. When he had finished, the Prince said, 'You know you can eat the leaf too.' Hanok tried it and it was very different but just as tasty as the fruit.

Then, he lay down on the soft grass. He looked up and a puzzled expression came across his face. This new sight did not make any sense at all. The tree they were under was extremely high and it branches spread right across the wide River of Life. On the other side was another massive similar tree trunk. At first, Hanok thought he saw two trees. Branches from both reached up and stretched over the water to join and become one tree.

A Glimpse of the Future: Hanok's Story

He asked his royal Tour Guide. 'How can this be? Is this just one tree?' The Prince explained, 'This is a special one called the Tree of Life. And like the River of Life, anyone who eats of it will live forever. And what's more, every month, the fruit is different.'

Hanok was lost for words and shook his head in amazement. How good could Ouranos get! He was very satisfied from his drink of water, the fruit and its leaf. Still lying down, he closed his eyes and thought about the past week. He had left the Heart of Grace, his wife, family and friends, flown through the planet's atmosphere, journeyed seven days through deep outer space, been rewarded with a grand welcoming ceremony, enjoyed a personal royal tour of parts of the city, and had climbed the highest mountain. It had been about a week ago since he had eaten the manna that P-A had given him. But the little he had eaten and drunk was enough to fill him with new strength and vigour to keep on going. And he had not slept a wink for a week. He seemed to have twenty times more energy than ever before. His whole body was still full of the electricity and power from the Great Love Energy Source. And he had not once felt the least bit tired.

This new body really was mega-super sensitive. Whatever he tasted, touched, saw, heard and smelt was sooo beautiful, sooo alive and indescribably glorious. This was the bliss of eternal life. It was a totally new feeling for Hanok and gave a whole new meaning of the phrase, a healthy life. Oh yes, Ouranos was all health, wealth and life. No sickness and death whatsoever. And it was SO cheap–all was for free! There was no money or currency system in Ouranos. Yes, Hanok was very, very happy here.

His day-dreaming was soon interrupted when he heard the Prince's voice say, 'Come now, my friend, I'll show you inside my home, the Temple of Meqqidas, the Heart and Headquarters of the government of all Basileus.'

And that's the end of the third panorama.

Panorama 4 – The Temple Of Miqqedas

The Grandest Musical Welcome: Prince Yehosua and Hanok continued up the rest of the path to the very top of Mount Siyon. A majestic fanfare of trumpets could be heard announcing their arrival. They came to a series of large steps leading to a massive area with many levels of very wide platforms. Myriads of cherubims and angelos had already assembled there and eagerly waited to greet their beloved Prince and His newcomer companion. This was a very special occasion. It was the first time a human being had come to the Temple.

The massive orchestra and choir stood in crowded but orderly groups on the platforms. No-one felt squashed together. There were so many, yet there was plenty of room for everyone. An aisle had been left leading up to the entrance of the Temple. As Prince Yehosua and Hanok stepped up through the aisle, the angelos took off their crowns, lay them down and bowed low in adoration.

The leading musician cherubim conducted a music anthem especially composed for the grand entrance to the Temple. He was the first to touch his harp and strike the first note. The choir joined in by singing words full of praise, while others played their harps and wind instruments. Every face beamed with pure joy. They loved making music from the depths of their hearts to their cherished Theotes Royal Family. They wanted to sing the love language of Ouranos and express their deep emotions and heartfelt thanks.

Hanok thought the music he had already heard on the Sea of Glass was perfect. But this was even more perfect—if such a thing were possible. But with the Theotes family, <u>all</u> things were possible. This superb ceremonial music of hosts of celestial beings was another magnificent new sound experience.

Like Hanok's mega-supersensitive ears and eyes, the rest of his new body was also mega-supersensitive. It was designed to be filled with the vibrations of the wonderful love language of music. His ever-expanding brain absorbed all the sounds like a sponge and once again, thrills surged through his entire body. The music fired up more electrical charges and Hanok tingled all over with exhilaration and ecstasy. His

A Glimpse of the Future: Hanok's Story

whole being was meant to respond to the pulses of Great Love sent through music by the Theotes Creators. Hanok experienced this electrical circuit of Great Love in all its fullness.

Music was the royal Theotes language of Great Love, a mixture of words of praise and glory, and the powerful sounds of majestic melodies and rich harmonies. After all, it was Theotes Word and language which had created everything in the very first place. Word, Word everywhere; oh, wonderful Word of Great Love!

Hanok was so humbled by the size of a second welcome and the sheer numbers of cherubims and angelos who were there. Never had he ever experienced such royal treatment or heard such superb language before. He stood trembling and unable to move. He had to stop himself from falling over. Prince Yehosua looked ever so lovingly down at Him and said, 'Come my beloved one. Welcome to my home! You are part of my Royal Family. And please, please call me your Brother.'

What an honour for humble Hanok to have the great Prince Yehosua as a Brother! In a most respectful and ever-so-grateful voice he quietly replied, 'Thank You. Thank You.' He paused and looked adoringly into the Prince's face. A lump welled up in his throat and tears came into his eyes. Then he smiled and softly whispered the word, 'Brother.'

The Prince held out His hand and Hanok held it tightly. The two brothers proceeded up the last few steps to the top of the platforms. The Temple of Miqqedas glowed in all its glory and radiated light in all directions. It was gi-normous and far too big to see the whole building. The Temple was supported by seven colossal columns. Each column was made of pure transparent gold and studded with large lustrous pearls.

The Holy Place—*The Table of Bread and Juice; The Candlestick; The Altar of Perfume*

The entrance to the temple was a wide magnificent curtain. It was made of a thick cloth covered with beautiful blue, purple and scarlet designs. The Prince parted the curtain in the middle and they entered a huge chamber called the Holy Place. This great spacious room contained three stunningly beautiful pieces of furniture which were all made of polished, solid, pure gold. All three objects shone and glittered and were intricately decorated with exquisite shapes and patterns.

The Prince paused to let Hanok take it all in. Naturally, Hanok asked what they all meant. So, the Prince briefly explained how each one had special meaning. They were all important in the great Plan of Salvation to help rescue humans from sin and bring them home to Ouranos. One day, He would give Hanok more lessons and he would learn what they all represented. There was so much to study and Hanok looked forward to spending more time with his new Teacher.

To the far right was a golden table with gold plates and gold goblets neatly arranged. To the far left stood a beautiful golden candlestick with curved arms pointing upwards. It was decorated with flowers and almonds. Straight ahead in the distance, in front of a massive superbly decorated curtain, sat a square altar with hot coals and incense fumes rising up giving out subtle perfumes. The two brothers flew over to the altar and gazed at it. Hanok sniffed and closed his eyes to enjoy the new aroma.

The Prince explained, 'Dear brother, our precious trusting faithful ones still on the Heart of Grace below, who are talking to us right now, don't always realise how their words and thoughts actually reach up to this Altar of Incense. Their words are now floating as sweet perfume up and over that curtain you see behind the altar. Their songs of praise and their requests go to the other side and the Father-King is listening to them this very moment.'

Hanok was amazed to realise that his own words had reached into Ouranos in real life. He thought about all the times he had gone alone into the forests and spent hours talking with his invisible King and Lord. His pleas and cries for help had all drifted upwards to Ouranos to this very altar in the Holy Place in the Temple of Miqqedas. Even the times when he was lost for words, his groans and moans were understood and heard by the Royal Listeners. Feelings of guilt, regret and sadness he felt when he admitted he had done something wrong, were all covered over by this beautiful fragrant incense. And the Father-King had understood and forgiven him, always drawing his heart closer with beams of Great Love. Forgiveness was a Theotes miracle and only something the

A Glimpse of the Future: Hanok's Story

Royal Family could do. No humans had the power to forgive like this. Of all the pieces of furniture in the Temple Hanok had seen so far, this one was the closest to the King, right next door in His Most Holy Place. What this Altar of Incense stood for was truly astonishing.

'Oh, my dear brother,' continued the Prince, 'I have so much I want to teach you! We have designed this Temple so thoughtfully. We use the purest solid gold for our furniture because it represents perfect Theotes character. Everything in this Holy Place teaches about our Great Love for all of our children down on the Heart of Grace. It teaches what My role is in our mighty Rescue Plan. The Table of Bread and Juice tells a story about Me. The Candlestick speaks of Me. The Altar of Incense is also about Me. They all reveal what I will do one day in the future when I go to the Heart of Grace as the Promised Seed. This whole Temple of Miqqedas is all about bringing our human children back close to us and rescuing them from that dreadful battlefield. You, dearest Hanok, are proof that our rescue plan works perfectly, and that free will always wins over force. Always. One day, you will understand much more. You have eternity to learn about this subject.'

Hanok turned and gazed around the huge Holy Place. He looked forward immensely to studying more about this amazing Temple of Miqqedas, its furniture and what it had to do with the rescue of humans.

Then, the Prince pointed to the thick absolutely gorgeous curtain behind the altar. It was the only thing which separated them from the Father-King. It was massive and hung from a long strong rod which lay across four colossal gold pillars. A silver socket or hollow was on the top of each pillar for the rod to lie in. The golden curtain was superbly embroidered with pictures of huge cherubims in vivid colours of purple, blue and scarlet. It spread in one massive piece right across the giant room with no division in the middle.

Then the Prince said, 'Now it's time! This is the moment you have waited so long for! Please come and meet My Father–your Father-King.'

In the next panorama of the story, we will get just a glimpse of what is behind this massive curtain.

Panorama 5 – The King And His Story

The Most Holy Place and the Throne: The pair flew to the side of the great curtain and passed around it into the next gigantic room called the Most Holy Place. In here, Hanok was at the very heart and core of the Theotes Trio, the ultimate Source of Great Love. It was also the Prince-Chief Commander's Headquarters for the Great War. This was the most glorious of glorious places in Ouranos, indeed of all Basileus. Its brightness and light surpassed everything Hanok had seen so far. Once again he wondered, 'How bright can bright get?' His eyes were dazzled for a few seconds at the incredible glory of all glories. What he saw could not be fully described with human words.

In front of him was a huge pure white throne with a large cherubim standing on each side. They had three pairs of wings and the top pair spanned out widely across the back of the throne with their tips touching high. The other wings hung loosely by their sides. With the great white seat of the throne across the bottom, they made a giant frame. The two heads of the cherubims were bowed down in deep respect as they looked intently downwards. Hanok noticed that they were looking at a large gold box underneath the seat. The box had a stunning border of golden crowns right around the top. And around the whole frame of the throne, there was a very large curve, like a rainbow of beautiful shiny emerald green. The throne in all its fullness was a most magnificent sight to gaze upon.

Of course, inside the frame, the almighty, all-powerful King of Basileus sat in His glory and majesty. His form was so dazzling that it was difficult to see Him clearly. But He, like His Son, had a similar body to Hanok's with arms, hands, feet, head, ears, eyes, nose and a mouth. Like the Prince, the King was much bigger and taller than Hanok. Hanok noticed that His hair was pure, white, long and curly like His Son's. The Father-King's garments were the whitest white possible. Dazzling light radiated all around Him and the room was fully lit up even brighter than in the Holy Place.

At last, after 365 years, Hanok was presented face to face with his beloved Father, the One who had assisted His Son in all creation, and the One he had talked with so often. What a privilege! The King's shining,

A Glimpse of the Future: Hanok's Story

burning bright eyes looked deeply into Hanok's as He smiled the most welcoming, loving smile, just like Prince Yehosua's on the Sea of Glass. Once again, Hanok was greatly humbled and overwhelmed. He took off his crown, carefully laid it on the shining golden floor with his palm leaf and harp. Then, he bowed his head low and lay down flat in deep reverence and adoration.

The King's Song The King was extremely pleased to greet His child. Like everyone else in Ouranos, He loved singing the wonderful love language which He had created. So, He rejoiced with his own beautiful love song. With his perfect melodious voice, He sang these words.

'I am the Lord your King,
who has brought you out of the land of bondage,
out of the place of sin.
You have no other King but Me.
I have loved you with an everlasting love.
With loving kindness have I drawn you up to Me.
You have risen and come to Mount Siyon,
Oh, precious child of Mine.'

Then the King said in His very special Theotes voice, 'You may stand up now and come boldly to My throne. And—you may call me Father.'

Hanok felt a new energy pulsating within. He arose and confidently stepped closer towards his Father. He felt exceeding great joy in the presence of the mighty King. Prince Yehosua had presented his loyal trusting servant, not as a feeble, weak and weary human warrior, but instead, as faultless, blameless, perfect in character and exactly as he was originally designed to be. Back on the Heart of Grace, a wall of sin had separated human beings from their Royal Family and made the King and Prince invisible. But now, Hanok was on the inside behind the great dividing curtain and was able to see and hear the Father-King one on one. Oh, communication was so much easier.

Of course, the Mystery Holy Spirit was also present in this Most Holy Place, but was still invisible as always. There was no greater joy for Hanok than to be with the full Theotes Presence like this. There was no greater pleasure for the Holy Spirit than to see a human child united with the Royal Family. Oh, He had many more surprises planned for young Hanok. And there was no greater thrill for the Father and Son than to have their wonderful electrical current of Great Love flowing like this. The Most Holy Place was charged and fired up with the light, power and energy of Theotes Great Love.

A Royal Meeting Prince Yehosua sat down on the large throne at the right side of His Father. At the same time, He and the King both beckoned to Hanok inviting him to sit on the left side. The Prince said, 'Dear Hanok, you are an overcomer. You have earned the right to sit on this throne with us.' Hanok was speechless and climbed up onto the great white seat. It was big! There was plenty of room for the three of them. What an honour!

Hanok felt enormously privileged to have an even closer and greater relationship with the Royal Family than the cherubims and angelos had! This was amazing. But he felt no superiority over them. In Ouranos, there was no reason at all for anyone to feel better than others. His body tingled all over with life at its very fullest. Being a royal family member and such a close intimate friend was indescribable. He felt truly like royalty, simply because he <u>was</u> royalty. All his efforts, struggles and tears fighting in the Great War were well worth it.

The King and Prince let Hanok have a few minutes silence to take everything in. The superhuman mind was racing. Hanok stared around in awe and enjoyed the exact same view as the King and Prince had seen for eons upon eons as they watched over their metropolis, and indeed of all Basileus. Hanok could see through the golden transparent walls of the Temple and looked way down past the platforms. The cherubims and angelos were leaving and his eyes watched them descend from the mount. Some were flying and others were walking. He traced the path of the mighty River of Life as it wound its way down the mountain to form smaller rivers and streams which branched out to all parts of Ouranos. He saw the huge buildings way below and the spread-out gardens with animals freely wandering around.

Hanok noticed how Theotes glory and light from the Temple lit up every corner of the city. It never went out. There was no night-time here at all, just eternal daytime. Everyone below could look up and see the Temple and know their Theotes Rulers were with them. They were perfectly safe

A Glimpse of the Future: Hanok's Story

and free from all fear. And it wasn't as if the Royal Family was spying and prying on everyone. No! There was nothing for anyone to hide or keep secret, because they were all totally honest, and they naturally kept the faith and obeyed the Law of Great Love. No-one had a guilty conscience because they never ever did anything bad. All hearts were completely clean. The Law with its ten rules were unspoken. Love, trust and obedience came so easily and weren't even discussed because everyone naturally lived the perfect life they were designed for.

The King and Prince smiled at each other knowing what was going through the mind of their beloved child. Then the King explained about the symbolism in His throne, and how the gold box underneath contained two tablets with the ten Royal Rules on them. He had written the Rules with His own hand and with His ultimate supreme authority. They could never be carved over or changed.

The Prince explained, 'One day, I will teach you more lessons about these Rules and the government of Basileus. But for now, all you need to know is that our enemy Satan, was once called Lucifer. He was a cherished chief cherubim who stood with Me right beside this throne. He was on one side and I was on the other. He knows all about the Royal Rules. But to our deep grief, he became jealous of Me and decided he wanted the highest authority in Basileus. He knows every Rule and has broken every single one. He has been doing his utmost on the Heart of Grace to force our human children to break them too. He tells lies that the rules are too difficult to keep.' Hanok nodded in agreement. He knew all about that!

The King said sadly, 'We tried many times to talk with Lucifer and persuade him to come back to us. But he was cleverly manipulating many angelos to think like him. He formed an army against us. So, we had to change his name to Satan which means adversary and opponent. It was such a tragic time when we had to banish him from Ouranos. But it had to be done. None of The Bad of sin is ever allowed into this sacred city. Before Satan left, the pearl gates were always open, but then we had to close them so he could not come back inside. So now, we have angelos stationed at the gates to open and shut them when our messengers come and go taking instructions to other worlds, especially to the Heart of Grace.

The Greatest War Ever

The Prince-Chief Commander went on to say, 'Dearest soldier, mighty warrior, true and trusting loyal servant—this very throne and the gold box with the Royal Rules, are what you fought for in the Great War. Your efforts are being rewarded right now by you being here and seeing the very centre of our theocratic government. Others are still down there fighting on the battlefield. They are still helping defend our Theotes family as being the rightful Rulers of Basileus. They are defending us simply by choosing to use their gift of free will to stay on our side and by obeying our rules. They might only be a minority, but they are proving to all our children in the other worlds and to other human beings that our ways are fair, just, right and best. One day, when the Great War is over, multitudes of My human soldiers will come and be here with us too.'

Hanok suddenly felt a strange twinge of longing to return to the Heart of Grace and to fight again with his old friends. He had so much more to tell everyone—many more stories to share of the good news and great hope of Ouranos. And the people had to know right now before it was too late. Oh, how he wanted so many more people to join the Prince's army, to live the perfect life of The Good, and be strong and fit for Ouranos! This place was so real and he was so alive to tell the absolute truth.

The Prince read his thoughts and smiled. He asked, 'Are you happy here, my beloved?'

Hanok grinned and replied, 'Oh yes, of course. I'm perfectly happy. Thank You!' Then he hesitated before saying, 'But, please, please may I return to my old home for a while and fight in the Great War again? I have a new body, endless energy—and I can handle whatever Satan fires at me. I have new word-weapons to fight back with. I have so many more stories of Your truth and Great Love to share. I want to tell everyone how real you are! Our enemy and his army of demons are lying when they say you don't exist. That's such a terrible crime! There are so many more who need to come and be where I am now - with You in Miqqedas and Ouranos.'

The Prince laughed and said, 'It's wonderful and noble that you have such enthusiasm. But no, you cannot go back. Once you have eaten the food of Ouranos, you stay here forever. And besides, we have many

A Glimpse of the Future: Hanok's Story

more human soldiers down there fighting for us. We will place billions more on the planet-stage in the future.' Hanok was somewhat disappointed. But, at the same time, he never wanted to leave this paradise. Yes, to answer the Prince's question—he was perfectly happy here.

The King's Message Of Hope The King closed the meeting with wonderful words of hope. He said, 'My precious child, do not worry about your family and friends back home. All is under our control. We know the plans we have for our children and will take away cold, hard, stony hearts and replace them with warm, soft, fleshy, loving ones. We will bring many more from all ends of the planet—the blind, the lame, the sick, the old, the young, the exhausted mothers and their little babies, the over-worked fathers, and the poor as well as the rich. Our Holy Spirit is always working in most powerful and unfathomable ways. When our human children call to us, we always hear them. We will open the eyes of those blinded by sin. We will bring those prisoners who sit in the darkness out from their prisons. Great multitudes will come to Ouranos.

And just like you, they will eat and drink our life-giving water and food so they too can live forever. They shall also sing together with us here in the heights of Mount Siyon. And they shall be filled to overflowing with our Great Love and goodness. Their mourning will turn to joy, and their sadness into rejoicing. Their weeping will stop, and their work shall be rewarded. And they shall be rescued from the land of the enemy. There is great hope in the end that our children will come out of the darkness into the light here. We shall wipe away all tears from their eyes. And there shall be no more death, nor sorrow nor crying. Neither shall there be any pain. The old will pass away and all will be made new. We promise all these things. And you can be certain that we keep our promises.

The Father-King added, 'My dear son, You can come back here to visit any time you like. We can talk about whatever you want, and I will answer any questions you have. Farewell my precious child, until next time. There's just one thing to remember—in Ouranos we never say goodbye, only farewell. Welcome home, my dear child!'

Prince Yehosua added, 'Yes, dear brother, it's time for you to go now. I have prepared a very special place for you—your own personal mansion down in the city below. I'm sure you will like it.'

The Greatest War Ever

Hanok climbed off the great throne and bowed deeply to his Father-King and said, 'Thank You. Thank you ever so much for rescuing me and bringing me here. I feel very much at home in this place.' The Prince helped him put on his crown and handed him the harp and palm branch. There were parting smiles and waves as Prince Yehosua led his young brother around the thick curtain and out of the Most Holy Place. They passed through the Holy Place with its beautiful golden furniture. It was quite a distance, so they flew the whole way. Then they were at the front of the Temple at the top of the steps again.

What awaited Hanok next? That will be seen in the next and final panorama.

Panorama 6 – A Personal Assistant, The Mansion and a Surprise

Personal Assistant: The pair were now standing on the outside of the Temple of Miqqedas on the top platform. Prince Yehosua said, 'Now it's time for your Personal Assistant to take you to your mansion. But—remember you can come and see me anytime you like.' 'Oh, thank You, dear Brother,' replied Hanok. He liked saying the word, Brother. The Prince smiled His ever-loving smile.

Then a nearby angelo who had been waiting outside, stepped forward. It was none other than Hanok's own Protector Angelo, P-A, the one who had been with him since he was born on the Heart of Grace, and had travelled with him through the journey to Ouranos.

The Prince said, 'You no longer need a protective angelo because you have no danger here to be sheltered from. But he is still called P-A, and is now your Personal Assistant. P-A will help you with whatever you want. He will also take you to parts of Basileus and show you around the kingdom and introduce you to new Basileite friends. But for now, I must return to My Father. There is the Great War to fight. And, the greatest show on the Heart of Grace must go on. There is still much to be done.'

The Royal Tour-Guide, Brother-Prince, Chief Commander and Producer of the show, hugged his younger brother again and said, 'Farewell for now my dear brother—trusting, loyal and obedient servant, mighty war-

A Glimpse of the Future: Hanok's Story

rior, leading player in the greatest show on the planet, and now, a new title of 'Citizen of Ouranos.' They both laughed and the Prince turned and went back into the Temple.

Hanok and P-A laughed and hugged. They already knew each other extremely well. P-A said, 'Come. I'll take you a different route down to your mansion. Let's fly!'

The happy pair sprung off the platform and flew upwards leaving the beautiful Temple of Miqqedas and Mount Siyon behind. They soared way out high above the mountains and city below. A huge powerful eagle passed them going in the opposite direction. Hanok marvelled again at his own natural ability to fly. He shouted across to P-A, 'I'm flying just like that eagle. Never, ever, ever will I grow weary or feel faint again!' Hanok knew such a freedom he had never known to exist in his old home. He was free from being bound and tied up by space, time, gravity, human pressures and enemy attacks. At last, he was truly free– free as a bird.

The two flyers soared in great circles and Hanok gazed at superb views over hundreds of kilometres. He looked down upon rolling hills with rivers meandering through the valleys. He saw flat plains and forests. There were shimmery green grassy pastures, fields of purple heather, and meadows filled with yellow buttercups. There were blue lakes, green lakes and in between aqua-marine lakes. And of course, there were the masses of glorious clean, shiny, golden city buildings— nothing like the hazy, smoky, dirty cities back on the old planet which were covered with clouds of grey-brown smog.

Far in the distance in outer space, Hanok saw the countless scintillating lights of all the galaxies and nebulas with their other worlds hiding inside just waiting for him to explore. It truly was a bedazzling sight to behold and the best birds-eye view of Ouranos possible.

A group of angelos passed them at super speeds. Hanok asked P-A where they were off to. P-A replied, 'Oh, they are going on an urgent mission to the Heart of Grace. Angelos are always going to and from that planet with specific missions to carry out, or to bring back reports for the Chief Commander.'

Hanok felt a wave of sadness as he remembered there was a Great War still going on. But there was no time for such sorrow at this moment. P-A led him down to the ground and they landed on the soft piece of grass next to a shiny gold-paved street. P-A announced, 'Here we are. Here is your new mansion specially designed and prepared for you by the Prince.'

The Mansion, the Wreath and a Furry Friend: Hanok looked across the street and saw the house of his dreams, his permanent abode. In fact, it was far beyond his dreams. This glorious mansion was made of a silvery-golden coloured building material he had never seen before. It was supported by four strong pillars with pearls set in them. Beside the beautifully carved front door was a large stone with Hanok's new name engraved on it. This name described his character in the language of Ouranos and he would be known by this name from now on. Yes, this was definitely <u>his</u> home.

P-A said, 'Dear friend, I must go to my own place now. It's just around the corner if you need me. Farewell. See you soon.' He paused a second and added, 'Oh, and there's one more thing–just be aware–there is a very special surprise waiting for you.' He smiled knowingly, but said no more. Hanok grinned and waved, wondering what it could be.

Then, he crossed the street holding onto his prizes and walked up the garden path to his new home. It was lined with perfectly shaped low hedges and rows of deep red roses bordering immaculate lawns. There was not one weed or prickle, not even a thorn on the roses. He picked a ruby red rose and smelt its strong sweet perfume. Oh, he exclaimed, 'This will never fade!' Then, he walked up the golden steps across the wide verandah to the door. As he touched the carved handle, the door gently opened automatically. There was no need for keys and locks or fences here because there were no thieves or criminals to keep out. Ouranos had no crime record at all.

The new homeowner stepped into a large welcoming entrance hall furnished simply and elegantly. To the right was a golden shelf and he knew what that was for. He took off his glittering crown and gently placed it on the shelf as he had seen angelos do earlier. Then, he put the red rose down next to it. Beside the shelf was a beautiful white ring of leaves

A Glimpse of the Future: Hanok's Story

hanging on a gold hook. It was a wreath and on each leaf was written the word PURITY. Around the wreath were stones of many colours which shone vividly. Like a magnifying glass, they made the letters of the word seem even bigger. And at the back of the wreath was a curved bow which had the word, HOLINESS, written on it. This must be the surprise P-A referred to.

To the left was a plain but stunning bronze table and Hanok laid the palm branch on it. Then he tried on the wreath. It fitted his head perfectly. He removed it and placed it back on its hook ready for some very special occasion in the future.

Suddenly, a strange but familiar loud noise sounded. Someone—or something—was inside. A huge ball of fur burst through a large archway, bounded up and put its large paws on Hanok's shoulders. It was none other than the lion he had befriended just after his arrival. The lion had been attracted to him and, unbeknown to Hanok, had adopted this human as his master! Hanok was shocked and thrilled at the same time. He had always wondered what it would be like to have a pet lion. And now he did.

So, <u>this</u> was P-A's big surprise! Apparently, the Prince had noticed the bonding between lion and human at that first meeting. He had organised for P-A to take the lion to the mansion. Hanok immediately gave his new pet the name, Leopold. In his old earthly language, Leopold meant brave people and lion-hearted. But he might just sometimes call him Leo for short. The word Leo meant to roar. But Leo's roar was more of a loud, happy, friendly, contented purrrrrr. Leo, the lion, sounded a good name for his furry friend.

With Leo close behind, Hanok continued his exploration. The mansion was obviously designed specifically for him and satisfied all his wants and needs. There was nothing he did not like. All the furnishings were his favourite colours. They were not overdone and elaborate, but practical and useful with plain, tasteful styles. He knew he would never tire of them. Marble staircases led to several stories above the bottom level. Each room seemed to have a different purpose. He wasn't sure what and would have to ask P-A what to do in them. He thought the largest room would be perfect for social events, because there were plenty of gorgeous silver and gold carved chairs around the walls. He looked forward to having many angelo friends over to visit.

Hanok noticed there was no bedroom to be found and straight away realised why. There was no need for rest and sleep. And there were no light-switches or man-made lights either because Theotes light filled every corner of every room.

The Thinking Room: Up on the top floor was an empty room except for a chair and a table in the middle. The table was made of silver and decorated with carvings of fruit and flowers, but not overdone. Beside it was a large silver armchair with a soft but firm cushion covered with a blue velvety type of material. It was embroidered with patterns of silver fruit and flowers to match the table. Blue was Hanok's favourite colour. But this blue was different to the many shades of blue he had seen on the old planet. It was the most beautiful blue he had ever seen.

He sat down in the chair and felt extremely comfortable as if it was designed specifically for him—which it was. He thought this would be the perfect place to come and have quiet times alone, to ponder and to think. Oh, yes, there were so many things to ponder and think about. He decided to call this quiet, peaceful room, the Thinking Room because he could come here, be alone and simply—think.

Hanok remained in his comfortable Thinking Chair for quite a while. Leo had flopped down beside him and was purring contentedly beside his new master. Hanok closed his eyes and thought about recent events. He had met so many people. Uh oh! No, he had not met any people at all. He was the one and only human in Ouranos. He had met so many angelos, cherubims, and the King and Prince.

Amazing thoughts sprang into his new, alert, never-tiring mind. It wasn't that long ago that he was transformed in the earthly forest, he had met P-A, left the Heart of Grace, flown to Ouranos, had a grand welcome on the Sea of Glass, met his new Brother Yehosua, had a royal city tour and had a picnic with the Prince under the Tree of Life beside the River of Life. Then he had gone inside the Temple of Miqqedas, was taken into the Holy Place and the Most Holy Place and had seen the great white throne with the golden box of Royal Rules underneath. He had seen his

A Glimpse of the Future: Hanok's Story

Father-King face-to-face and sat down on the throne with Him and His Son. Finally, he caught up with P-A again, had an exhilarating flight, and was settled in his own mansion—with a pet lion. Phew!

The deep thinker opened his eyes and suddenly wondered, 'Why aren't I tired? I should be exhausted by now. So much has happened in such a short time, yet it feels like I've been here forever. Time just doesn't matter here. Oooooh, I feel so satisfied and happy. This is where I truly belong.'

Hanok was in his eternal home at last! He was at the new beginning of a new life in a new world. No longer was he playing his role in the great drama on the Heart of Grace. No longer was he on the battlefield in the thick of the Great War. Here in Ouranos, there were no curtains to close on any dramatic scenes of darkness, because everything was completely exposed to the brilliant light of glory and Theotes Great Love. Far, far away, on the tiny speck of the old blackened planet, the tragedy of the controversy between good and evil continued. But life here in Ouranos went on without end for loyal, trusting, transformed and rescued Hanok.

The story of his life on the Heart of Grace had the perfect happy ending of the perfect life with no end. For Hanok, we can truly say, 'And he lived happily ever after!

The End

There is a beautiful quotation from the last paragraph of The Great Controversy page 679. It reads, 'The great controversy is ended. Sin and sinners are no more. The entire universe is clean. One pulse of harmony and gladness beats through the vast creation. From Him who created all, flow life and light and gladness, throughout the realms of illimitable space. From the minutest atom to the greatest world, all things animate and inanimate, in their unshadowed beauty and perfect joy, declare that GOD-IS-LOVE.'

Conclusion:

In conclusion to this final talk, I really hope and trust you have enjoyed Hanok's Story. We have pictured in our minds sitting in outer space and looking at the world as an outside, objective observer. But in real life, we have just had a few minutes of an intermission, a break, a time to rest and get our breath back, in the greatest show on Earth.

Hanok's Story has been my Grand Finale for this series of talks. But God's Grand Finale is yet to come and will be the most spectacular sight ever. This real show is almost over and the invisible stage curtains will soon draw together for the very last time. But for now, unlike Hanok, we must return to the battlefield. Hanok has already eaten the food of Heaven. But, praise God, we have the great wedding feast to look forward to in the very near future when the Bridegroom, Jesus, comes to claim His bride, the trusting, courageous minority, the loyal soldiers in His Church. By God's grace and mercy, we will soon be home at last forever and ever and ever and ever and ever. And like Hanok, we will be able to say, 'And we all lived happily ever after.'

Thank you so much for listening to these talks. Originally, it was going to be a single one-hour talk. But—one thing always leads to another and here we are at the end of eight. My prayer for all the listeners is that, you have been blessed and encouraged to hold on tightly to the cords of faith and to do what is right by God.

I trust that you now have a greater perspective of what has been in the past, why the world is like it is today, and what is in store for us in the near future. 1 Corinthians` 13:12 says, *'Now we see through a glass darkly; but then, face to face. Now, I know in part; but then shall I know, even as I also am known.'* I hope you have experienced even more of the Great Hope of Heaven because Heaven <u>is</u> real and God, Jesus and the Holy Spirit <u>really</u> do exist!

Let's close with a short prayer. 'Our dear heavenly Father, words fail us to comprehend your power and might and love for us. As we prepare to go back onto the battlefield of the Great War of Words, we need You more than ever before. Father, I claim all twenty promises in Psalm 91 for myself and for the listeners, especially these ones. Verses 2-3 *'I will say of the Lord, He is my refuge and my fortress; my God in Him shall I trust. Surely He shall deliver me from the snare of the fowler and from the noisome pestilence;* vs 5 *'Thou shalt not be afraid for the terror by night, nor for the arrow that flieth by day;* vs 10 *'There shall be no evil*

A Glimpse of the Future: Hanok's Story

befall thee, neither shall any plague come nigh thy dwelling, for He shall give His angels charge over thee to keep thee in all thy ways; and vs 16 'With long life will I satisfy him and shew him my salvation.' Thank You, Father-God. In the almighty power of the name of Jesus Christ, we pray. Amen.

'Christ is coming with clouds and with great glory. A multitude of shining angels will attend Him. He will come to raise the dead, and to change the living saints from glory to glory. He will come to honour those who love Him, and kept His commandments, and to take them to Himself. He has not forgotten them nor His promise. There will be a relinking of the family chain. When we look upon our dead, we may think of the morning "when the trump of God shall sound, when the dead shall be raised incorruptible, and we shall be changed."
1 Corinthians 15:53

A little longer and we shall see the King in His beauty. A little longer and He will wipe all tears from our ours. A little longer and He will present us "faultless before the presence of Hs glory with exceeding joy." Jude 24 Wherefore when He gave the signs of His coming, He said, "When these things begin to come to pass, then look up and lift your heads, for your redemption draweth nigh."

Desire of Ages 362

www.ingramcontent.com/pod-product-compliance
Lightning Source LLC
Chambersburg PA
CBHW050308010526
44107CB00055B/2147